THE POLITICS OF VALUES

THE POLITICS OF VALUES

Games Political Strategists Play

Jo Renée Formicola

ROWMAN & LITTLEFIELD PUBLISHERS, INC.
Lanham • Boulder • New York • Toronto • Plymouth, UK

ROWMAN & LITTLEFIELD PUBLISHERS, INC.

Published in the United States of America
by Rowman & Littlefield Publishers, Inc.
A wholly owned subsidiary of The Rowman & Littlefield Publishing Group, Inc.
4501 Forbes Boulevard, Suite 200, Lanham, Maryland 20706
www.rowmanlittlefield.com

Estover Road
Plymouth PL6 7PY
United Kingdom

British Library Cataloguing in Publication Information Available

Library of Congress Cataloging-in-Publication Data:

Formicola, Jo Renée, 1941–
  The politics of values: Games political strategists play / Jo Renée Formicola.
    p. cm.
  Includes bibliographical references and index.
  ISBN-13: 978-0-7425-3973-0 (cloth : alk. paper)
  ISBN-10: 0-7425-3973-3 (cloth : alk. paper)
  ISBN-13: 978-0-7425-3974-7 (pbk. : alk. paper)
  ISBN-10: 0-7425-3974-1 (pbk. : alk. paper)
    1. Christianity and politics—United States.   2. Christian conservatism—United
States.   3. Values—Political aspects—United States.   4. United States—Politics and
government.   5. United States—Religious life and customs.   I. Title.
  BR517.F577   2008
  320.520973—dc22   2007035985

Printed in the United States of America

∞ ™ The paper used in this publication meets the minimum requirements of American
National Standard for Information Sciences—Permanence of Paper for Printed Library
Materials, ANSI/NISO Z39.48-1992.

To Allan, my husband, who continues to be my staunchest supporter and my best critic.

To the students in my Senior Seminar during 2005 and 2006, for their enthusiasm in examining and debating the politics of values.

Contents

Acknowledgments

E VERY BOOK IS LIKE A BABY—easy to conceive, but hard to deliver. *The Politics of Values* was no exception. I was always interested in how values, morality, and ethics impinge on the political process and how different religious organizations work to advance them in the political arena. In fact, I have spent my entire professional career researching and writing on various aspects of the same overarching question: What is the appropriate role of religion in politics?

I began to pursue this concern with renewed vigor during the Bush administration. It encouraged greater input from conservative religious denominations through the president's support of the Faith-Based and Community Initiative, as well as other public policies that reflected traditional moral agendas and views. The standard way to understand and evaluate such political activity was through my own personal research and discussions with colleagues, but another more interactive one was through dialogue and debate with the students in my seminars on "The Politics of Values," specifically in 2005 and 2006. They were enthusiastic and anxious to work on a variety of thesis topics that had become critical moral and political issues and a significant part of what I defined as "the politics of values." To them, I owe a debt of gratitude for listening to my evolving theories and for sharing their own views and analyses with me. Special thanks, then, to Michael LaRosa, John Grey, Matthew Steele, Michael Ricci, John Paul Yates, Marie Bianchi, Renee Smith, Joseph Krause, Onel Lopez, Gina Paulk, Amanda Grybko, Katie Cerak, Chase Pepper, Gregg Demers, Brian O'Malley, Laura LaSota, James Wilson, Michael Muldowney, Jennifer Bruder, and Brittany Wallis.

Research, of course, is also only as good as the researcher. There were so many times in the writing of this, and previous books, that the librarians at

Seton Hall University saved me: They found long-lost volume numbers and esoteric quotes. They miraculously turned up legal citations and websites. So, thanks to Richard Stern, Sister Anita Talar, Beth Bloom, and Alan Dozier, as well as everyone else on the reference desk at Seton Hall University who were always available to assist with their special expertise and infinite patience.

Finally, every author gets tired, burned out, sick of his or her project, and needs a supporter. For that, I would like to thank my husband, Allan, who read this entire manuscript with a critical eye, who talked out salient points with me, and who always made me feel as though I was writing the next, most important political bestseller in America. He helped me through all my long days of research, my hours of writing, and never reminded me of my all too often, forgotten promise that "this is the last time I will ever write another book!"

Introduction

THIS BOOK EXAMINES the emergence, climax, and gradual erosion of the symbiotic relationship between the Republican Party and the evangelicals from 1998 to 2008. It will argue that their similar, conservative, social values tied them together in moral, ideological, and partisan ways during the last decade, thus jeopardizing the principle of the separation of church and state and doing irreparable harm to the American political process.

Ultimately, the interdependence of evangelicals and Republicans led to a new way of doing the business of government through what this author calls "the politics of values." The term, as used here, is a way to describe their political strategy, one that is driven by four basic tactics. First, the politics of values exploits divisive or "wedge issues" by targeting values voters and incorporating their moral agenda into Republican policy initiatives. Second, the politics of values is about identifying, preparing, and supporting conservative leaders for the future. Third, it is concerned with framing and controlling the political debate within its own moral parameters. And fourth, the politics of values clearly articulates the values of its candidates and assertively defines the moral flaws of its opponents.

This strategy, then, has many nuances. The politics of values uses social and cultural "wedge issues"—namely, those moral matters that divide rather than unite people—to solidify its electoral base. These concerns include, but are not limited to, public controversies over abortion, gay marriage, stem cell research, cloning, death with dignity, evolution, birth control, and divorce. It also plays on a myriad of personal issues related to character, integrity, and honesty as part of American politics today.

Within the context of the politics of values, then, moral conflict festers continually and any one or some of the issues can be brought to the fore at any given time. This is a tactic that has been used to deflect attention from larger political issues such as foreign policy, the economy, domestic reform, or political performance.

In the past ten years, the politics of values has become the strategy of choice for the Republican Party. It has become the preferred means of campaigning to secure the religious and socially conservative base—the "values voters"—and to assure the political dominance of the GOP. Just as significantly, the politics of values has also become the critical method of advancing the evangelical moral agenda in public policy, legislation, and judicial decisions.

How were the Republicans and their religious supporters able to gain so much power, manipulate the principle of separation of church and state, and elect George W. Bush twice?

Originally, the evangelical political presence was only a specter, much like the Communism that Karl Marx described in the *Communist Manifesto*. Evangelical voters were part of an ephemeral, coalescing constituency, one that became increasing significant within the American political process during the latter part of the 1970s. Although the evangelicals were in the forefront of an emerging religious-political movement, only a few could see the specter, as it appeared only at certain times and in particular places.

In 1982, while doing research at the White House about the U.S. Catholic bishops and their role in trying to influence U.S. public policy, the author's first true understanding of the merger of conservative evangelicals and Republican politics became real. At the time, it seemed as though the Catholic bishops were taking the lead in bringing the moral dimension to politics in a number of critical areas; specifically nuclear disarmament, economic justice, and abortion. As the leaders of the largest religious denomination in the United States as well, it appeared to the author that they would have had enough clout to exert some positive influence on the Reagan administration—but they did not.

In fact, it was just the opposite. Officials in the Reagan White House maintained that the Catholic Church in the United States had the body of a lion but the voice of a mouse. This was in contrast to evangelicals, who in spite of their smaller numbers were considered much more valuable to the Republicans. They were registering hundreds of thousands of new voters a year and bringing them into the party.

Hundreds of thousands of voters, the numbers seemed astronomical; it had to be an exaggeration. But soon thereafter the demographics spoke for themselves: The new relationship between the administration and the galvanizing Christian right could be seen in meetings and other interactions between the Moral Majority and government power brokers in Washington, D.C.

In the early 1980s the evangelicals were just beginning to emerge from the political shadows. Their religious identity, ideology, and cultural beliefs, which had been misunderstood, were becoming more pronounced. They were no longer a vague and disparate group of religious revivalists, folks who spent too much time praying in tents and declaring too many "Amens." They were, unbeknownst to many, creating Christian alternatives to the society in which they lived, establishing political offices in the nation's capital, and developing a slow, but symbiotic relationship, between the religious right and the conservative wing of the Republican Party. As they registered more voters, their connection with the GOP became stronger and more meaningful, until, by the next quarter of a century, the evangelicals would be able to make the critical difference in two very close elections for George W. Bush.

In about 1998, George W. Bush, the governor of Texas, and as yet an unannounced Republican presidential candidate, began to be tutored deeply in the ideology of conservatism and neoconservatism by Karl Rove, his political mentor. Rove brought in experts in areas that might be crucial in developing a political agenda that would help the younger Bush understand policy choices, expand his own approaches to political quandaries, energize the base, and make a successful run for the presidency.

Within the context of this political education, evangelical thinkers were also invited to discuss spiritual ideas, their moral agendas, and to present solutions that could be applied in the creation of public policies that would reflect the traditional values of America. It was anticipated that their biblical views and input might help to create Republican responses to the cultural divide that had emerged in the United States in the aftermath of the Great Society of the 1960s. By the time George W. Bush was elected to the presidency in 2000, the moral influence of the evangelicals had morphed into solid partisan support for the Republican Party and the basis of the GOP's political platform that reflected conservative social and cultural views.

As a result, a nexus between religion, ideology, and politics emerged within the new administration—an iron triangle based on a consensus of similar *values*. Corresponding beliefs in God, home, family, prayer, individual responsibility, and hard work were quickly transformed into public policies based on "compassionate conservatism" and translated into executive actions for faith-based and community initiatives.

Similar constituent and party concerns became part of the overarching, morally consistent public policy based on the "culture of life." Support for a more moral foreign policy eventually encompassed a justification for a pre-emptive military strike and support for regime change. And they were part of a larger evangelical and Republican commitment to doing the Lord's work to advance democracy and capitalism around the globe.

The deepening religious-political symbiosis was jarred, however, by a number of events and trends in the decade between 1998 and 2008 that led to a paradoxical dynamic. It led to both the strengthening and weakening of their close relationship. First, the tragedy of September 11th forced the president to reconsider much of his original agenda in light of the terrorist attack on the United States. Nonetheless, he still cast his military policy in moral terms—the sacred duty to preserve U.S. security in light of suspected weapons of mass destruction, a way to liberate oppressed people, the obligation to make regime change, and the need to support human rights. It would be a conflict led by a commander-in-chief of proven integrity and fought by brave young men and women dedicated to this nation's highest ideals. These moral values of character and commitment underscored and justified the moral values that impelled Americans to respond to the heinous acts perpetrated on them by violent fanatics.

Second, the culture wars, as a result of the invasion of Afghanistan and the engagement in Iraq, had to be led increasingly by the evangelicals acting as surrogates for the conservative Bush government. With help from the president in his bully pulpit by his executive actions, and by some legislation designed to advance traditional values, evangelicals, with their megachurches and charismatic leaders, preached to the values voter against the materialistic, liberal policies of the recent past. They provided an alternative to the lifestyle that had preceded the Bush presidency, entered the public debate, and engaged in the politics of values with a conservative fire and zeal not seen in the political arena since the Reagan administration. They worked tirelessly to support the case for Terri Schiavo, the Partial-Birth Abortion Ban, the Violence Against the Unborn Act, and the vetoes of embryonic stem cell research funded by the federal government. They opposed Plan B—the morning-after pill—and registered voters, got people out to the polls, did direct mailings, created voter guides, and issued report cards on candidates for political office.

Third, the beginning of opposition to evangelical power also began during the first Bush presidency. As a reaction to their growing Christian moral agenda, the religious left and center in America led the backlash against the evangelical, biblically inspired public policies.

By 2005, progressive religious groups realized how Christianity in the United States had been "hijacked" by conservative denominations; it had become partisan and too politically involved. New and charismatic ministers began to demand a return to values that were broad rather than dogmatic, prophetic rather than literal, aimed at the common good, and inclusive of all.

Their power, growing quickly in the liberal media and in disenchanted segments of society, began to pose a threat to the continued control of evangelicals in the public arena. Even more critically, the possibility arose that the progressive religious left and center had the potential to ally its fledging movement with liberal, Democratic politicians seeking office in 2006 and even in the coming national election in 2008. Thus, the pendulum began to swing.

Finally, the Republican Party lost sight of its political prize and the fact that reelection was the reward of a political job well done. Instead, it had a significant political comeuppance, particularly in the midterm election of 2006, a surprise to those who were busy playing the politics of values and being caught up in their own self-righteousness. As a result, an implosion occurred. The war in Iraq started to go from bad to worse, corruption plagued the party, and scandals within its evangelical partnership helped the spiritual/political symbiosis to unravel.

This book will show how evangelical moral influence morphed into public policy and partisan political support for the Republican Party. It will show how the politics of values were used as a means to gain and hold political power, and it will articulate how those who tried to implement the politics of values in campaigns and public policy began to fall into disrepute. Due to their own arrogance and scandalous behavior, many were voted out of elective office, losing significant races in the 2006 midterm elections, and leaving the Republican Party severely compromised for the 2008 presidential election.

Many evangelicals and Republicans, however, refuse to recognize these realities. They continue to believe that recent political losses only represent short-term responses to local, rather than national, issues. They believe that traditional values and the values voters that support them will continue to thrive in the future because of the strong symbiosis they have formed based on similar values.

This book will argue that the ensuing erosion of the evangelical-Republican symbiosis will soon become more visible and powerful as demands grow for an emphasis on new spiritual values and adjusted political priorities. In short, the nexus of conservative ideology, religion, and politics is imploding. In its place, progressive alternatives are developing; in fact, some are already being presented to the voter by candidates who are motivated by new challenges and cultural directions.

Peace will emerge as a critical value in the future, while wedge issues and the politics of values will be less dominant. In some cases, Democratic candidates are already replacing divisive concerns with an emphasis on environmental stewardship, immigration reform, social justice, equalizing economic disparity, and responding to the global AIDS crisis.

Religious progressives are also looking to change the politics of values, espousing prophetic notions of teaching truth to power, finding solutions based on universal, transcendent notions, and providing innovative solutions to society's problems. Indeed, they are increasingly becoming committed to providing a broader, pluralistic vision for a new type of socially progressive moral and political agenda. If these political and religious trends continue, the possibility of a politics of unity may yet reappear and reassert those values that made America great.

1

The Emergence:
Traditional Values Become Politicized

Introduction

"Is conservatism finished? What might have seemed an absurd question less than two years ago is now one of the most important issues in American politics. The question is being asked—mostly quietly but occasionally publicly—by conservatives themselves as they survey the wreckage of their hopes, and as their champions in the Republican Party use any means necessary to survive this fall's elections . . ."[1]

E. J. Dionne, Jr., asked this provocative question about the future of conservatism in his column in the *Washington Post* in the summer of 2006. To liberals, it was spot on: a foreshadowing of the ideological shift and party realignment that would actually occur during the midterm elections in November. To conservatives, however, the question was totally invalid, a query into cyclical aberrations and even rumors—like those about the deaths of Mark Twain and God—clearly premature and exaggerated.

Conservatives believed this because they recognized that a new, solid relationship between politics and values had emerged since 2000, a symbiotic connection that had grown and matured after the election of George W. Bush. It was a special relationship that had strengthened the power of the Republican Party, social conservatives, evangelicals, and other traditional Christians, the result of a common connection: a value structure based on the teachings of the Bible and a commitment to implement its message in America through the political process.

Together, the Republican Party, social conservatives, and traditionalist Christian denominations have forged a special "iron triangle," an impenetrable political bond based on biblical standards, political goals, and public policies, all of which have been reinforced by the continual interactions of their constituencies. This chapter tells the story of how that political-religious symbiosis came to be—from the 1980s to the present—and the many disparate events, ideas, and commitments that made it happen.

Creating the Symbiosis

Conservatism in America was once cast by liberals as nothing more than the reactionary thought of closed minded anti-intellectuals. The Republican Party was patronized by elitists as a WASP bastion; social conservatives were painted as heartless, uncaring reformers; and traditionalist Christians were viewed as nothing more than country bumpkins, holy rollers, papists, and political bunglers. Yet, the cohesive, similar *values* of all three constituencies have become the solder that holds together the most unified ideological force in America today.

As a result, values, which were once an *end* in themselves, and something to be pursued because of their intrinsic worth, have now become a *means*—a new way—to frame campaigns, win elections, create public policies, advance legislation, and secure major judicial appointments. Values, now, are being used to give a sense of *moral* cohesion to all things political in the eyes of major segments of the American population.

The use of traditional values in the political process has left many liberal politicians trying to figure out how the ideological earth shifted beneath their feet. They are asking why the conservative appeal to values and personal character helped to create a whole new political landscape since 2000.

If values were, indeed, the key to winning the presidency, what values were important enough to get formerly phlegmatic, religious voters out to the polls? What strategies did the social conservatives use to make moral values so important? Why did progressive ideas seem less clear to the electorate? Why didn't they appeal to the average voter any longer? What happened to America's core values—the values that were the essence of the American experiment, the justification for democracy's expansion and destiny? What happened to tolerance? What happened to compromise? What happened to civility? What happened to unity? In short, what happened to classical liberalism? And perhaps, more importantly in the eyes of progressives—can it come back with the force and vigor that once characterized the American dream? Can it re-emerge and save the United States?

The search for America's core values has become the Holy Grail of U.S. politics today. Academics, religious leaders, policymakers, and media gurus are in a desperate competition, a race to define and reclaim America's intrinsic values. They were the beliefs that included and inspired diverse peoples to become part of a society and a culture that recognized and protected their equality, freedom, and hope.

It seemed so clear when Thomas Jefferson wrote in the Declaration of Independence that "All men are created equal and endowed by their creator with certain inalienable rights, among these are life, liberty, and the pursuit of happiness." The Constitution reiterated those ideas, proclaiming that the U.S. government was founded to "secure the Blessings of Liberty to ourselves and our Posterity." And yet, these principles became blurred since their inception by the realities of economics, politics, cultural changes, interests, wars, and religious diversity.

Elites today are busy debating, reporting, analyzing, and trying to make sense out of the current relationship between politics and values, but their attempts are too late. They have missed the bigger picture: the symbiotic realignment that has already occurred between the religious right, social conservatives, and the Republican Party.

Instead, the pundits would be better served by attempting to understand *how* values are being used to create new types of campaigns, political behavior, and public policies that reflect the moral standards of that segment of the American population that wants to return to its roots. Its heritage is its Protestant beginnings, and its goals are to try to reclaim it all in the name of God and partisan politics.

Everything in the political process has changed since the 1980s. Candidates need to start their campaigns earlier, raise more money, be better connected, and have flawless pasts in order to even get into primaries. The critical political questions are no longer about a candidate's stand on foreign policy, social justice, or government reform. Instead, they revolve around moral issues. Is the candidate pro-life or pro-choice? Does he/she favor gay marriage? Where does the candidate stand on embryonic stem cell research? How does he/she feel about death with dignity and physician-assisted suicide? What is the candidate's view on creationism, evolution, and intelligent design? What about sex education?

Political campaigns are but one example of this new set of criteria for elections. Efforts to pass specific pieces of legislation, to implement executive orders, to lobby on behalf of special interests, and to make choices of judicial nominees and other government appointees are all being decided on the basis of values, as well. Even more astounding is the fact that the values that are gaining greater acceptance in the public arena are not just the "traditional" ones—God, home, and family. Instead, in many cases, they are *countercultural* ideas. That is to say that the current political values of a growing number of Americans represent a backlash against the educational, sexual, racial, and ethical values that have dominated American culture since the l960s.

Which Values? Life and Death

It's hard to pinpoint the beginning of the values wars. Some say they began with the election of the first Catholic president, John F. Kennedy, in 1960. Protestant fears of the candidate's loyalty to Rome and papal influence on American politics were put to rest by the young Democratic senator from Massachusetts during the campaign, but Kennedy's presidency opened a decade characterized by many curious political turns. From the president's involvement in the Bay of Pigs and Vietnam to his assassination and the tenure of Lyndon B. Johnson, the new and vocal liberal calls for "flower power" and "power to the people" resonated among Americans by middecade.

Along with the desire to "make love not war" came legislative and judicial actions for civil rights, the movement toward "black power," women's rights, and major entitlements granted by the programs of the Great Society. Shocked social and religious conservatives reacted quietly against what they viewed as "the welfare state," "radical feminism," "acid heads," and "pacifism" by slowly distancing themselves from the mainstream and embracing a cultural divide that was developing in the United States. Their responses were simple: give people a hand up rather than a handout; protect the institutions that had made America great—support the family, serve God, and vote for the Republican Party.

Life issues became the lightning rod that first prodded conservatives into political action. Religious groups and social/economic traditionalists, along with leaders in the Republican Party, began to take stock of the results of the liberal, Democratic changes that had occurred in American culture and politics after the decade of the 1960s. In 1973, when the Supreme Court ruled in *Roe v. Wade* that a woman had the right to terminate a pregnancy, religious and social conservatives realized that the fetus's right to life would be trumped legally by the mother's right to privacy in a test of medical, economic, social, and quality-of-life priorities. According to conservatives, the right to life was no longer a value that could be taken for granted or expected to be protected by the government.

Religious leaders had more or less avoided the judicial battle in *Roe*, most in denial that the case could be won by progressives and feminists. They did little to inform or rally their congregations to oppose the coming change in values that would soon be sanctioned by the Court. Instead, only groups such as the National Right to Life Committee, a coalition of lay individuals, filed *amicus*, or friend of the court, briefs upholding the principle of the right to life of the fetus.

The loss of the pro-life supporters came as a shock to the religious establishment. As a result, it energized evangelicals, Catholics, and other traditionalist religious groups who proceeded to commit their future efforts and resources towards intense political action in the public arena to limit abortion and make it the most significant litmus test for all future political candidates.

Through the 1970s and up to the present, the debate over abortion has remained the most volatile and contentious issue separating values voters from more progressive constituencies in the United States. The election of George W. Bush and a Republican Congress in 2000 became the catalyst for government policies that shifted the former emphasis on privacy rights toward a broader moral perspective that included the right of the fetus to exist.

Supported under the Catholic rubric of the "culture of life," the first major change in government policy came on the new president's first day in office. At that time, George W. Bush reinstated the Global Gag Rule, a policy of Ronald Reagan and his father that grew out of the 1984 Mexico City population conference. It prohibited any U.S.-government-funded international entity from using its own private funds or public monies to perform or provide abortions. It banned such organizations from lobbying their own governments for a change in abortion laws or conducting public education campaigns about abortion. Further, it prevented the referral of women to abortion providers or giving them counseling about abortion.

By 2002, the president declared a "Sanctity of Life Day" and directed states to classify a developing fetus as an "unborn child." With this new fetal designation, funds for State Children's Health Insurance Programs (SHIP) could cover children from conception to age 19. At the same time, the Bush administration also withheld congressionally approved funds for the United National Population Fund, specifically because the UNFPA provided educational services about reproductive health and contraception.

Other pro-life actions came out of the White House. In 2003, the president signed the Partial-Birth Abortion Ban. Originally ruled unconstitutional by the Supreme Court in *Stenberg v. Carhart*[2] in 2000, the Nebraska ban on partial-birth abortion had been struck down by the justices because it lacked a health exception to save the life of the mother, was too vague in its description of what was meant by a fetus, and put an undue burden on a women's choice to have an abortion.

In 2006, the Supreme Court reconsidered its decision because the Congress had passed a new, federal Partial-Birth Abortion Ban Act in 2003. It was different from the Nebraska law in several ways and ruled legal the second time around. The congressional enactment required abortion providers to prove that the procedure would be safer than other alternatives, give specific information about the abortion procedure itself to those requesting it, and leave other alternatives open for women considering late pregnancy termination.

In 2004, the president showed his further commitment to pro-life policies by signing the Unborn Victims of Violence Act. That law elevated the rights of the fetus and recognized them as distinct from those of its mother. Thus, the murder of a pregnant woman and the resulting death of her fetus would be considered as a double homicide in all states under the new federal law.

Strengthened by the enactment of that ban, candidates who had pro-life views began to speak out more loudly in the public debate. In 2004, the election of more social and religious conservatives to the Congress, such as Senator Tom Coburn, a physician from Oklahoma, occurred, along with the defeat of the pro-choice Democratic minority leader, Senator Tom Daschle of South Dakota. Senator Arlen Specter, (R-PA), the then incoming chairman of the Judiciary Committee, promised speedy votes on the president's judicial nominees, a particularly important statement because the justice candidates' views on abortion had become the most important consideration for final approval.

This change within the congressional mentality as well as the thinking in the White House brought an intensified values-oriented approach to the politics of abortion. Vice President Dick Cheney articulated it when he spoke before the National Right to Life Committee in 2004. He called the organization "a great movement of conscience" that "reflects the compassion of our country, and our commitment to equality and dignity for every life."[3]

That said, actions continued to speak louder than words. In September of 2004, the Bush administration also offered federal employees a Catholic health plan that specifically excluded payments for contraceptives, abortion, sterilization, and artificial insemination. Two months later in November 2004, House and Senate conferees added an anti-abortion provision known as the "Federal Refusal Clause" to an omnibus spending bill. Reflecting the growing political power of the religious and social conservatives, the rider had language that barred federal, state, and local agencies from withholding taxpayer money from any group that refused to provide or pay for abortions, denied abortion counseling or referrals, or would not force its health care providers to undergo abortion training. The latter expanded "conscience protection," to *all* health care providers, an exemption formerly only given to Catholic physicians or those working in Catholic health care facilities.[4]

Other executive actions reflected the president's pro-life stance. He pressured Congress to support the denial of federal funds for women in the military seeking abortions in the case of rape or incest. At the same time, he signed the Teen Endangerment Act, a piece of legislation that prohibited anyone other than a parent from transporting a minor across state lines for an abortion. And in a major political coup, he nominated two Supreme Court justices who held similar traditional views on life issues—Chief Justice John Roberts and Justice Samuel Alito—both of whom were confirmed without major political difficulties.

Of all the Bush administration's pro-life policies, only one has been challenged successfully by opponents. That was the ban on the over-the-counter sale of emergency birth control known as Plan B, or the "morning-after pill." Although the reproductive technology existed for a number of years to prevent unwanted pregnancies at their very earliest stage, religious conservatives cast the dispensing of Plan B in moral terms. They argued that access to the pill was a form of early abortion and that its use would only promote greater sexual promiscuity. In fact, some pharmacists even became "conscientious objectors," refusing to fill prescriptions for Plan B.

Feminists and social progressives, however, saw the availability of Plan B in pragmatic, legal terms: as a critical, new aspect of personal freedom and privacy. They argued that its use could reduce the chances of unwanted pregnancies by as much as 89 percent[5] and would have a major impact on women's lives.

The issue turned political during the Bush administration. Right to life senator Rick Santorum (R-PA) led the fight in the legislature to oppose Plan B. Senator Mike Enzi (R-WY) introduced a bill to override state laws that would require health insurance companies to pay contraceptive costs. And, in a high-level attempt to kill the morning-after pill, Lester Crawford, a Bush appointee who was commissioner of the Food and Drug Administration, tabled consideration of the over-the-counter sale of Plan B in August 2005. But, his actions backfired.

Staff scientists had declared the pill safe, and the FDA's women's health chief resigned in protest. Morale was reported as having "plummeted."[6] At that point, Senators Patty Murray (D-WA) and Hillary Clinton (D-NY) took the congressional lead to save Plan B. They vowed to block the president's nomination of Andrew von Eschenbach for the embattled position of FDA commissioner left vacant by the surprise resignation of Crawford a month after his ban of Plan B. Murray and Clinton had told the secretary of Health and Human Services, Mike Leavitt, that unless the FDA reconsidered the denial of the over-the-counter sale of Plan B, the von Eschenbach nomination would face a serious confirmation challenge. Their strategy worked. The White House capitulated and got its nominee, and women over the age of 18 were allowed to buy Plan B over the counter. Minors could purchase it with a physician's prescription.

Politicians, religious activists, and scientists in the values wars have also tied stem cell research to questions of the value of life and death. The issue came to the fore in 1998 when researchers at the University of Wisconsin and Johns Hopkins University were able to isolate stem cells in a laboratory. Those cells had the potential to develop into any kind of tissue, but the process was considered controversial because the technique used to accomplish this would require destroying human embryos.

It became political when President Bush declared that federal funding for such research could only be used on existing stem cell lines, that is, colonies derived from leftover embryos at fertility clinics. Public monies, according to his policy pronouncement, could not be used to create new stem cell lines that would be used only for research purposes and then deliberately destroyed afterward.

It became frightening to social conservatives and others, however, when scientists in Massachusetts performed the first cloning of human embryos in 2001 and attempted to generate replacement tissues that patients' bodies would not reject. High profile individuals such as Nancy Reagan, Christopher Reeve, and Michael J. Fox supported such research, hoping to raise awareness about the positive potential of stem cell research and the possibilities of finding cures for Alzheimer's disease, spinal cord injuries, Parkinson's disease, and other debilitating illnesses.

In 2004, Californians enacted Proposition 71, a bill that authorized the spending of $3 billion over ten years to fund stem cell research. The next year, New Jersey's governor announced the funding for a $150 million stem cell research center and the intention of allocating another $230 million for research. Connecticut followed suit, earmarking $100 million, and the governor of Illinois issued an executive order authorizing $10 million for stem cell research in his state as well.

With the states taking the initiative to advance stem cell research, Congress approved funds in a landmark bill, which the president ultimately vetoed. Incidentally, this was the first piece of legislation that Bush vetoed. At a White House event with children born from adopted frozen embryos, his words were clear: "These boys and girls are not spare parts. They remind us of what is lost when embryos are destroyed in the name of research. They remind us that we all began our lives as a small collection of cells."[7]

Within the whole question of the value of life and stem cell research is another critical issue that has further polarized religious and social conservatives: the question of death. Most recently, the political battle became starkly real as the media reported on the battle to save the life of Terri Schiavo, a young and vital married woman from Florida who suffered severe brain damage at the age of 26. Her heart stopped beating one night in 1990 due to a potassium deficiency, most likely the result of an eating disorder, bulimia. For fifteen years, she was kept alive in a hospital by artificial means: breathing tubes, intravenous fluids, and other life-sustaining apparatus. During that time, Terri's husband, Michael, relying on the professional opinions of physicians, eventually came to accept that she had no brain function and wanted to exercise his right as her legal guardian to allow her to die. Terri's parents, however, vehemently opposed this and claimed that she responded to their voices when they visited her in the hospital. They wanted her to be kept alive, believing in their hearts that she could improve with therapy in the future.

The clash between Terri's husband and her parents, the Schindlers, was filled with acrimony. The problem began when Michael won a $1 million malpractice settlement on Terri's behalf and intensified when he fathered two children with his live-in girlfriend during the mid-1990s. The Schindlers accused him of adultery and argued that he should not be allowed to serve as the legal guardian for Terri.

Her parents, on the other hand, were portrayed by the Schiavo camp as meddling, religious fanatics who refused to accept medical reality. It was simply a matter of time before their personal attacks escalated from words to judicial challenges as both sides tried to control the ultimate fate of Terri Schiavo.

In 1998, Michael Schiavo filed the first petition to remove his wife's feeding tube, and eventually in 2000, he was granted that right by the presiding circuit court judge, George W. Greer. After a significant number of legal challenges during the next two years by Terri's parents, countersuits by Michael Schiavo, and a decision by another circuit court judge, Frank Quesada, that the tube be reinstated, the case finally ended up again before Judge Greer in 2003. He reiterated his former decision: that the feeding tube could be removed from Terri Schiavo. By then, all judicial appeals were exhausted.

However, the Republican-controlled Florida legislature, which had been cautiously watching the case, jumped into the dispute a week later and passed "Terri's Law." It authorized Republican Governor Jeb Bush to intervene in the case, and soon thereafter, he ordered Terri's tube to be reinserted and rehydration to begin. Now, the battle for the life of Terri Schiavo became a public and political spectacle—based on the contradictory life values of her husband and parents.

In September 2004, the Florida Supreme Court struck down "Terri's Law," ruling it to be unconstitutional and an encroachment on the power of the judiciary. As a result, in February 2005 Judge Greer again gave Michael Schiavo the right to remove Terri's feeding tube.

But, just as the end was in sight, the value of life became politicized yet again in a case that was considered a "great political issue," one that "resonate[d] with Christian conservatives," and one that had the White House providing "talking points about how to respond to requests to the Schiavo case . . ."[8] In short, it became a cause celebre and a means to win political points for many in Congress. The *New York Times* reinforced this dilemma by reporting that "conservative lawmakers took up her case as a symbol of the sanctity of life."[9]

As soon as the decision was handed down by Judge Greer, Rep. Tom DeLay (TX), the Republican majority leader in the U.S. House of Representatives at the time, announced that the Congress would take up the case of Terri Schiavo. He said, "we are trying to protect her constitutional right to live," and then added that the Congress was looking to protect her from having someone else "control her future by pulling out a feeding tube and letting her starve for two weeks."[10]

A Congressional inquiry was also justified, according to Rep. Tom Davis (R-Va) chair of the Government Report Committee. He proceeded to subpoena a number of Terri Schiavo's physicians and ultimately required them to maintain certain pieces of evidence, namely, records on the condition of the *medical equipment* that was keeping Terri alive. This stalling tactic prevented the removal of her feeding tubes until the congressional hearings were completed.

The media loved the drama of it all. Outside Woodside Hospice, where Terri Shiavo lay in what was hotly debated by various physicians as "a persistent vegetative state," people gathered with signs supporting and opposing the removal of her feeding tubes. Jugglers came one day. Television cameras were present twenty-four seven. Her parents gave interviews. They released tapes of Terri "responding" to them. Priests prayed. Senator Bill Frist (R-TN), a physician and at the time the majority leader of the Senate, declared at one point that "Terri is alive. Terri is not in a coma."[11] The Internet was filled with bloggers examining every aspect of every word that was uttered by each side. Randall Terry of Operation Rescue, an anti-abortion interest group, carried the fight beyond the hospice by lobbying Congress and the Florida legislature. CNN and FOX debated the issue on the air, talking to all sorts of "experts" on the matter during their continuous news cycles. Bioethicists and medical commentators kept ringing the alarm bells, calling the entire situation a "counterrevolution" on one hand and an "erosion of a very hard-won multiple-decade process of agreeing that the decisions belong inside families."[12] The Reverend Jesse Jackson came in support of the Schindlers and Terri.

Within days of the last ruling by Judge Greer allowing Terri Schiavo's feeding tube to be removed (March 18, 2005), the political theatre began, with congressional politicians now playing major roles. The Senate passed a rare "private relief" bill that allowed a federal court to intervene on Schiavo's behalf. The House Republican leadership called a special Sunday night session in the middle of Easter recess to vote on the Schiavo measure.

The final House bill was broader than the Senate version because it was an attempt to advocate on behalf of all incapacitated persons, rather than simply to resolve the case of Terri Schiavo. But quickly, Congress compromised and negotiated a final bill that dealt only with the comatose Floridian and made only nonbinding recommendations for broader legislation in the future.

In preparation for a positive vote, President Bush cut his Easter vacation short and flew back to the White House from his ranch in Crawford, Texas, to sign the Schiavo bill of relief. But soon after, a federal judge in Florida again refused to allow the reinsertion of Terri Schiavo's feeding tube. Last-minute desperate appeals by her parents to higher courts were also denied. Terri Schiavo passed away peacefully on March 31, 2005, with her husband at her side and within days of all the extraordinary judicial, legislative, and executive attempts to save her life.

In the immediate aftermath of her death, Rep. Tom Delay hinted that the judges who refused to intercede in the case would have to answer for their behavior. And, James Dobson, founder of the evangelical group Focus on the Family, said that such judges were "guilty . . . of judicial malfeasance . . . [and] the extermination of an innocent human life."[13]

What makes her case so compelling, besides trying to do what was best for Terri Schiavo, are the politics behind the frenzy.[14] A network of social and Christian conservatives in Florida, led by the Schindlers and Terri's brother, had been working to build religious and political support for her cause for almost two years. They were backed by Catholics, evangelical lobbyists, and a variety of spiritual advisors. In the political arena, they were helped by Ken Connor, the well-connected trial lawyer who had previously represented Governor Jeb Bush before the Florida Court on the case. Connor got Rep. Dave Weldon (R-FL), a physician and old friend, to raise the issue in the House. He, in turn, enlisted the support of Mel Martinez, the newly elected Republican Florida senator, who incidentally, was Connor's former college roommate. Thus, Connor seeded support in both the House and the Senate; the Florida elected officials did the rest.

This was the first time that the value of "death with dignity" was challenged as mere "euthanasia" by the adherents of what has come to be known as the "culture of life" in the political arena. Governor Bush was one of those political actors who had "prodded the Florida Legislature"[15] to act on behalf of Terri Schiavo. Clearly seen as an ally of Christian conservatives, his actions were seen as posturing for a future presidential bid.

The case also opened a national debate about the value of life and death and the role of government in both. What had always been a personal or family matter had now become a public, social, cultural, and religious issue based on values. Although it was recognized by most Americans as a gut wrenching and complex decision, the case revealed that a majority of the members of the House felt that a patient's rights at the end of his/her life required guidelines and that they should be legislated by Congress. Such thinking has left open the door to a potential constitutional clash between privacy rights and due process on the issue of death with dignity.

Current law allows individuals to decline "extraordinary measures" to save their lives, and they may request a DNR (do not resuscitate order) in a living will. Such a document is clear about how an individual wishes to die. However, most young people have not considered filing such written instructions. They are, therefore, the most vulnerable and susceptible victims of family clashes about how to resolve the end of life—questions that inevitably emerge in tragic situations. In many cases, the courts are called on to adjudicate such problems, with the standards varying from state to state.

The same is true regarding assisted suicide. It is legal in Oregon, the Supreme Court having ruled that the federal government did not have the right to overrule the state's Death with Dignity Act[16] approved by voters in 1994 and affirmed in 1997. The law allows physicians to help their mentally competent, terminally ill patients to end their lives; similar legislation is being considered in both California and Vermont. Thus, the further possibility of federal action and interpretation on a variety of other "life" rights—those dealing with conception, birth, cloning, and stem cell research—still exists on actions that could easily be interpreted as a personal intrusion by some and a protection of medical abuse by others.

In the longer term, the Schiavo case also helped to create closer ties between evangelicals and Catholics in the United States since both religious denominations are committed to Pope John Paul II's teaching on the "culture of life." The Pontiff, incidentally, had intervened in the case indirectly while giving a speech in Rome, saying that providing water and food are "natural means of preserving life, not a medical act"; that it is "ordinary and proportionate," and thus, "morally obligatory. . . ."[17]

But, even before such support was publicly given, a détente of sorts had begun between Catholics and evangelicals eleven years earlier when leading theologians from both groups held a series of meetings and wrote a document entitled "Evangelicals and Catholics Together."[18] The statement recognized a "pattern of convergence and cooperation" between both groups and a commitment to secure the truth of politics, law, and culture with the moral truth. The Christian conservatives called for greater religious freedom, a defense of human life, particularly for the old and the radically handicapped, along with the resistance of euthanasia, eugenics, and population control. The theological differences between the Christian denominations were recognized, but the document stressed the social issues where they were alike, calling on their followers to support a nonpartisan, religious agenda oriented to the common good and based on public reason. Evangelicals seemingly accepted the way that Catholic theologians framed moral issues within a political context,[19] and later were able to oppose Senator John Kerry, the Democratic presidential nominee in the 2004 election, on some of those views.

Terri Schiavo's parents, the Schindlers, are Catholics and worked with members of their church as well as evangelicals to save their daughter's life. People close to the case were reported to have said that "evangelicals were the first to take a stand in their support."[20] It is clear that the case helped to strengthen the bond between both groups who appear to continue to have a growing relationship.

The political fallout continues. It has been reported that Michael Schiavo, who "remains furious at lawmakers in Tallahassee and Washington who intervened in [his wife's] case,"[21] has been working though TerriPAC, a political action committee that he established, to fund and campaign against the politicians who tried to stop the removal of Terri Schiavo's feeding tube. He offered help to James Webb, the successful Democratic challenger to Senator George Allen of Virginia; Claire McCaskill, the successful Democratic challenger to Senator Jim Talent of Missouri; State Representative Jim Davis, who ran to replace Governor Jeb Bush in Florida; and Ned Lamont, in his unsuccessful quest to unseat Joseph Lieberman for his Senate seat in Connecticut. There are rumors that Schiavo has been asked to run for public office but that he has declined. He has also written a book entitled *Terri: The Truth*.[22] In yet another response, the Schindlers have established a foundation called the Terri Schindler Schiavo Foundation Center for Health Care Ethics to protect "the rights of disabled, elderly and vulnerable citizens against care rationing, euthanasia and medical killing."[23]

Questions of life and death still remain the critical values that divide people in the United States, not just morally, but politically as well. They do so because they are issues that lack inherent, authentic compromise—

demanding pragmatic solutions in concrete situations. During the Republican primary debates of 2007, Wolf Blitzer of CNN asked the presidential candidates what was the most important moral issue in America today—and they all answered it was still abortion. That response continued to show that there is no escaping the chronic quandary of American politics: how to craft a political position that adequately reflects the conflicting moral positions of voters today, or to find a way to reconcile the politics of values with personal conscience.

Which Values? Education

The public education system was one of the places where the values wars began to fester during the 1960s. At that time, many evangelical Baptists and Methodists began to feel a sense of political unease, particularly as they perceived certain Supreme Court rulings as a challenge to two of their most important social values: education and religious liberty. These had both been intertwined with the significant Protestant contribution to the establishment of the common school in America—particularly in the context of curriculum and values instruction.

The invocation of the Lord's Prayer for daily guidance, the reading of the King James version of the Bible, and the traditional use of Christian examples for living reflected the influence of Protestantism in American education. Indeed, they helped to create a *de facto* Christian system functioning within the required public one. So, when the Supreme Court struck down the practice of state sponsorship of prayer and Bible reading in the public schools in *Engle v. Vitale*,[24] *Abington Township School District v. Schempp*,[25] and *Murray v. Curlett*[26] in the 1960s, evangelicals began to believe that they had to unite to save America's schools from godless liberals.

Part of that fight revolved around continued challenges to public school curriculums, particularly with regard to the debate between the biblical story of creation and the scientific approach to evolution. Having been vindicated in the Scopes case in 1925, liberals believed that Darwin's theories would forever remain the accepted norm in teaching biology in public schools. But since that decision, evangelicals have steadfastly challenged the Court's holding even after it struck down creationism in *Epperson v. Arkansas*[27] and *Edwards v. Aguillard*.[28]

States such as Pennsylvania, Kansas, Georgia, and Utah are still fighting the creationism battles in order to retain a semblance of the biblical curriculum in science classes. For example, in Cobb County, Georgia, members of the conservative school board insisted, as late as 2004, that anti-evolution stickers with the message that "evolution is a theory, not a fact," be placed on all textbooks. Subsequently, Judge Clarence Cooper of the Federal District Court ruled that the message was simply a way to convey an endorsement of religion and held that the stickers were to be removed.[29]

In Kansas, the school board went even further. New standards were voted to define the notion of "science." In 2005, the Board of Education attempted to broaden the definition by saying that science does not have to be explicitly limited to natural explanations. It also voted to retain its recommendations that teachers instruct students on the specific questionable points in evolutionary theory when they teach it. Minnesota, New Mexico, Ohio, and Pennsylvania continue to allow some form of this kind of critique of evolution as well.

A more recent attack on evolution has been mounted by evangelicals through their support of "intelligent design." The Institute for Creation Research in California credits Dr. Phillip E. Johnson as being its founder and marks the publication of his book, *Darwin on Trial,* in the early 1990s as the basis and justification for a new understanding of creationism. Johnson is supported in his intelligent design theory by the Discovery Institute in Seattle, which funds much of his work. The scientist and his followers contend, in the most simple of terms, that every watch must have a watchmaker, and that by extension, the universe must also have some intelligent force that has directed its creation and development. Intelligent design theory also has the support of Pope Benedict XVI and the Dalai Lama, both of whom reportedly feel a sense of "unease with Darwin."[30]

In 2005, the battle between the modern forces of creationism and evolution were joined in Pennsylvania. At that time, the Dover School Board voted six to three to require ninth grade biology students to be told that there was a controversy over the theory of evolution, that intelligent design was a competing theory, and that books on the subject were available at the school library.[31] In response, several parents in the Dover district brought suit against the school board and argued that intelligent design was simply creationism masquerading as science, that it was inherently religious, and that it had no place in a science class. Before the case could be heard, however, the conservative school board was voted out of office.

But, the many liberal public interest groups that had already joined in the legal fray still wanted a judicial decision that would definitively decide whether or not intelligent design was constitutional. Among them, the ACLU and the Americans United for Separation of Church and State filed motions opposing intelligent design in the U.S. District Court for the Middle District of Pennsylvania, while the Thomas More Law Center, a Christian public law firm, took up the position in favor of it.

In the subsequent case, *Kitzmiller v. Dover Area School District*,[32] Judge John E. Jones III, ruled that the Dover School Board's mandate to its teachers was unconstitutional. In his decision, Jones maintained that intelligent design was simply the child of creationism rather than scientific theory; that it invoked supernatural causation, was flawed and illogical and without merit in the scientific community.

While evangelicals have been disappointed in the curricular loss over the battle to teach intelligent design, they have continued to challenge public school policies on two other teaching fronts: the right of schools to provide what they believe to be "liberal" sex education and tolerance of nontraditional sexual orientation. These issues, seen in broad terms of morality and within the purview of parental guidance, have impelled evangelicals and other social conservatives to become involved in the political process to win control of local school boards, and in turn, to gain influence over the design and budgeting of curricula and specific programs.

Indeed, education was one of the values in contention among conservative voters in the 2000 and 2004 elections, ultimately giving impetus to candidate Bush's support for school choice during his first run for the presidency. His subsequent rejection of the policy, though, and his work with Senator Ted Kennedy (D-MA) for the more pragmatic and bipartisan law known as "No Child Left Behind" gave the impression that the White House and congressional Republicans were seeking creative ways to reform the American education system. The current policy, however, still remains fraught with testing and reporting problems, leaving social and religious conservatives to continue to pursue other avenues to provide better instruction for their children.

One of the policy strategies pursued by evangelicals is coalition building among a variety of educational reformers. Most favor authorizing the use of public money for private instruction—particularly for parents who want to home school their children or send them to specialized, charter, or magnet schools.

This movement gained momentum during the 1990s and still has legs today. It had a variety of options, from tuition tax credits to the use of vouchers for educational fees that would allow parents the ability to shop around for the right school for their children. The argument behind it is quite simple: Americans have choices of every kind of product—cars, refrigerators, clothing, houses, and even lipstick. But—one of the most important consumer products of all, education, is an absolute monopoly. It assumes that "one size fits all" and that government bureaucrats know better than parents what is best for their children.

In 1999, Hubert Morken and this author analyzed this policy alternative in the book, *The Politics of School Choice*.[33] Having interviewed and surveyed leading educational reformers in the United States, it was found that there were a wide variety of educational and political approaches to school choice in different parts of the country—a disparate movement that had the potential to alter public education as we know it today. The spectrum of responses on the school choice continuum went from retaining the status quo to giving each family a certain amount of public educational funds or "financial credits" that could be spent at any school, anywhere, for the education of its children. In Cleveland, for example, students were given vouchers and were allowed to use them, even in a parochial school, if their families were below a certain poverty level. That principle was tested in *Zelman v. Simmons-Harris*,[34] and in a narrow decision, the Supreme Court held that under certain conditions a state may provide such financial assistance in failing school districts where students have no other options for a decent education.

In response to schools that do a poor job at educating and schools that do not teach the values that families want their children to learn, parents are increasingly instructing their children at home. They are tested by the particular school district in which they live; some let the home schooled students attend the local public school for scientific experiments in laboratories and to participate in extracurricular activities when the school day is done. In other districts there is a total separation among the different types of education. But, in the home school situation, parents control the venue, the curriculum, and the values instruction of their own children.

In some cities, such as New York, Chicago, Jersey City, Indianapolis, and Washington, D.C., wealthy professionals have established scholarship funds to supplement student tuitions at nonpublic schools. Some states have attempted to do the same thing using public funds.

The state of Florida, for example, had experimented with an Opportunity Scholarship Plan that would be implemented through the public sector. It allowed the use of public monies to be expended to help families pay for whatever kind of education they wanted (including private/parochial school) if their children were in school districts that had failed to make adequate progress after state performance audits. In 2006, the state supreme court decided that such funding was illegal[35] because it allowed the money to be used in any school—private, parochial, or public ones—and that such funding essentially subverted the public system.

Magnet schools and charter schools have been the most successful means by which parents have gained greater school choice. Such schools are technically under state control and are considered as public schools, but they operate within state financial guidelines and with public monies. They have specialized and/or experimental curriculums and a highly competitive, selective student body. In many cases, there have been fierce political battles over establishing charter schools, as the National Education Association and others see them as diluting the financial resources, faculty, and the best students from the public system.

Politically, the views of social and religious conservatives about the value of school choice are being implemented quietly now through the Bush administration's turnaround and renewed support for educational options. This is being done, for example, by its support for charter schools in New Orleans. Secretary of Education Margaret Spellings announced in June 2006 that the federal government would give $24 million to the state of Louisiana to develop such schools in the aftermath of Hurricane Katrina.[36] Doubling the amount of money that the state received initially after the tragedy, the federal funds were supposed to be used to "jump-start the state's educational recovery" and provide a "laboratory for the widespread use of charter schools,"[37] particularly in the dysfunctional public school system in New Orleans.

Thus, the freedom to choose an effective—as well as a values-oriented— education remains a vital part of the social and religious conservatives' agenda and a matter that continues to be pursued by many local Republicans and other party candidates for national office. Concomitantly, concerns over curriculum, public funding, and the teaching of Christian morality are still major considerations for values voters and will play a part when they walk into the voting booth and choose political candidates for public office in the future.

Which Values? Marriage

Finally, the need for traditional family values remains a major concern of social and religious conservatives who only accept a biblical definition of marriage. They perceive it as being assaulted in the courts due to the fact that Massachusetts recognizes gay marriage and that a number of other states have legalized civil unions or some type of domestic partnership. Having galvanized evangelicals and others, this issue has given rise to numerous organizations committed to defending marriage. The most significant of these is Focus on the Family, founded in 1977 by Dr. James Dobson, an evangelical psychologist.

His organization is committed to six principles to advance traditional family values. These consist of recognizing the preeminence of evangelism, the permanence of marriage, the value of children, the sanctity of human life, the importance of social responsibility, and the value of male and female. The organization's website explains that in response to the challenge of changing roles within the workforce and the family, Focus on the Family helps "to reconcile the pressures for careers, liberation, and material goods with Christian principles to encourage men and women to embrace their traditional family roles."[38]

The Family Research Council grew out of Focus on the Family and works politically to influence public policy, legislation, and judicial decisions to maintain traditional family values. Since definitions of marriage have been reconsidered judicially, the institution is no longer understood, *de facto*, to be between a man and a woman. In fact, Massachusetts broke new ground in 2005 when it legalized gay marriage, prompting a number of other judicial challenges since then. Several states have adjudicated the issue, with Washington and New York both opposing any changes in the traditional institution of marriage. Just recently, however, the issue regarding the legality of gay marriage again resurfaced in Massachusetts with the legislature defeating a proposed constitutional amendment to return to a traditional legal definition of marriage. The measure needed fifty votes to be defeated, but lost 151 to 45.

In 2006, Washington state's Supreme Court upheld the validity of its Defense of Marriage Act banning same sex marriages. The court ruled that its decision was supported by the essential need for procreation; a decision that was hailed by the Faith and Freedom Network and Foundation, a religious interest group within the state. In New York, the state's highest court also found that century-old laws limiting marriage to a man and a woman were based on legitimate social goals, primarily the protection of the welfare of children. The court held that the plaintiffs, the [American] Civil Liberties Union and the Civil Liberties Union of New York, which consolidated four separate cases, did not prove that this restriction was "irrational . . . [or]based solely on ignorance and prejudice against homosexuals."[39] The Family Research Council filed an *amicus* brief in the case as well.

In 2006 the Georgia Supreme Court also overruled its lower courts and reinstated a ban on same-sex marriage.[40] The Vermont and Connecticut courts have held that the legal benefits of marriage should be provided to same-sex couples and have led to legislation legalizing "civil unions" in those states.[41]

Traditional family values are a means to garner political support for both political parties and an essential component of the politics of values. Politicians such as Bill Clinton and George W. Bush, taking different values positions, know the importance of one of the first tactics of the politics of values: how to appeal to large segments of the population. Clinton's support for the Defense of Marriage Act was a positive stance, and although Bush's opposition to gay marriage was a negative one, he was able to parlay the moral divide to attack "activist judges and some local officials [who] have made an aggressive attempt to redefine marriage in recent years."[42] Further, the Bush administration has been accused of using the issue of gay marriage politically to garner the support of black ministers who are "lukewarm" about tolerance for gays and are in a position to influence black voters.[43]

> The debate about homosexuality that has roiled predominantly white mainline churches for years has gradually seeped into African-American congregations, threatening their unity, finances and, in some cases, their existence.[44]

The question of homosexuality now also implies questions about the value of traditional marriage, families, and stability that must be reconciled within many black evangelical and mainline churches. Committed to the Bible, its teachings, and congregational/individual interpretations of these issues, black churches have been in the forefront of fighting for personal liberation, civil rights, and political equality throughout American history. To deny the same opportunities to homosexuals is a source of moral strife within black congregations, causing a splintering among parishioners who are conflicted both spiritually and politically—and caught within the politics of values.

The fight over what marriage really is, culturally, socially, and religiously, may be decided by the government in the end. The Senate has been attempting to open this matter for debate, raising concerns that same-sex marriage and/or civil unions will raise new questions about the legality of homosexual relationships as well as gay adoption, custody battles, divorce, and health and death benefits. Twenty-seven states have adopted legislation recognizing marriage as a relationship between a man and a woman, and the question can be expected to turn up as propositions and/or initiatives in other states in the 2008 presidential election.

Trying to Make Sense of It All

In many ways, the rise of ethnic diversity, religious pluralism, multiculturalism, globalization, and the terrorism of 9/11 have all helped to nurture the growing conservative social and political culture of the last quarter of a century. In its wake is left an eroding liberal one. And, while people try to simplify the reasons for the vast change that has occurred and continues to take place in America today, the reasons are so complex that trying to understand it can only occur in small doses, if at all.

Diversity is one of the reasons why the current conservative culture is so much more appealing to large segments of the American population. While everything else is in flux, conservatism is coherent, optimistic, and antimodern. It is an attempt to return to a culture that is simple, unified, secure, and known. It is, indeed, ideological comfort food for many within society who are hungry for the good old days, that old-time religion, and the way we were.

Obviously, the drive for this return to the past is built on values that are the direct opposite of many of the beliefs that have propelled America forward and that have created the divided and disconcerting current cultural climate in the United States. It is also, in the minds of many, the only way to stave off the excesses and abuses that American liberal thinking has created along the way.

While there are many reasons why the American ideological divide between liberalism and conservatism has occurred, this book will make the case that a shift from socially pragmatic to values-oriented politics is the result of three critical factors. The first is the fruition of a mature, unified, aggressive, and conservative religious culture in America. This is characterized by an all-pervasive, public way of thinking and acting that is optimistic—based on a coherent message of the good news of Jesus Christ and the development of a haven for those who have felt alienated by the prevailing materialism and secularism of postmodern America. The second reason for the ideological divide is due to the increased involvement of conservative religious groups in the American political process. No longer simply trying to find their place in American society, evangelicals in particular have consciously and organizationally decided to participate in the political process in order to advance their traditional "values" agenda. And third, the election of public officials and the appointment of government personnel committed to these same conservative and religious values have created a *changed relationship between religion and government,* in the guise of traditional values intertwined with public policies designed to change the principles of American social and political culture.

One of the unintended consequences of using values for political purposes is that individual moral concerns have supplanted the public agenda. By using values-based politics, officials are advancing policy choices and making decisions based on inviolable, sacred religious principles rather than on political ones whose very essence is based on compromise, pragmatism, and social justice. Today's politics, based as they are on values, have become a zero sum game—if my values win, yours lose. There is no middle ground on which political principles can develop and mature. Toleration is eroding. Respect for diverse ideas is lessening, and the American public is the loser—losing its collective ability and will to work together to bring the nation to a higher level of strength and unity. Yes, everything is different now, but the critical question is whether or not the politics of values will enable the United States to attain a higher level of social justice for the attainment of the common good—at home and abroad.

Notes

1. E. J. Dionne, Jr., "The End of the Right?" *Washington Post,* August 4, 2006, A17.

2. *Stenberg v. Carhart* 530 U.S. 914 (2000).

3. Robin Toner, "Cheney Addresses Anti-Abortion Group," *New York Times,* April 21, 2004, A21.

4. Sheryl Gay Stolberg and Carl Hulse, "Negotiators Add Abortion Clause to Spending Bill," *New York Times,* November 20, 2004, A1.

5. Phoebe Connelly, "Contraception in the Crosshairs," *In These Times,* March 26, 2006, www.inthesetimes.com/article/2558.

6. Associated Press, "Commissioner Under Fire for Vioxx Scandal, 'Morning After' Pill Delay," September 23, 2005, www.msnbc.msn.com/id/9455426.

7. Dana Bash and Deirdre Walsh, "Bush Vetoes Embryonic Stem-Cell Bill," September 4, 2006, www.CNN.com.

8. Robin Toner and Carl Hulse, "A Family's Battle Brings Life's End into Discussion," *New York Times,* March 20, 2005, Al.

9. Abby Goodnough and Carl Hulse, "Judge in Florida Rejects Effort by House," *New York Times,* March 19, 2005, A1.

10. Goodnough and Hulse, "Judge in Florida Rejects Effort by House," A12.

11. Carl Hulse and David D. Kirkpartick, "Moving Quickly, Senate Approves Schiavo Measure," *New York Times,* March 21, 2005, A14.

12. Sheryl Gay Stolberg, "A Collision of Disparate Forces May Be Reshaping American Law," *New York Times,* April 1, 2005, A18.

13. Carl Hulse and David D. Kirkpatrick, "Even Death Does Not Quiet Harsh Political Fight," *New York Times,* April 1, 2005, A1.

14. See the full story on this in David D. Kirkpatrick and Sheryl Gay Stolberg, "How Family's Cause Reached the Halls of Congress," *New York Times,* March 22, 2005, A1.

15. Adam Nagourney, "In a Polarizing Case, Jeb Bush Cements His Political Stature," *New York Times,* March 25, 2005, A1.

16. See *Gonzalez v. Oregon,* 546 U.S. 243 (2006).

17. John Paul II, "Life Sustaining Treatments and Vegetative State: Scientific Advances and Ethical Dilemmas," March 20, 2004, www.vatican.va.

18. "Evangelicals and Catholics Together," *First Things* 43 (May 1994): 15–22.

19. Laurie Goodstein, "Schiavo Case Highlights Alliance between Catholics and Evangelicals," *New York Times,* March 24, 2005, A20.

20. Goodstein, "Schiavo Case."

21. Abby Goodnough, "Husband Takes Schiavo Fight Back to Political Arena," *New York Times,* August 16, 2006, A15.

22. Michael Schiavo, with Michael Hirsh, *Terri: The Truth* (New York: Dutton, 2006).

23. Goodnough, "Husband Takes Schiavo Fight Back to Political Arena."

24. See *Engle v. Vitale* 370 U.S. 421 (1962). It disallowed state sponsorship of prayers in public schools.

25. See *Abington Township School District v. Schempp* 374 U.S. 203 (1963). It disallowed state sponsorship of Bible reading and recitation of the Lord's Prayer.

26. *Murray v. Curlett* was combined into the analysis of the *Abington* case.

27. See *Epperson v. Arkansas* 393 U.S. 97 (1968).

28. See *Edwards v. Aguillard* 482 U.S. 578 (1987).

29. *Selman v. Cobb County School District.* Civil Action No. 1:02-cv-2325-cc (December 20, 2005).

30. George Johnson, "For the Anti-Evolutionists, Hope in High Places," *New York Times Week in Review,* October 3, 2005, wk3.

31. Specifically, *Of Pandas and People* published by the Foundation for Thought and Ethics.

32. See *Kitzmiller v. Dover Area School District,* Case No. 04cv2688, Cited as: 2005 WL 578974 (MD Pa. 2005), Decided December 20, 2005.

33. Hubert Morken and Jo Renee Formicola, *The Politics of School Choice* (Lanham, Maryland: Rowman & Littlefield, 1999).

34. See *Zelman v. Simmons-Harris,* 536 U.S. 639 (2002).

35. See *Holmes v. Bush* FSC Case Nos. SC04-23323/2324/2325 (2006).

36. Susan Saulny, "U.S. Gives Charter Schools a Big Push in New Orleans," *New York Times,* June 31, 2006, A19.

37. Saulny, "U.S. Gives Charter Schools a Big Push."

38. www.focusonthefamily.com/aboutus/A000000408.

39. See *Hernandez v. Robles,* 2006 NY Slip Opinion 05239. Decided July 6, 2006.

40. Georgia State Supreme Court S06A1574, *Perdue v. O'Kelley et al.*

41. In Vermont civil unions were held to be legal by its state Supreme Court in 2000 and have been institutionalized by the legislature. In February of 2007, however, H275 was introduced in the legislature as a step to legalize gay marriage. In Connecticut, the state legislature legalized civil unions without a court order in 2005.

42. Jim Rutenberg, "Bush Calls for an Amendment Banning Same-Sex Nuptials," *New York Times,* June 4, 2006, A30.

43. Yolanda Young, "Black Clergy's Silence Hurts Gays," *USA Today,* March 10, 2006, A16.

44. Neela Banerjee, "For Some Black Pastors, Accepting Gay Members Means Losing Others," *New York Times,* March 27, 2007, A12.

2

The Nexus: Evangelicals, Social Conservatives, and Republicans Come Together

Introduction

IN HIS BOOK *American Theocracy*, Kevin Phillips characterizes the role of religion in American politics today with two words: "*widely underestimated.*"[1] Indeed, regardless of what the press says, or hopes, it is safe to say that religion is alive and well and plays a critical role in every aspect of life in the United States today.

The Pew Forum on Religion and Public Life, which gathers statistical data, especially demographic information, reports that 76.7 percent, or 208 million American adults, overwhelmingly self-identify as Christians (see table 2.1 for a breakdown by denomination). Non-Christians include Jews (1.4 percent), Muslims (0.5 percent), Hindus (0.4 percent) and Unitarian Universalists (0.3 percent). Surprising, those who said they had no religion, or did not declare a religion, were only 14.2 percent of the population.[2]

It is easy to see then that Christians, because of their sheer numbers, would be able to have the most significant impact on politics and public policy in the United States. Add to that their economic clout, cultural influence, and history, and it is possible to understand why many people claim that, for all intents and purposes, America is a Christian country.

Those who look deeper, however, see that even with their huge population and social influence, Christians are still unable to control the entire political process. Protestants themselves are composed of a number of different faith

TABLE 2.1
U.S. Demographic Profile

Christian Subgroup	Percentage	Population (million)
Protestant	49.8	103.58
Roman Catholic	24.5	50.96
Mormon	1.3	2.70
Jehovah's Witness	0.6	1.25
Eastern Orthodox	0.3	0.62
Other	0.2	0.42

Source: The Pew Forum: "United States Religious Demographic Profile." Accessed at
http://pewforum.org/world-affairs/countries/?CountryID=222.

communities, many of which are splintered for theological and ideological reasons. Catholics, who represent the largest single denomination in the United States, traditionally do not vote as a bloc due to the wide diversity of adherents in their church. While the rest of the religious groups are essentially too small to have a critical impact on all of the divergent public policy issues that exist in the United States, they bring the element of pluralism to the political debate and offer a counterbalance to Christianity in the United States.

Evangelicals, alone, have been able to use their growing numbers to make a real impact on American society and the political process. Although their numbers are hard to discern because of how they self-identify, the one thing that the last twenty years has shown is that evangelicals are united, clear, and certain, not just in their religious beliefs, but in their political views as well. This chapter looks at how their values became the basis for a religious-political symbiosis in America, one that has flourished in spite of the culture wars, legal strictures, and the principle of the separation of church and state.

The Religious Connection

To explain the changed relationship between politics and values, it is important to understand the influence of *religion* in American society today. In fact, there is almost general consensus that this is the underlying phenomenon responsible for the red and blue mentalities that dominate political thinking in the United States now.

No discussion of politics and values today can get beyond one sentence without mentioning either the "Christian Right" or the "evangelicals." Both terms are often confused and tell very little of the back stories that have contributed to their growing mystique in the United States.

It's hard to start at the beginning, because religion in America is such a long and complicated chronicle. However, the bare bones of the story start with the Spanish. Their missionaries were quick to follow Columbus and the conquistadores; plant the seeds of Catholicism in the western part of the New World, convert the indigenous people to Christianity, and instill loyalty to the crown. The Puritans who came seeking religious freedom in 1620 settled in Massachusetts Bay and ironically established a colony based on their own tightly circumscribed religious principles. Only members of their church could vote and hold office, while all individuals were taxed to support their church and pay for their schools.

Economic incentives lured other English settlers to establish colonies as well, but whether for religious or financial reasons, all adopted a way of life in the colonies based on the teachings of Jesus and the scriptures, belief in individualism, and respect for the consent of the governed.

The English colonists encouraged hard work and adopted the Protestant work ethic, recognizing it as the basis of capitalism, financial success, and a sign of being predestined to eventually be called to heaven as part of God's elect. They represented white, Anglo-Saxon thought, culture, and theology, all of which continue to be represented in the various Protestant denominations of today—along with the rich tradition of the historically black Christian churches that emerged after the Civil War as well.

John C. Green, a well-known political scientist and expert in religion and politics, claims that within American religious history, Protestantism has gone through a number of evolutionary stages trying to find its appropriate place in American political life.[3] According to him, the first stage is what he calls "movement politics," or that period of time when Protestantism attempted to challenge the legitimacy of most political institutions. The second stage was one of "quiescent politics," or that time when Protestantism detached itself from political institutions and attempted to create its own culture and sense of values. And the third stage, according to Green, was a time he calls "regularized politics," that is, when Protestantism attempted to function within established political institutions and processes for policy advantages. What happened in each of these stages helps us to understand the phenomenon that is evangelical politics today.

During much of the early twentieth century Protestantism was in competition with Catholicism for resources and power in the United States. This revolved around Catholic efforts to challenge the *de facto* Protestant educational system that was synonymous with public education. Establishing schools and colleges of their own, Catholics lived in ethnic ghettos, were loyal to a foreign pope, and obeyed their clergy on matters of religious and public policy. As their numbers began to grow with increased immigration at the turn of the century, competition for government "favor" became more pronounced as Protestantism began to fragment.

Some denominations were able to adapt their theologies more easily to modern ideas. Those groups came to be known as "mainline" Protestant churches: the Methodist, Episcopalian, Presbyterian, and Church of Christ Congregational denominations. Originally predominant in the northeast, these churches were led by the best of educated men, who in many cases were political as well as religious leaders. They espoused new ideas, such as the Social Gospel, which accepted notions of public welfare and economic reforms.

A second offshoot of mainline Protestantism was "fundamentalism." It encompassed those who literally followed the biblical message in their daily and political lives. Their ranks were peopled with individuals who were committed to personal transformation and a dedication to preserving Christian civilization in the United States.

Most fundamentalist Protestant groups had emerged by the end of the eighteenth century. Baptist preachers in particular followed settlers to frontier areas and worked for little pay. They held meetings rather than services. They appealed to those who stressed individuality and rejected the European notion of "confessional" Christianity, which is the government profession of a specific religion. Eventually the more fundamentalist Protestants emerged as Southern Baptists, Pentecostals, and members of the Holiness Churches of Christ, the Church of the Nazarene, and the Assemblies of God. They developed their own identities and separated from more progressive, mainline Protestant churches. Later, Seventh-Day Adventists, Mormons, and Jehovah's Witnesses, along with "holiness" Methodists, grew into an organizationally disparate, but different, group of conservative religious groups as well.

Fundamentalist religious groups functioned primarily in the rural areas of the South and America's heartland, each being led by a minister who carried out social and religious duties for the advancement of his congregants. David Gushee, a theologian, professor, and expert on Protestantism, claims that fundamentalist involvement in politics was seen "as a worldly, or even sinful, activity."[4]

Religiously and culturally, they opposed many modern ideas. They even became politically involved to challenge the teaching of evolution in the public schools. Fundamentalists worked to pass legislation on the state level to support creationism, and by the 1920s were strong enough to get William Jennings Bryan, the former Democratic presidential candidate, to bring suit against the state of Tennessee for teaching evolution in its schools.

The Scopes Monkey Trial, as it has come to be known, was the high-water mark of fundamentalist political involvement in the United States up to that point. However, when the case was decided and the court allowed the teaching of evolution, it became a profound blow to their religious beliefs and political activity. The trial ushered in a "period of political detachment," an "intense focus on individual redemption," and an emphasis on building fundamentalist religious institutions—a pragmatic means by which to influence American culture in the future.[5]

It was this notion of establishing institutions of their own that gave rise to the third prong of Protestantism: the evangelicals. They were active mostly in the north, and they began to coalesce around the need for greater Bible study.

It was the Reverend J. Elwin Wright of the New England Fellowship who brought many northern evangelical congregants from his region together with fundamentalists. By inviting influential religious leaders such as the Reverends Will Houghton, Charles Fuller, Walter Maier, and Ralph T. Davis to speak at summer Bible conferences, Wright developed a network of similarly committed ministers who shared his vision of a unified evangelistic movement.

This interaction spurred Houghton, the president of the Moody Bible Institute in Chicago, to bring together over one hundred evangelical religious leaders for a national conference in 1942. These included Harold J. Ockenga, Stephen W. Paine, and Robert G. Lee, ministers who sought to organize and articulate the message of Jesus in a united voice.

Eventually a group of 147 ministers signed off on a document in which they committed to work together for the common good, thus founding the National Association of Evangelicals (NAE) in April 1942. They started a major evangelical movement, bringing together religious fundamentalists as well as social conservatives in America. Reenforced by moderate thinkers such as Carl Henry, who brought fresh ideas to the religious table, the NAE began to gain momentum in the evangelical community.

Its leaders stressed social engagement rather than separation and established a blueprint for a political agenda. It included a strong sense of American nationalism and the rejection of Communism during the period of the Cold War. Both commitments were outgrowths of biblical notions of political loyalty and obedience to secular power. Spurred on by other evangelists such as Billy Graham, new periodicals such as *Christianity Today*, and emerging religious/political organizations such as the Christian Freedom Foundation, evangelicals were on the social, cultural, and political rise in America after World War II.

Today the NAE claims to represent from 52 to 60 (depending on various reports and time frames) like-minded denominations. The organization works in partnership with religious coalitions, commissions, affiliated churches, and schools. While it is difficult to state definitively how many evangelicals there are in the United States, sociologists think they represent about 25 to 30 percent of the population, a percentage that could include up to about 80 million people.

Their political beliefs are predicated on evangelical religious beliefs: the literal interpretation of the Bible; the need for personal transformation, religious revivalism, and the turning away from sin; the enduring, healing salvation of Christ; the apocalyptic belief in His second coming; and the obligation of each individual to evangelize and witness to Jesus's message in every aspect of one's life. Its tenets remain rooted in a credo that accepts the "good news" of the Gospel, its attendant teachings, and the need to spread Jesus' message—everywhere, even in the political arena.

During the 1960s the evangelicals opposed the election of John F. Kennedy, the civil rights movement, and women's liberation. Their ministers rejected the "God is dead" thesis, the use of psychedelic drugs, and the social revolution that was occurring in every segment of American life. Supreme Court rulings against prayer and Bible reading in public school, along with the 1973 ruling in favor of a women's right to choose in *Roe v. Wade*,[6] soundly awakened evangelicals to the world of politics.

A missionary zeal to communicate the literal and optimistic word of the Lord has been the basis for informing and directing all aspects of the evangelical public, private, and political life. In fact, today, some evangelicals even believe that America is destined to become a Christian nation and that they must be personally committed to spread the word of Jesus to non-Christians at home as well as abroad. Thus, foreign as well as domestic policy and the values on which their policies are designed and implemented are important to the advancement of the religious and political agenda of evangelicals.

The election of Jimmy Carter in 1976 was the first campaign in America in which a born-again Christian won the White House. It seemed like the perfect opportunity to inculcate fundamentalist Christian values into U.S. politics, to overturn Roe, and to get the country back to its traditional, biblical core.

Carter's commitment to a foreign policy based on human rights originally appealed to traditionalist Protestants who hoped that conservative, Christian values would pervade American international relations. But Carter's inability to find success in dealing with the Soviet Union and Iran disappointed many traditional religious groups. His failure to advance pro-life issues on the public agenda, curtail calls for social change, and support a more rigorous respect for religion in American public life caused a negative reaction to the Democratic president in many constituencies.

Because Carter could not deliver, evangelicals and other religious traditionalists realized that they had to step up to the plate to save America's eroding values. Among those willing to lead was Phyllis Schlafly, a conservative Catholic woman who had written the bestselling *A Choice Not an Echo* in 1964. Among the values she fostered were those of the traditional family, a response to the growing feminist movement during the decade. In 1972, she founded the Eagle Forum, a national organization of citizens who participated as volunteers in policymaking. A Phi Beta Kappa lawyer with a masters degree in political science from Harvard, Schlafly led the political fight against the Equal Rights Amendment, becoming a heroine to many women committed to traditional family values and their gender roles in American society at the time.

The woman described as "Karl Rove's Godmother" by *American Heritage Magazine*[7] has published the *Phyllis Schlafly Report* for the past forty years, has been syndicated in over one hundred newspapers, and has done commentary on over 460 radio stations. She continues her weekly radio program "Phyllis Schlafly Live" on forty-five stations currently, at the age of eighty-one.

James Dobson, mentioned previously, who also believed that most societal problems were a result of the breakdown of the American family, founded Focus on the Family in 1977 as a nonpolitical group designed to foster traditional family values. However, it eventually became political as it started calling for the formation of community committees in local churches to deal with family values at the grassroots, political level.

As Focus on the Family became more political, it established the Family Research Council in Washington, D.C., under the leadership of Gary Bauer. The political activist entered the presidential primary in 2000 in an attempt to bring concern for traditional family values into the public debate. Since then, the Family Research Council has established the Alliance Defense Fund and Focus on Family Action. Dobson remains extremely active, having recently held a values-voter summit in Washington D.C. and criticizing the Republican Party for failing to deliver on the evangelical agenda.

Jerry Falwell also made a major contribution by moving evangelicals into politics. A Baptist minister who originally founded his fundamentalist church in an abandoned bottling plant in 1956, Falwell was able to grow it into the 22,000-member Thomas Road Baptist Church. He televised his ministry on the Old Time Gospel Hour and established Liberty University in Virginia, Christian elementary schools, homes for unwed mothers, and a shelter for alcoholics.

Falwell had energized the political debate during the Carter administration by attempting to create an activist role for Protestant traditionalists in politics. In 1979, approached by Paul Weyrich, a young Catholic social conservative, Falwell agreed to lead a coalition of individuals who believed that America's morality was under attack. They were, according to Falwell and Weyrich, the Moral Majority—members of American society whose values were being eroded, in part, due to their own lack of political engagement on moral matters.

Establishing the Moral Majority, then, was supposed to give support to religious denominations that wanted to pursue a moral agenda in American politics. Falwell's organization was the first to call on pastors to organize their congregants on the grassroots level and to get them to register to vote. With the help of Richard Viguerie, another Catholic, the Moral Majority highlighted the voting records on moral issues of elected officials and began the use of direct mailings to make candidates' positions known to the public.

Other religious organizations with political commitments were beginning to come into existence around the same time, too. The National Christian Action Council emerged in 1977, Christian Voice in 1979, the Religious Roundtable in 1980, the National Affairs Briefing in 1980, the Council on Revival in 1980, the Council for National Policy in 1981, the American Coalition for Traditional Values in 1984, were but a few.

Thus, the establishment of evangelical and evangelical-like organizations began to become influential within American politics. Shored up by the rise of televangelism, charismatic preachers, and the eventual presidential bids of the Reverends Pat Robertson and Jesse Jackson in 1988, traditional family values, along with religion and politics, began to develop a symbiotic relationship. Each began to feed off the other.

Robertson's candidacy was the start of the political involvement of evangelicals in the political process as national *candidates*. Many were already running for local office as "stealth" or "under the radar" contenders, hiding their true identities and values out of fear that they would cost them elections. Robertson's overwhelming loss seemed to bear this out, and on the surface, it appeared to have stunted the viability of other aspiring evangelical candidates who might consider running for national office.

Evangelical involvement in the American political process also took a direct hit from the problems brought about by clerical scandals, like those involving Jimmy Swaggart and James Bakker. Further, rumored legal reprisals for alleged allegations of partisan political activity, disallowed by the IRS for religious organizations with a 50l(c)3 status, also led to the demise of the Moral Majority. By the end of the decade, traditionalist Protestant political activism was in shambles.

In 1989, Robertson and others picked up the political pieces of the Moral Majority and energized other traditional, religious activists by launching the Christian Coalition. Its mission was, and remains—according to its website—the development and defense of America's godly heritage.

Originally organized by Ralph Reed, Robertson's presidential campaign manager, the Christian Coalition was an attempt to offer people of faith a way to become actively involved in shaping public policy. It attempted to do this primarily through education, supporting a pro-family agenda, and raising awareness about the critical issues facing American society.

Today, the organization is essentially involved in voter education, issuing voter guides, lobbying, holding grassroots training schools, hosting events, and organizing community activities. But it has also been instrumental in serving as a model of religious involvement in the political process by giving birth to such public law firms as The American Center for Law and Justice. Currently, the Christian Coalition is also involved in outreach to Mormons, blacks, populists, and others who accept most of their religious principles.

Thus, it is possible to see how traditional values are tied to religion, particularly evangelical Christianity. But, the nexus is not complete. Those values are connected to *ideologies* as well.

The Ideological Connection

Generally speaking, an ideology is a worldview, a means of providing a picture of what the world is and what it should be, a means of organizing complexities into a simple, cohesive pattern of understanding.[8] In political terms, an ideology is the lens through which we view, filter, and interpret our support or opposition to government actions, policies, legislation, and politics.

Many social movements in the United States and abroad have been tied to ideologies: Communism to Marxism; fascism to national socialism; feminism to women's liberation; civil rights to black politics; communitarianism to liberation theology, jihad to radical Islam. Despite all these worldviews, some historians, such as Francis Fukuyama,[9] have argued that ideology has come as far as possible in the form liberal democracy, while Daniel Bell,[10] who had argued that ideology is dead, has now reconsidered his position and claimed that the ascendance of new beliefs has resurrected Pandora from her ideological box.

One of the assertions among political theorists today is that we are living in a postmodern age, a time that is undermining notions of truth, human rights, gender, nationality, race, ethnicity, and religion. Different cultures are bringing new connotations as well as definitions to ideas that used to seem safe, that had been "worked out" in the cultural and social marketplace of American thinking. But now the changing nature of the fundamental tenets that have characterized the American way of life is precisely the catalyst that has created the new, Christian ideology that is taking over the United States today.

The most common American political ideologies are still conservatism and liberalism, although many variations of these exist in different regions. Socialism, Communism, and fascism have lost the ideological wars in America, and although libertarians, neoconservatives, feminists, and ecologists are still vocal and vital on the ideological spectrum, they do not have the same influence or clout as the "right" and the "left." Even the "center" is floundering.

During the French Revolution in the late eighteenth century, when those who supported radical change sat on the left side of the National Assembly, liberals or progressives were known as being on "the left." Those who supported the status quo or who wished to return to more traditional social and political notions sat on the right side of the chamber, so that conservatives, today, are still said to be on "the right."

Having a particular ideology in the United States, that is, holding views that are a variation of a liberal or conservative worldview, used to be different than belonging to a particular political party. But today, both the Democrats and the Republicans are sinking deeper and deeper into ideological holes that have been dug by their own grave-diggers: their political bases. The Democratic Party is increasingly controlled by liberals, and the Republican Party by conservatives. Moderates or centrists are finding it more difficult to find an inviting place for themselves under what used to be all-inclusive party umbrellas. What was once a healthy ideological divide that allowed for inter party debate on a variety of issues has now become a chasm, demanding ideological adherence that is also *tied to religious beliefs*, thus creating more and more polarizing positions.

To complicate the picture, ideology has also become the key factor in the decision-making apparatus of the government. Political actors, who in many cases are Christian and/or conservatives, are the people providing the government justification for various judicial, legislative, and executive decisions. This new relationship is what Michael Walzer referred to in a recent article in *Dissent Magazine*.[11] He argues that ideological certainty and zeal have now migrated from the left to the right and that a relationship between conservative intellectuals and the government is now common.

At the same time, Walzer maintains that ideological uncertainty and skepticism about all-out solutions to social problems have migrated from the right to the left. He also points out that progressives lack an infrastructure that can be compared to that of conservatives; that instead, they have single-issue identities and conflicting interests and that they lack the ability to work together. In short, he represents the thinking of some liberal intellectuals who believe that religious conservative ideology has challenged liberalism both intellectually and pragmatically in American government today because it appears to be more coherent. What does it all mean?

The Political Connection

The complexity of why and how certain religious groups have allied themselves with particular ideologies, and in turn with specific political parties, is the focus of this book. In the United States, the culture wars have turned into a higher level of internal political conflict, which can be called *the politics of values*. It is a battle, in fact, that is characterized by the conscious conservative religious struggle to control the public debate, to advance traditional Christian values, to get like-minded candidates elected, and to influence both the domestic and international political policies of the U.S. government.

It is this religious, conservative pursuit of power that the Republicans understood and exploited in the elections of 2000 and 2004. The GOP's chief strategist, Karl Rove, consistently appealed to the Christian, conservative base as he planned the presidential campaigns for George W. Bush and many other national candidates.

Rove was the first to articulate and engage in the *politics of values* and to put its basic principles into practice. These were to (1) exploit the values divide politically by targeting "values voters" and incorporate their moral agenda into Republican policy initiatives; (2) mold the candidate ideologically into an acceptable conservative political leader; (3) frame and control the debate within moral parameters; and (4) articulate the candidate's values clearly while contrasting and assertively exploiting the moral "flaws" of the opposition. Taken together, the tactics of the politics of values became the successful Republican strategy to win and hold the White House in 2000 and 2004. What remains to be seen is if they will remain viable and relevant enough to win the presidency for the Republicans in 2008, if the politics of values can withstand challenges from its political and religious counterparts, and if it can serve as a blueprint for the party as it faces the myriad of challenges that will arise in the future. What lessons can be learned now for both the Republicans and the Democrats that can be applied later?

Targeting Values Voters and Incorporating Their Moral Agenda

Rove played the politics of values like a master from his earliest days as George W. Bush's political consultant. From the beginning, he targeted a specific segment of American Christians—evangelicals, Catholics, and Mormons—thus co-opting a specific religious and ideological base: conservative constituencies that would support the president in 2000 and could be counted on to assure his 2004 reelection as well. Was it brilliant or divisive? It all depends on your point of view—or ideology.

The politics of values is so volatile and remains that way today because it is a zero-sum game. It is committed to focusing on the voting strength of a particular religious group, like the evangelicals, and promising to advance their moral values in the political process. But, in so doing, the politics of values must be played out to its ultimate end; that is, the views of other members of diverse religious constituencies must be rejected.

If one religious group wins politically on a crucial moral value, such as a pro-life public policy, then another must lose. There is no middle ground given or accepted by either side in the abortion battle. There is no room for an incremental, evolutionary policy understanding or compromise. There is only continued policy polarization—a phenomenon that is in contradistinction to an American political theology that previously worshiped civil religion in the form of tolerance and pluralism. Instead, the politics of values operates on a strategy of applying literal, conservative, Christian, "god-given" principles to politics.

Currently, every Republican political advance is followed by a policy initiative to implement the moral values of the Christian conservatives. This is the underbelly of American politics today and the game that must be understood and played in order to be successful in the political arena. Take for example the incorporation of the principle of "compassionate conservatism" into a Republican policy initiative. It became the religious-political linchpin that pulled together disparate policy ideas and created a major political change that reflected the conservative way that the Bush government was going to do business with religious and charitable organizations during his administration.

On January 29, 2001, within a week of his inauguration, President Bush signed two executive orders, one giving bureaucratic life to a new White House Office of Faith-Based and Community Initiatives, and another setting up similar centers at five cabinet agencies. Based on the premise of allowing public funding for faith-based providers of social services, it was designed to respect religious integrity, to protect the beliefs (or nonbeliefs) of their clients, and to maintain the principle of separation of church and state. Although this was eventually to become a major political battle between the White House and Congress, it represented the first executive implementation of the new evangelical, Republican symbiosis that was going to characterize the Bush White House in the future.

Rove continued to target religious conservatives while he served as the president's political strategist. In fact, it has been reported that he began planning for the 2004 reelection campaign after Bush's first inauguration by putting together a "72 Hour Task Force," designed to find bits and pieces of constituencies that had been overlooked in the contested 2000 race. Rove had prepared a doomsday scenario—in case Bush had to win another hypothetically close race, even if it came down to the last *three days*. Bolstered by strategy seminars and demographics, Rove and the members of his "Breakfast Club" (chief campaign leaders) were able to identify several constituencies that needed more attention: women, Latinos, and Christian evangelicals.

Of these three, Rove recognized that there were about four million votes up for grabs among Christian evangelicals, a large number who had failed to vote in the election of 2000.[12] He emphasized and courted this special, but almost dormant, part of the Republican base. In so doing, he made a strategic change in the way that presidential politics was going to be played in 2004. He was going to deemphasize the usual once-every-four-year campaign of outreach to independent voters. Instead, he was going to put the campaign's emphasis on the true believers—giving the evangelically committed a real reason to go to the polls and be loyal to the Republican Party in the future. Rove would give the evangelicals what they wanted most: a choice among meaningful personal, political issues that could be voted on in light of their *moral* values. Apparently it worked in 2000 and 2004.

The president heaped praise on his political strategist and his future policy advisor for the way that he implemented what is referred to here as the politics of values. Bush dubbed Rove "the Architect," acknowledging the strategic thinking and work of his longtime friend, the man with the plan. Rove is reported to have said that the title was "a deep embarrassment,"[13] but most Washington insiders, whether or not they agreed with his campaign strategy, recognized Rove's genius: getting the president reelected in light of an unpopular war, a sagging economy, and a values divide.

Being called "the Architect" could be interpreted to mean that the president recognized Rove as the person who best played the "politics of values." He was the one who developed the religious and conservative policies that helped Bush to win elections, to frame and control the political, as well as the moral, debate, and to define the values that would win the White House. Various press accounts portrayed Rove as both the mastermind and the micro-manager of state electoral tactics during 2000 and 2004, a fact borne out by accounts that he even controlled the president's itinerary in order to get the best results from Bush's appearances.

However, in pragmatic rather than ideological terms, it is important to point out that Rove identified and went after the vital constituency that encompassed all of the Christian conservatives, a voting group that had been ignored by the Democrats. Speaking of Rove, Mike Allen, formerly a political reporter for the *Washington Post*, said, "His hand was in all of it."[14]

Matthew Dowd, who was a campaign strategist for the Bush-Cheney campaign in 2004, worked with Rove and contends that the Moral Majority and the Christian Coalition, which were politically successful in the 1980s and 1990s, were "basically . . . gone" by the millennium,[15] leaving a question as to whether or not they could even deliver the evangelical vote. He maintains that Rove was keenly aware of this and worked to rebuild the Christian base through the Republican Party, getting lists of activists and recruiting volunteers until 1.6 million religious adherents could be counted on in the battleground states.[16]

The pollsters point out that the campaign and its outreach to evangelical groups were factors that were able to change the political "culture" and the way that a certain religious segment of the population looked upon their political responsibilities in the elections of 2004.

Rove's tactical maneuver to target values voters enabled the Republican Party to mobilize and motivate close to three million votes for George W. Bush—three million votes among the evangelicals that the Democrats had overlooked or ignored in the 2004 presidential race; the votes that many believed made the difference in the outcome. Strategically, Rove shifted from persuasion to mobilization to motivation.[17] But, most important, he moved to winning.

Molding the Candidate Ideologically

In many ways, Rove's back story is as interesting as his professional biography. He had catapulted himself from a college dropout to the position of "the Architect" during a thirty-year odyssey that took him from Colorado to Utah to Texas and then to Washington D.C.

Over the years, Rove had become the intellectual mentor of George W. Bush. He had begun educating the future presidential candidate by opening his mind to ideas, ideology, and people that would expand and deepen his understanding of conservatism. One of Rove's earliest must-read recommendations to Bush was a book entitled *The Dream and the Nightmare: The Sixties Legacy to the Underclass*[18] by Myron Magnet. A Columbia Ph.D. with a scholarly background in Charles Dickens, Magnet is a fellow at the Manhattan Institute for Policy Research, a conservative think tank in New York City. His book and a subsequent one critiqued the liberalism of the 1960s, the sexual revolution of its elites, and their alternative lifestyles.

He argued in *The Dream and the Nightmare* that liberals created an underclass that was chronically poor and apt to remain that way due to repeated left-leaning liberal court decisions, legislation, and public policy. The nation's social problems, according to Magnet, were being left unsolved by government efforts and public attempts at welfare, both of which were having the effect of destroying incentive in America. On reflection, Bush said that Magnet's book "really helped crystallize some of my thinking about culture, [about] changing cultures and part of the legacy of my generation."[19]

Later, it was Rove who introduced Bush to Marvin Olasky, the University of Texas journalism professor who articulated the notion of "compassionate conservatism" in his book, *The Tragedy of American Compassion.*[20] In an intellectual relationship that has lasted more than a decade, Olasky brought new ideas to Bush's thinking. He challenged the premise of the Great Society, arguing that government bureaucracies could not do as good a job at providing social services as individuals, that they were incapable of bringing about moral change for those who were plagued by social ills. Olasky maintained that compassion was a "process" and that charity had a theological component. Therefore, he called for charity to become compassionate again, for people to *suffer with* their neighbors in need and to help create a sense of community as well as jobs. Olasky believed in accountability and called for a reappraisal of what it means to be made in God's image.

Bush's relationship with Olasky significantly influenced his ideological development and the adoption of compassionate conservatism as a viable approach to public policy. In fact, Bush was so committed to Olasky's ideology that he wrote the foreword to the professor's second book, *Compassionate Conservatism*, noting that compassion could provide hope and that conservatism could provide prosperity, and that taken together compassionate conservatism could create the basis for a policy agenda to promote social progress through individual change, one person at a time. Bush wrote: "Government will not be replaced by charities, but it can welcome them as a partner."[21]

It was also Rove who invited Stephen Goldsmith, the Republican mayor of Indianapolis in the late 1990s, to come to the Bush ranch when he was on a tour though the state to promote his book *The Twenty-First Century City: Resurrecting Urban America.*[22]

"Hizzoner" was the poster boy for personal responsibility and fiscal conservatism as well as the founder of the Front Porch Alliance, an organization that connected city agencies, religious and community leaders, and businesses. Goldsmith's ideas about running large cities were simple: "People know better than government what is in their best interest. Monopolies are inefficient. Government monopolies are particularly inefficient. Wealth needs to be created, not redistributed. Government should do a few things well. Cities must not raise taxes or price themselves out of competition with excessive regulations."[23] Some of his program innovations in Indianapolis could be construed as concrete applications of the notion of compassionate conservatism. They were so close to Bush's vision, in fact, that Terry Neal of the *Washington Post* called Goldsmith the presidential candidate's "intellectual soulmate," his twin in endorsing smaller government, less taxes, and encouraging community solutions to urban problems.[24]

Rove also brought John J. DiIulio, Jr., to meet Bush, participate in a policy discussion, and to theorize and legitimize the notion of the "faith-based initiative." A "public intellectual" with a Harvard Ph.D. in criminology, DiIulio was a big fish in the academic pond. A former Princeton University professor, he had been recruited to the University of Pennsylvania where he was given a prestigious endowed chair in political science. He was also a member of the Brookings Institution, a think-tank counterpart to the conservative Manhattan Institute. As the author of several important books in his field, DiIulio had impeccable credentials and had been courted by Rove for several years to come to Texas and discuss policy ideas with Bush. With the additional cajoling of Goldsmith, who became domestic policy advisor to the Bush presidential campaign, DiIulio agreed to attend a meeting on the faith-based initiative in 1999.

DiIulio talked[25] about the actual first visit and the Rove-Bush treatment. He recounted the whole experience with excitement to this author. He was impressed by Bush and felt that he acted in a genuine way toward him—giving him a bear hug on his arrival. Bush made it a point to sit DiIulio next to him and took notes on his comments. Bush deferentially turned to DiIulio for advice as controversial matters were raised, and at the end of the policy discussion session, asked him to stay in touch. Rove reinforced the offer and followed up by asking the Ivy League professor to screen position papers and to "be the true voice of compassionate conservatism" on the new policy effort. But DiIulio said he only ended up editing the text of some speeches during most of the campaign, that is, until the presidential candidate came to his hometown of Philadelphia for a political rally in June of 2000.

DiIulio was genuinely surprised[26] when the Bush campaign suddenly reconnected with him. When the candidate invited him to come to Carpenter's Hall, where the campaign event was to take place, he jumped at the chance and was even more intrigued when the candidate asked him to walk along with him and shake hands in the crowd. Finally, Bush asked DiIulio to ride with him in his limo and got down to business: What would it take, he asked, to make the faith-based initiative work? They had a frank discussion and, although DiIulio was impressed with Bush's sincerity, he waited for the next several months to see how the policy would evolve. The transition team led by Rove decided that the faith-based initiative would be the signature policy effort that would best identify and advance the principles of the new administration, and sometime after the election, when DiIulio was offered the position of the first faith-based director, he immediately understood it as the chance to level the playing field between public and sectarian organizations to provide social services.[27]

Intellectually, then, it was Rove who helped to create the George W. Bush that the American public knows today. He was, in many ways, "Bush's brain" as James Moore and Wayne Slater contend in their biography of the same name. By 2000, "the Architect" brought conservative theory into the marketplace of political ideas—in a totally new way. He made its notions viable and respectable, and he made those views real through the advancement of public policies that reflected social conservative thinking. Rove did all this through his own keen political understanding of both campaign strategy and his unique ability to manipulate meaningful public issues, in short, by playing "the politics of values."

Framing the Political Debate in Moral Terms

One of the most critical tactical moves in the politics of values is the ability to frame and control the parameters of the public debate during a campaign. In essence, the *political strategist* who can do this best can inspire party loyalists and force his opponents to respond to his challenges during the process.

Many modern political strategists are legendary for this. Pat Caddell, the first to use polls and focus groups, was able to identify ethics, values, and human rights as the most meaningful campaign issues for Jimmy Carter to pursue in his race for the 1976 presidency. Lee Atwater often bragged about his ability to change George H. W. Bush from a lap dog to a pit bull a few years later. And James Carville focused the first Clinton campaign with his now-famous slogan: "It's the economy stupid."

Karl Rove also added something new to the political strategist's arsenal: framing the debate in moral terms through the use of "wedge issues." Rove was able to use those concerns that separate people and the "magnet issues"—those concerns that bring people together—in new ways during the 2004 campaign. Rove took the initiative and defined the wedge issues as abortion, gay marriage, and stem cell research. In other words, he framed the debate around conservative and religious social values. In the same way, he aggressively defined the chief magnet issue as one of leadership, framing it as a referendum on the president's character and morality.

While the Democrats tried to make the economy and the war in Iraq the critical components of the campaign, their attempts to debate health care, jobs, social security reform, and the war on terror were eventually trumped by intangibles. These were questions of leadership and character; attributes that the Republicans were able to equate with the larger issues of preserving America's national security and the ability to serve as its commander-in chief.

While the country seemed deadlocked on values, it became clearer as the election loomed and as the war continued that the Republican campaign would focus on leadership and character and then hit at the social wedge issues to complete the victory.

Rove was able to do this: to clarify, simplify, and offer the evangelicals personal choices about the president's political and moral values. Gay marriage, stem cell research, abortion, creationism, faith-based initiatives—they would all be up for a moral referendum in the presidential election of 2004. With a clear choice, Rove would change the cultural wars into political ones and really begin to play the *politics of values*, the trump card in the high stakes game of the presidency.

Now Rove would use values as a means to attain political ends, rather than as an end in themselves. Virtue would no longer be its own reward; instead, values in the guise of moral, political issues would become a major cog in the wheel that drove the political machine on to the election of 2004 and the midterms in 2006.

Defining and Exploiting the Values of the Opposition

In 2004, a lot of the work on the Rove-defined "wedge issue" strategy was done for him by the Democratic candidate, Senator John Kerry. To many people, the Democratic senator from Massachusetts seemed at a loss to articulate where he stood on values as well as unable to explain how his personal Catholic views informed or reconciled his political and moral standards.

Kerry had followed three other Democratic Catholic candidates in their pursuit for national office: Governor Alfred E. Smith (NY), Senator John F. Kennedy (MA), and Rep. Geraldine Ferraro (NY). They each had differences with their church on matters of faith and politics, and each tried to reconcile their consciences in different ways. Smith, a presidential candidate in 1928, defended his support of "Rum and Romanism" but staunchly defended the separation of church and state. He lost. Kennedy, a presidential candidate in 1960, simply said that he was a Catholic who was a candidate for the presidency, not a Catholic candidate for national office. He pledged that if his religion conflicted with his duties as president he would choose to fulfill the responsibilities of his office. He won. Geraldine Ferraro, the first woman candidate nominated by either major political party for vice president, who ran with Vice President Walter Mondale, said that Catholics could hold a variety of beliefs on abortion and signed off on a congressional document supporting women's reproductive rights. She found herself reprimanded by the cardinal of New York, John O'Connor, for making an incorrect statement of dogma. Later, the powerful religious leader wondered how believing Catholics could vote for such a candidate. The Mondale-Ferraro ticket went down in flames.

Kerry, then, had only one winning model to emulate: the Kennedy one in which he insisted on being his own man. Therefore, Kerry would have to go it alone and face a double challenge in 2004: to take on his church *and* beat the opposition party on questions of values. This would be difficult to do, since the church hierarchy was an entirely different body than the one that led the church during the Kennedy run in 1960. It was stronger, much more politically active, more conservative, and involved in a variety of national moral issues, specifically since its loss of political clout in the aftermath of *Roe v. Wade.*

After that Supreme Court decision in 1973, the bishops emphasized that Catholics and Catholic candidates should be consistent in their religious beliefs and political practice. They had been demanding it for years, first in a variety of documents that reflected a similar Vatican call for moral coherence, and later in their political efforts to impact public policy on moral matters.[28]

Kerry decided to deal with his church as an independent candidate, taking a liberal approach to substantive, values-oriented issues. In effect, he opted to reject the church's continual call for spiritual and political unity, ignored the admonitions of the hierarchy's leadership, and in general took a pluralistic approach to major social problems. The Democratic nominee claimed that he opposed abortion morally but supported the right to choice and privacy for each woman politically and legally. As a U.S. senator, he had voted against the Partial-Birth Abortion Ban and the Unborn Victims of Violence Act in 2004 and opposed the Defense of Marriage Act (1996).

His views on abortion, same-sex marriage, and stem cell research were in conflict with Catholic social teachings and, according to some of the Catholic hierarchy, indicated a lack of moral coherence between his church's teachings and his civic stances. As a result, a small number of conservative Catholic bishops threatened Kerry with punitive actions, specifically the denial of the sacrament of Holy Communion as a way to stifle his opinion and the ideas of other Catholic politicians who held public attitudes that differed from the religious views of the church.

The refusal of the sacrament rests with individual bishops who have authority under established canonical and pastoral principles, and consequently there were different judgments among the bishops as to what to do. In Colorado, Bishop Michael J. Sheridan said that he would deny commu-

nion to Catholic politicians and voters "until they have recanted their positions and been reconciled with God and the Church in the Sacrament of
Penance." In New Jersey, threats by Archbishop Robert Meyers resulted in
then Democratic Governor James McGreevy announcing that he would
abstain from taking communion. In other places, such as Missouri,
Nebraska, and Colorado, Catholic politicians, including Senator Kerry, were
put on notice to reexamine their consciences before taking communion in
order to reconcile their personal consciences with church teachings.

As a result, most of the Catholic leadership was essentially very cautious in
its discussion of the candidates, remaining quiet and passive with regard to
their moral stands during the campaign. Karl Rove attempted to capitalize
on this perceived hierarchical ambivalence to appeal to the more conservative
elements in the Catholic Church. In fact, when President Bush was in Rome
in June of 2004, he asked the Vatican secretary of state to pressure the American bishops to speak out about more political issues, including same-sex
marriage. The president sought greater activism from the Catholic hierarchy
in the United States, and in turn promised Pope John Paul II, the pontiff at
the time, that he would be more aggressive in his approaches to the cultural
issues that they both shared.[29]

Pope John Paul II praised President Bush for his promotion of moral values and his concern for international terrorism. And, even though the pope
opposed the war in Iraq, Bush was able to demonstrate his personal moral
coherence to the pontiff and to cast a shadow over the spiritual inconsistency
of his adversary, Senator Kerry.

The Catholic vote was an area where Rove had also hoped to make inroads.
The U.S. Catholic bishops had focused on the abortion issue and the nuclear
debate, but their political involvement and policy pronouncements had been
limited by Pope John Paul II during the 1980s. In fact, the Catholic Church
in America had been characterized by a White House official as a constituency that had the body of a lion but the voice of a mouse.[30] Translation: It
could not turn the religious beliefs of Catholic adherents into a meaningful
voting bloc.

Traditionally, Catholics had voted Democratic, but with the election of
Ronald Reagan in 1980, they began to switch their allegiance and realign
themselves in greater numbers with the Republicans, gradually emerging as
a constituency cross-pressured by economic concerns and a desire for social
mobility. As a result, Catholics had changed dramatically in their participation in the political arena by the end of the twentieth century.

The size of the Roman Catholic population, nearly a quarter of the U.S.
total demographic today, represents the largest single denomination in the
United States. That breadth, which includes a significant number of Latinos

and immigrants, plays a part in its growing concern for a variety of social justice interests and needs that span the political spectrum. As a result, Catholics, who are ethnically and ideologically diverse because they are made up of immigrants and others, have become known for their continued inability to vote as a bloc or be a major force in U.S. politics. Instead, they represent a significant part of the "swing vote," that is, an independent, uncommitted part of the electorate.

Kerry's inability to crystallize a sizeable part of the Catholic vote opened the door for Rove to make electoral headway with this vital religious constituency. Further, he was also able to define the "Catholic" side of Kerry to the electorate better than the candidate could define himself, until Rove was eventually able to "drive up Kerry's negatives with harsh attacks questioning Kerry's leadership credentials."[31]

In the end, Kerry was only able to garner 47 percent of the Catholic vote, while Bush took 52 percent,[32] a switch in the trend of rising Catholic support for the Democrats in recent years. In contrast, Rove was also able to clarify Bush's stance on the wedge issues and to fold Bush's opposition to abortion and stem cell research into a neat values package that he identified simply as support for a "culture of life."

This notion had been floating around in a variety of iterations within Catholic theological circles for a long time and had been a topic of discussion among pro-lifers and pacifists for a number of years. Joseph Cardinal Bernadin of Chicago had preached the idea that all human life is sacred and had argued for a coherent social policy to protect the right of the weakest and most vulnerable in society. John Paul II, the late pope, had advanced a similar but more forceful notion in a 1995 encyclical, or official teaching letter, entitled *The Gospel of Life.*[33] In it, he argued that life has always been jeopardized by poverty, hunger, disease, violence, and war, but that now it was under even worse attack from contemporary political policies. He identified these as legal actions that allowed genocide, abortion, and euthanasia; policies that supported subhuman living and working conditions and advanced medical research that compromised the most vulnerable (embryos) in society. This modern culture, John Paul II contended, attacked the very dignity of every human being, and in so doing created a "conspiracy against life," a "culture of death." He exhorted everyone to reaffirm the value of human life, an argument that Rove took up and consciously or unconsciously used to present the Republican presidential candidate as being in sympathy with the beliefs of conservative Catholics as well as most evangelicals and Mormons.

The question of gay marriage became a bit more problematic to handle. The judiciary of Massachusetts, Senator Kerry's home state, had interpreted its constitution as being required to give equal status to the marriage of gay citizens under its equality statutes. The legislature, in fact, was under judicial sanction to provide legislation to assure such rights. How could this burning issue be framed to give the presidential incumbent the edge? Rove simply let the president piggyback on the Defense of Marriage Act—pointing to it as the law of the land. Additionally, Bush supported a constitutional amendment to protect heterosexual marriage and rallied behind state attempts to adopt legislation to limit gay marriage. Kerry took a stance that was unpopular and questionable to many, both Democrats and Republicans alike. With no clear consensus on the issue across America, Kerry was left to defend a position that had not been resolved in the minds of many voters.

Thus, by the election of 2004, the battle lines were drawn and the strategy set—essentially by the political strategist, "the Architect" Karl Rove. He was carried out by the president and followed by his administration. The issues would include moral questions and give voters moral choices. In turn, questions of personal values would be turned into questions of leadership. He would help define Bush, but more importantly, he defined *Kerry*, who was having difficulty making his personal views clear to the public. In doing so, Rove framed the election in his terms, in terms of intangibles—personal beliefs and commitments, consistency, loyalty, truth, leadership, and character.

The politics of values won the day, but by the 2006 congressional midterm election, many of the Republicans' formerly winning tactics began to erode. The party suffered a stinging defeat and lost its majorities in both the House and the Senate by unexpected scandals and abuses, the war, and a Democratic backlash. The biggest question that remains, then, is whether or not the politics of values can again become a winning strategy for the Republicans in 2008 and beyond. Political strategists will come and go, and Rove has made his exit, but will playing the politics of values as a campaign and policy tool still have relevance for the Republican Party? Or will it have to focus more on domestic reforms, security, and peace abroad?

Just as important, will the Democrats have to adjust to the politics of values in order to win national office in the future? Or is the political symbiosis between the Republicans and evangelicals so strong that it cannot be weakened by short-term political setbacks such as in 2006?

The next chapter looks at the saturation of the American culture by the evangelicals and questions whether or not their all-pervasive presence and values can be defeated in the political arena. This, along with their strong sense of consistency, witness, and mission in the political arena as well leave many questions to be answered about the politics of values in 2008 and beyond.

Notes

1. Kevin Phillips, *American Theocracy* (New York: Viking, 2006), 121.

2. The Pew Forum on Religion in Public Life, "United States Demographic Profile," http://pewforum.org/world-affairs/countries/?CountryID = 222.

3. John C. Green, "Seeking a Place," in *Toward an Evangelical Public Policy*, ed. by Ronald J. Sider and Diane Knippers (Grand Rapids: Baker Books, 2005), 15.

4. David P. Gushee, ed., *Christians and Politics Beyond the Culture Wars* (Grand Rapids: Baker Books, 2000), 16.

5. Green, "Seeking a Place," 18–19.

6. *Roe v. Wade* 410 U.S. 113 (1973).

7. See the review of *Phyllis Schlafly and Grassroots Conservatism: A Woman's Crusade*, by Donald Critchlow (Princeton, NJ: Princeton University, 2005) written by Frederick D. Schwartz, senior editor of *American Heritage Magazine*. November 2, 2005, www.americanheritage.com.

8. Lyman Tower Sargent, *Contemporary Political Ideologies* (Belmont, California: Thompson, Wadsworth, 2006), Chapter 1.

9. Francis Fukuyama, *The End of History and the Last Man* (New York: Free Press, 1992).

10. Daniel Bell, *The End of Ideology* (Cambridge: Harvard University, 2000).

11. Michael Walzer, "All God's Children Got Values," *Dissent*, (Spring 2005), www.dissentmagazine.org.

12. The Institute of Politics, John F. Kennedy School of Government, *Campaign for President: The Managers Look at 2004* (Lanham, Maryland: Rowman & Littlefield, 2006), chap. 3. See also Sam Parry, "Bush's Incredible Vote Tallies," *Consortiumnews.com*. November 9, 2004, www.consortiumnews.com/Print/2004/110904.html.

13. Howard Fineman, "Rove Unleashed," www.msnbc.msn.com/id/6596809/site/newsweek.

14. "Karl Rove: The Architect," Interview with Matthew Dowd, www.pbs.org/wgbh/pages/frontline/shows/architect/interviews/dowd.html.

15. "Karl Rove: The Architect."

16. "Karl Rove: The Architect."

17. "Karl Rove: The Architect."

18. The information on this book and other works is drawn from Jo Renée Formicola, Mary Segers, and Paul Weber, *Faith-Based Initiatives and the Bush Administration* (Lanham, Maryland: Rowman & Littlefield, 2003), Chapter 1. Reference here is to: Myron Magnet, *The Dream and the Nightmare: The Sixties: Legacy to the Underclass* (New York: William Morrow and Company, 1993).

19. Alison Mitchell, "Bush Draws Campaign Theme from More Than 'The Heart,'" *New York Times*, June 12, 2000, A1.

20. Marvin Olasky, *The Tragedy of American Compassion* (Washington, D.C.: Regnery Publishing, 1992).

21. Marvin Olasky, *Compassionate Conservatism* (New York: The Free Press, 2000), xii.

22. Stephen Goldsmith, *The Twenty-First Century City: Resurrecting Urban America* (Washington, D.C.: Regnery, 1997).

23. Goldsmith, *The Twenty-First Century City*, 7.

24. Terry M. Neal, "Midwestern Mayor Shapes Bush's Message," *Washington Post*, June 5, 1999, A6.

25. This was an interview conducted by the author and Dr. Mary Segers for the book with Dr. Paul Weber entitled *Faith-Based Initiatives and the Bush Administration* (Lanham, Maryland: Rowman & Littlefield, 2003). See the chapter, "The Ugly Politics of the Faith-Based Initiative" for a much fuller description of DiIulio's explanation of the implementation of the policy.

26. DiIulio interview.

27. This was a term used in the Personal Responsibility and Work Opportunity Reconciliation Act (Public Law 104-193) enacted August 22, 1996. It (a) encouraged faith-based organizations to expand their involvement in the welfare reform effort; (b) allowed the government to give public monies to sectarian agencies that were providing social services where the federal government could not or did not; (c) provided assurances that the religious integrity of institutions would be protected; and (d) would preserve the religious liberty of those whom they served. Charitable Choice, as an alternative or supplemental service, was never implemented by the Clinton White House but was seen as a potential new way to bring about more efficient and better social services by the Bush administration.

28. The most recent Vatican document dealing with Catholic politicians is *Sacramentum Caritatis* issued by Pope Benedict XVI on February 22, 2007. The most recent American hierarchical statement is "Catholics and Political Responsibility" updated and issued on June 12, 2007. Both documents are available at www.usccb.org.

29. David D. Kirkpatrick, "Bush Sought Vatican Official's Help on Issues, Report Says," *New York Times*, June 13, 2004, A38.

30. Interview with Linda Chavez, head of the White House Office of Public Liaison, January 14, 1986.

31. Sam Parry, "Bush's 'Incredible' Votes Tallies," November 2, 2004, www.consortiumnews.com.

32. Results of the Associated Press poll as reported by the Catholic News Service in Patricia Zapor, "End of 'Catholic Vote.' Other Categories May Predict Election Better," www.catholicnews.com/data.

33. Pope John Paul II, *The Gospel of Life (Evangelium Vitae)* (Boston: The Daughters of St. Paul, 1995).

3

The Culture Wars: Values,
Values Everywhere

Introduction

IF THERE IS ONE THING that distinguishes the values of American religious conservatives today, it is the fact that they have challenged—and have had a considerable impact on every segment of American society—its economics, education, politics, and culture. This influence reflects the power of the spiritual and *political* commitment of religious conservatives who follow biblical teachings, witness to Christ's message, and accept his personal salvation. Most importantly, their religious dedication can be seen in personal and institutional evangelization for public policy and political action that supports traditional values in the family, as well as in business and the nonprofit and public sectors.

The all-pervasive saturation of evangelical religious beliefs in American culture has also become affiliated with the Republican Party, creating a clear sense of partisan identification between religion and government in the United States. Indeed, that symbiotic relationship leads Kevin Phillips, the author of *American Theocracy,* to call the religious right, with its specific doctrines and huge number of followers, even a "pillar" of the present Bush presidential coalition.[1]

The willingness of religious conservatives to witness for Jesus has become a new way to pursue a values-infused politics and a more complete, pervasive approach to fulfilling the everyday needs of American society. It begins in the family and is nurtured by teaching children about the basic, core values of

Christianity. In some cases, Christian witness occurs though home schooling; in other cases, in religious academies. Even something like picking a summer camp for a boy or girl has now become a spiritual exercise. Simply go to www.beliefnet.com, click on "camp quest," and lists of spiritual summer camps will appear. In fact, www.CampJobs.com will even give anyone looking for a position as a counselor or a coach a placement choice of Christian camps in as many as 28 different states.

The latest trend, however, is what the *New York Times* calls "conservative boot camp."[2] A typical teenage camper was reported to have brought her sandals, camp gear, *The Politics of Prudence* by Russell Kirk, and a Bible to a retreat-like atmosphere filled with seminars and conferences. Many of the young campers who were living in the woods were actually getting ready to become first-year students at evangelical universities, of which there are now a significant number in the United States.

The summer camps are run by nonprofits, such as Young America's Foundation. Some are run with private money, and one has even been reported to have a $2.5 million dollar donation from the Ronald Reagan Leadership Academy.[3] Reportedly, such financial support helps the camps provide tuition for young, aspiring members of the Christian Right so that they can learn about the heritage of religious and social conservatism.

While it is becoming more apparent to public observers that virtually every aspect of American life now has a Christian alternative, these choices represent a challenge to the multicultural, liberal, modern way of living in the United States. In most cases, these religious alternatives are extremely well thought out, planned, financed, and often, supported politically by government programs and policies within contemporary society.

One of the main reasons for creating Christian options within American culture is due to the current evangelical concern about the lack of faith on the part of many of its younger members. The *New York Times* recently reported that youth ministers have been looking at data that predicts that if trends continue only "4% of teenagers will be 'Bible–believing Christians' as adults."[4] The fear that such a statistic could be true[5] has created alarm over increasing sexually pervasive and permissive music, divorce, dysfunctional families, and eroding religious values.

In fact, twenty years ago the possibility of losing a generation of young religious conservatives led to the establishment of Teen Mania, a youth ministry founded to deal with post-Christian America. It attempted to do this by staging its own kind of religiously inspired concerts and events in order to get teenagers to "clothe [themselves] with Christ, with his lifestyle."[6]

The kinds of activities that Teen Mania sponsors are a challenge to mainstream culture. For example, they recently sponsored a concert with Christian rock bands and inspirational speakers in San Francisco. In the fall of 2007, they held an event called "BattleCry," to bring attention to what organizers viewed as the current violent, sexually permissive culture in America. Some city supervisors were unhappy with the event, claiming that it was really an exercise in intolerance, especially toward homosexuals. They maintained that the event used overtly antigay rhetoric, while the organizers maintained that they were simply trying to call attention to the suggestive messages of the media and corporate world.[7]

Other activities have been ongoing to influence the social, cultural, and religious thinking of young evangelicals. For example, for questions and answers about sex, parents can augment their personal values and spiritual beliefs by sending their teens to an electronic concert with comedy skits and music videos about the importance of sexual abstinence. Known as the Silver Ring Thing (SRT), over 40,000 teenagers thus far have participated in its program by taking a pledge to refrain from sex until marriage, according to its founders, the Reverend Denny Pattyn and the Youth FORUM Southwest.

Pattyn, a minister from Sewickley, Pennsylvania, conceived Silver Ring Thing in 1995, has watched it grow, and has seen it receive over $1 million in federal and state monies since 2003. This has enabled him to provide an abstinence message to teenagers funded partially through President George W. Bush's faith-based initiative.

The organization's website tells how Silver Ring Thing can offer young people "protection from the destructive effects of America's sex obsessed culture."[8] It maintains that this can be done by saturating the United States with young people who have chosen sexual abstinence; a commitment to purity that "can only be achieved by offering a personal relationship with Jesus Christ . . ."[9]

Silver Ring Thing is designed to provide a Christian alternative to the pervasive sexual culture of today by providing concerts and offering a 12-point follow-up plan based on a commitment to Christ. Concert goers are also given the opportunity to purchase a silver ring to wear as a symbol of their sexual abstinence promise. Inscribed on the ring is "1 Thess. 4:3-4" a reference to the biblical verse "God wants you to be holy, so you should keep clear of all sin. Then each of you will control your body and live in holiness and honor." Along with the silver ring, young people at the concerts can also buy a Bible for about the cost of a CD.

In 2005 in response to Pattyn's ministry and the government funding for it, the American Civil Liberties Union of Boston brought suit in the U.S. District Court in Massachusetts[10] against the U.S. Department of Health and Human Services. The ACLU claimed that the *content* of the Silver Ring Thing's program was a violation of separation of church and state because the purpose of its outreach was to bring "unchurched" students to Jesus Christ. Its suit contended that federal dollars were being used to support religious activities, that the government grant provided direct aid to a sectarian institution, and that federal funds were underwriting religious activities as well as providing a message of governmental endorsement and preference to religion in general. In short, the ACLU argued that the message of Silver Ring Thing intended to advance Christianity rather than sexual abstinence.

In a settlement between the ACLU and the Department of Health and Human Services in February 2006, the government agreed to stop funding the religious activities of Silver Ring Thing *as it was structured*. And, it also agreed that future federal funding[11] would be contingent on the organization's adherence to the laws that protect the separation of church and state.

In an attempt to comply with the agreement, Silver Ring Thing quickly altered and removed the organization's religious content from its website and changed its follow-up activities by removing references to Jesus. It "sanitized" its message, according to the ACLU. Within a day, Denny Pattyn claimed victory for Silver Ring Thing. He contended that the settlement allowed SRT to pursue federal funds on the same terms and conditions as other organizations and that it could not be discriminated against because it was a faith-based organization. Pattyn claimed to be "ecstatic"[12] with the dismissal of the case and Silver Ring Thing's continued ability to obtain federal grants.

Silver Ring Thing also teaches that sexually transmitted diseases are rampant among sexually active teens, and that STD's have serious personal and social consequences including depression, alcoholism, and personal guilt. However, statistics gathered from the federally funded National Longitudinal Study of Adolescent Health, conducted by researchers at Yale and Columbia Universities, recently found that there was no statistical difference in the rate of sexually transmitted disease between those who took abstinence pledges and those who did not.[13] Nevertheless, President Bush asked for $206 million in federal funding for abstinence-only programs during 2005.[14]

Other organizations, such as True Love Waits (TLW), founded in 1993, also evangelize for sexual abstinence among young people. Estimates are that between 1 and 2.4 million youths have signed a pledge stating that ". . . I make a commitment to God, myself, my family, those I date, and my future mate to be sexually pure until the day I enter marriage."[15] TLW contends that it helps youth to find biblical solutions to life, a Baptist approach carried out through Life Way Ministry.

One means by which True Love Waits reinforces its virginity message is through the sale of a line of religious jewelry. Not to be outdone by Silver Ring Thing, which provides links to purchase Clarity, Serenity, and Purity Angel bracelets in amazonite, rose quartz, and peridot to empower Christian intentions, TLW offers its teen members purity rings and pendants ranging from $24.95 to $199.95. They can be purchased from the TLW website. And of course, everywhere else, the jewelry manufacturers of the world have jumped on the bandwagon and produced Guardian Angel pins, earrings, and bracelets in every variation thereof.

This type of jewelry is being used to complement religious clothing, particularly in new youth-focused markets like the ones in Southern California. There, several stores called C28, named after Colossians 2:8 (the Epistle of St. Paul, which warns against the love of temporal things), are selling religiously inspired t-shirts. The store's brand, "Not of this World," offers merchandise with Christian messages like, "Bad Company Corrupts" and similar messages on t-shirts.[16] C28 also markets religious jewelry for those who want to shop for their religious wardrobe all in one place.

Traditional Christian clothing and its message have also been augmented by new "rebellion" religious sportswear. One manufacturer, Extreme Christian Clothing, has a line of shirts that is "not about wearing faith subtly."[17] Instead, it claims it is about inspiring others, coming to know real life, taking up the cross daily, and risking it all for Christ. Extreme Christian Clothing sells t-shirts with messages like "Satan Sucks!!!," "My God Can Kick Your God's Butt," and "Got Jesus?"

If the purpose is to look good in Christian fashions, can Christian-inspired diet books be far behind? Any Christian bookstore worth its name contains the self-help publications of Don Colbert, M.D., a certified family practitioner. He turns to his faith and the Bible when marketing his own Divine Health Nutritional Products and his faith-based food books. *Walking in Divine Health* and *Toxic Relief* are two of his early publications; his most recent offerings are *Body by God,* the *Hallelujah Diet,* and *What Would Jesus Eat?* And, for the true believer, Colbert's *Bible Cure* series provides "ancient truths, natural remedies and the latest findings" for stress, headaches, PMS, mood swings, and other health problems. The same bookstores also carry *The Divine Diet* by Carole Lewis and *The Maker's Diet* by Jordan S. Rubin.

Stephen Arterburn is a Christian food guru, among other things. He is the founder and chairman of New Life Ministries, which Arterburn's website describes as "the nations' largest faith-based broadcast counseling and treatment ministry." Through his nationally syndicated radio show, "New Life Live!," Arterburn reports that he has sold over 113,000 copies[18] of his self-help book, *Lose it for Life,* written with Dr. Linda Mintle.

Arterburn, who attended Southwestern Baptist Theological Seminary, holds two honorary degrees, and through the Ambassador Speakers Bureau, a Christian-based talent and literary agency that he works for, he commands thousands of dollars per speech on the lecture circuit. He claims that his Christian counseling message has made a difference to a large number of people, particularly women. They are the major focus of his organization known as "Women of Faith," which he founded in 1996. According to Arterburn, attendance at these conferences has "exceeded 1.6 million" participants since then.[19]

But Jesus diets are only part of the appeal to religion in everyday life. Evangelicals are concerned about the environment too, and have opened up a whole new debate about global warming by asking, WWJD—What Would Jesus Drive? Reverend Jim Ball, a Baptist minister and editor of *Creation Care, A Christian Environmental Quarterly,* asked the question first. He believes that America has a moral obligation to reduce the pollution that causes global warming. Writing about this concern in 2002, Ball and his organization, the Evangelical Environmental Network (EEN), attempted to raise awareness about the ethical responsibility to lessen global warming, to challenge the automobile industry, and to encourage the Christian public to take action.

Advertisements on Christian radio and cable television stations in America's heartland were aired to get the moral environmental message across and were hit home by activists who drove hybrid cars to the homes of the CEO's of the major car manufacturers to deliver letters about the responsibility to lower greenhouse gases. The formation of an interfaith environmental coalition added to the legitimacy of Ball's efforts, catching the attention of the media and public relations gurus in the United States. General Motors, obviously recognizing the potential of the evangelical environmental message and the possible damage to its SUV market, responded with sixteen "Come Together and Worship" concerts sponsored by Chevrolet that featured Christian rock bands.

In 2005, this moral environmental message and its attendant publicity translated politically into the Climate Stewardship Act introduced by Senators John McCain (R-AZ) and Joseph Lieberman (D-CT) and Congressman Wayne T. Gilchrist (R-MD). The legislation was designed to limit greenhouse gas emissions and dependence on foreign oil, but to little avail. The separate bills, like so many other pieces of legislation, are still currently "under consideration" in the Senate Environment and Public Works Committee and the House Subcommittee on Environment, Technology, and Standards.

All of these religious experiences and attempts to impact American culture provide critical parts to the values background needed for the type of college experience that Naomi Schaefer Riley talks about in her book *God on the Quad.*[20] Riley traveled to a number of religious universities to look at how and why church schools were working to create a "missionary generation" as well as how they were attempting to change values in America. Her conclusions? Young men and women attend religious universities willingly and without parental pressure; the schools "devote an enormous effort to forming the intellectual and moral character of their students"; the schools try to insulate them from the broader culture; they instill in them a sense of vocation; and their graduates will be in the "vanguard of a more conservative generation."[21]

In sum, religious education and Christian alternatives are recognized as powerful tools in preparing the next generation of young religious and social conservatives. In fact, even in secular universities religion is on the rise. Just recently, Peter J. Gomes, the university preacher at Harvard, reported that "There is probably more active religious life now than there has been in 100 years."[22] Short-term political losses, like the Republican midterm debacle in 2006, are simply recognized as that—a temporary setback, lessons to be learned in order for evangelicals of all ages to go forward, a bump in the road on the journey to create economic, social, and *political* structures that reflect biblical models and gospel imperatives.

Put Jesus in the Workplace

Jesus, it seems, is everywhere and on everybody's mind, due to the all-pervasive evangelism of His adherents. Christianity is especially on the rise in the workplace. Groups like Billy Graham's Evangelistic Association and the Promise Keepers have always supported the notion that Christians should practice their faith on Sunday and infuse Jesus's principles on the job for the rest of the week as well. But that message has been redefined and updated to fit today's more complex work environment.

Os Hillman, who at one time owned and operated an advertising agency, has been called the "unofficial leader"[23] of the faith-at-work movement. Having attended an University of South Carolina and the Calvary Chapel Bible School, he later founded the International Coalition of Workplace Ministries and Marketplace Leaders. Its purpose is to help people apply their faith and its principles at work. To that end, Hillman's organization provides books, CDs, and DVDs to inspire and educate pastors and individuals on how to bring Christian values to the job.

Hillman lectures, consults, and has written a number of books including *The 9 to 5 Window, TGIF: Today God is First, Faith and Work: Do They Mix?* and *The Upside of Adversity.* He claims that his International Coalition of Workplace Ministries and Marketplace Leaders has more than 900 ministries, and his resource webpage provides sales information on such publications as *God Is My CEO* by Larry Julian, *Selling Among Wolves* by Michael Pink, *Exec-*

utive Influence: Impacting Your Workplace for Christ by Christopher A. Crane and Mike Hamel, and *Kingdom Companies* by Dr. Jorg Knoblauch.

After all is said and done, preaching, or evangelism, is what evangelicals do. And as long as conservative religious groups do not harass others or create a hostile work environment by using religion as the basis for hiring, promoting, or firing, their preaching is legal. General Motors is now dealing with a lawsuit by a group that is demanding the right to form Christian affinity-groups, such as Bible discussion clubs. Coca-Cola has agreed to establish such groups as part of a past settlement for racial discrimination charges, while Intel has allowed such meetings for close to a decade as part of its seventeen other diversity clubs.

Other groups such as the American Chamber of Christians in Business (ACCB) also influence the faith-based workplace. ACCB's purpose is to promote opportunities for networking, to increase employment opportunities, and to stimulate private enterprise and prosperity by instilling biblical ethics and accountability in business. Membership in the organization depends on the size and type of a business and the employment status of its individuals. Its website claims that Jesus Christ is the Chairman of the Board, but that members drive the organization.

Founded by Al Otero, the president of Trust House Mortgage, Inc., in Florida, ACCB is an outgrowth of Otero's involvement with the International Chamber of Commerce, the Florida State Hispanic Chamber of Commerce, and his role as co-founder of the Miami Christian Chamber of Commerce.

The Association of Christian Financial Advisors drives this point home even more. Dedicated internally to support others, the organization focuses on trying to understand the biblical principles of financial planning through prayer and fellowship. Externally, it helps its members to find Christian accountants, bookkeepers, brokers, and others who provide financial advice or service to those who will sign a statement committed to the Christian faith.

Of course, involvement in finances also means that Christian banking is not far behind. One financial institution likes to call banking the way to build the Kingdom, and another calls on its patrons to evangelize with their checkbooks. For example, the Reliance Bank donates a percentage of its profits each year to further the Salvation Army's evangelical and charitable work around the world. It is reported that over the last decade this has totaled about $20 million.[24]

Put Jesus in the Media

In 2006, "Heaven's Love Thrift Shop," a comic strip about finding Jesus, began to appear in American newspapers. The main characters were simple folks and designed to remind people that "there is a God and that God loves them,"[25] according to Kevin Franks, its cartoon creator. He sees the comic strip as part of his personal ministry, a special way to witness to Jesus in a medium that is "bending over backwards not to portray the beliefs of people of faith . . ."[26]

Clearly, the media is another area where conservative Christianity has made major inroads over the years. A case in point is WRMB, a Christian radio station in Florida. The station motto is "Think Biblically, Live Christianly, Serve Effectively, and Evangelize Consistently." One of the partners in WRMB is Janet Vigilante, who is also the current president of the ACCB. The station, in turn, is part of a larger conglomerate, the Moody Broadcasting Network. Vigilante, through her personal business, provides trips to the Holy Land Experience in Orlando.

The Moody Broadcasting Network, the parent company of WRMB, is the larger picture in this story. It illustrates the early recognition and significant impact of the evangelical commitment to establish Christian institutions to advance biblical principles and the gospel message—the Moody Broadcasting Network was the first to foster Christian broadcasting in American society.

The company is named after Dwight Lyman Moody, a Massachusetts-born shoe store worker who found Jesus after being visited and converted by the pastor of the local Congregational Church in 1855.

In 1887, Moody founded the Chicago Evangelization Society. Later the Society and his training school merged into the Moody Bible Institute, an official academic entity. Since then, the Institute has established a correspondence school (1901), an evening school (1903), and a radio station (1926). The first station was called the "Radio School of the Bible," and since that time, it has grown to almost 600 affiliates to become a major player in conservative, religious talk radio.

The Christian radio industry, of course, is a lot bigger than Moody Broadcasting. Moody is just one of over forty radio *networks* that control the major portion of about 2,500 radio *stations*, and a burgeoning number of over 90 internet radio *sites* like *Addicted2Jesus*.[27]

Organizations like the National Religious Broadcasters Incorporated help to unify their members' message, resources, and communications. With its own *National Religious Broadcasters Magazine*, the organization represents approximately 600 members to attain their goals.

Christian radio is a changing and growing phenomenon, saturating the secular media. Starting in the 1940s, radio networks had to offer free airtime to meet government requirements for religious and public affairs programming. Catholics and mainline Protestants received most of the airtime, and because denominations such as the Southern Baptists and the Assemblies of God were out of the mainstream, they were overlooked.

The marginalized fundamentalists formed their own umbrella religious organization known as the National Association of Evangelicals (NAE) in 1942, and as one of their first orders of business, established the National Religious Broadcasters Association. Eventually, the organization accepted members of the mainline Protestant churches into their own burgeoning organization, which became independent of the NAE soon thereafter.

By the 1980s the National Religious Broadcasters Association became the spiritual and *political* voice of many evangelicals, with broadcasting preachers like Jim Bakker, Oral Roberts, and Pat Robertson. During those days, it was estimated that the Christian radio and television industry provided $2 billion worth of revenue to the Christian media industry.[28]

It appears today that the 2,500 Christian stations, which are evangelical and mainline Protestant as well as Catholic, exist in a universe of nearly 13,000 media outlets in the United States. They represent a little less than ten percent of the total radio market but are able to provide a conservative, countercultural alternative to committed religious traditionalists. By saturating the airwaves with their religious *and* political ideas, a significant part of the purchasing power of evangelicals, which is estimated to be about twenty-five percent of the total population in America, is directed inwardly and used to reinforce its cultural, religious, and political *values through the media*.

The Christian music industry today is a critical factor in the success of Christian radio, since it serves as a way to evangelize for Jesus. Both gospel and Christian rock are more relevant and saleable today than ever before. Some say the move from traditional gospel to more popular Christian rock music began in the 1970s when a group known as Mind Garage recorded "Electric Liturgy." Others say it was when Larry Norman, an early Christian rocker, asked in his now prophetic song "Why Should the Devil Have All the Good Music?"

Traditional gospel music has its roots in African American spirituals and was brought out of the south after the Civil War. It acquired an urban sophistication, influencing blues and jazz, and was popularized by traveling singing preachers in the late nineteenth century. T. A. Dorsey, who wrote "Precious Lord Take My Hand," is credited with adding the element of entertainment to gospel music, advertising religious concerts, and charging admission to hear it. Choirs, quartets, and soloists such as Mahalia Jackson gave it a wide following, principally in the South.

Gospel has taken on a new life in the past decade. According to the Gospel Music Channel, a 24-hour, gospel/Christian music station, it has 80 million fans, is broadcast on 1,400 radio stations, and sells $1 billion in CDs annually.[29] The McDonald's Gospelfest in New York City, Gospel Jamborees at theme parks around the country, and even the first Gospel Dream competition—a takeoff on *American Idol*—attest to some of its growing mainstream appeal. The first Gospel Dream winner was Brian Smith, a DJ from Michigan, who won a recording contract from Sony BMG's Zomba Gospel Records. By 2006, the Gospel Music Channel again sponsored the event but held auditions around the United States and televised the finals on national television.

Christian rock is the hottest of the hot, now topping $4 billion[30] in total revenues in the United States. What is Christian rock? Definitions are as broad as claiming that only bands and singers that explicitly state their belief in Jesus and use Christian imagery qualify for the title to definitions that those who are influenced by their faith and believe that they should appeal to the general public are also Christian rockers. All the while, more and more entertainers are bringing the message of Jesus to religious conservatives—as well as mainstream American society.

There are an ever-growing number of categories of Christian music. They include, but are not limited to, urban gospel, rhythm and blues gospel, pop and contemporary gospel, modern Christian rock, country gospel, inspirational gospel, instrumental gospel, and praise and worship gospel. However, behind it all is the truism that Christian music is an alternative to contemporary heavy metal and rap that extols premarital and extramarital sex, lyrics that describe intimate acts, thematic exploitation, eroticism, the drug culture, pornography, gay and androgynous lifestyle, and Satan "sympathy," according to some evangelical critics.[31] It continues to be a reaction to, and a choice between, hope in Jesus and the violence of "gangsta" music and a means to inspire faith, to fulfill spiritual needs, and to provide simple enjoyment.

The current crop of Christian rock bands and singers is huge and growing. Groups such as the NewsBoys, Relient K, MXPX, and Plumb, for example, are part of the Revelation Generation giving concerts and singing for the Lord. Top groups include Third Day, a more mainstream group, and P.O.D.—Payable On Death. Other groups like U2, Creed, Thrice, and Blessid Union of Souls are made up of members who profess Christian values and use its influence in their music. Jeremy Camp Avalon, Ashla, Steven Curtis Chapman, Michael W. Smith, Jars of Clay, MercyMe, SONICFLOOD, Amy Grant, Faith Hill, Tim McGraw, and a host of other entertainers still bring audiences of all kinds to their Christian music experiences.

Television and radio have also been targeted as industries to provide Christian media alternatives. Pat Robertson and James Dobson have long been leaders in these endeavors. Robertson has parlayed his *700 Club*, which was originally a mix of Christian and secular shows on cable, into the Family Channel. It is probably the most successful of more than 250 full- and part-time Christian television stations on the air. James Dobson, the evangelical family psychologist and founder of Focus on the Family, is the leading radio personality among Christian fundamentalists. He reaches nearly two million listeners on 4,000 radio stations. Dobson provides Christian counseling, and within Focus on the Family is helped by media specialist Bob Waliszewski, who plans and tracks what is happening within the media markets. One of their most interesting findings is the fact that there is room for more Christian theatre. In response, Focus on the Family is not only in the business of evangelizing but also in the business of entertaining, but in a Christian way. The Father Gilbert Mysteries, a radio series about a policeman who becomes an Anglican priest, and other classics of literature and biographies are part of Focus on the Family's offerings.

Christian televangelists have also reemerged with a vengeance since the 1980s. They are even more powerful today than Jimmy Swaggart, Jim Bakker, and Oral Roberts was in the past. Well-educated, well-dressed, and well-spoken, today's televangelists are often the pastors and preachers at "megachurches" who command significant cable time on Sunday mornings.

These large worship institutions have been defined by the Hartford Institute for Religion Research as congregations that have over 2,000 adherents. According to their findings, there are 1,321 such megachurches in America, with the top ten all above 16,000 members.[32]

The largest is the Lakewood Church in Houston, Texas. Joel Osteen, a highly telegenic and charismatic preacher, is its pastor. He preaches to 42,000 attendees weekly at his megachurch, which used to be known as the Compaq Center when it housed the Houston Rockets. Osteen reaches an even bigger audience through his televised coverage. His website claims that he reaches 200 million households per week.

The son of a minister himself, Osteen began preaching after his father's death, taking up his dad's mantle and reaching the incredible success that he has today. Osteen is the author of the 2004 bestselling book, *Your Best Life Now: Seven Steps to Living at Your Full Potential*,[33] and the current self-help volume, *Becoming a Better You: 7 Keys to Improving Your Life*.[34] His new book had a first printing of three million volumes and purportedly could bring him a $13 million payday.[35]

Another incredible preacher is Bishop T. D. Jakes, who gives new meaning to the traditional role and influence of the black minister. Jakes began his ministry in small storefront churches as a young man, first in West Virginia and later in Texas. Probably one of the most successful of all the Christian televangelists, Jakes is committed to empowering women and ending domestic violence. His "Women Thou Art Loosed" conference in 1999 drew 85,000 women to the Georgia Dome in Atlanta and another 65,000 in 2000, while continuing to grow in influence and importance all across the United States since then.[36]

But Jakes is more than just a preacher; he is also the embodiment of T. D. Jakes Ministries and T. D. Jakes Enterprises as well. His ministries consist of a weekly U.S., European, and African television presence and occasional Latin American appearances as well. This exposure enables him to teach the Word of God: a message of spiritual restoration through Christ and a gift of survival and salvation through grace. Jakes also believes in the power of people's unity to overcome poverty, racism, and oppression. He claims that the ideal and the real must work in unison in order for people to overcome financial and cultural discrimination. He also stresses economic empowerment for all and prosperity for the poor.[37]

Along with seminars, gospel play tours, books, and music activities, T. D. Jakes Enterprises manages the for-profit part of the preacher's ministry—a huge business venture. T. D. Jakes Enterprises is the way that Jakes's evangelization gets out the Christian message. Through television, conferences, work with other pastors, lectures, CDs, DVDs, plays, music, and movies, he gives advice and biblical insight on how to integrate relationships, resources, and faith. He has had several books on the *New York Times* bestseller list, among them *Woman Thou Art Loosed, Maximize the Moment,* and *The Great Investment: Faith, Family and Finance.* Twentieth Century Fox even launched *Woman Thou Art Loosed* as a movie. Jakes, personally, is a multimillionaire.[38]

While Osteen and Jakes are apolitical ministers, others in similar positions in megachurches are not, and they represent a major potential political constituency for the Republican Party. Black and white preachers who have influence with large numbers of people are political targets for White House outreach, particularly as many are anxious to reap federal funds from President Bush's Faith-Based and Community Initiative. Take for example the Harvard-educated reverend Eugene Rivers of Boston, Massachusetts.

While he is not a television personality, Rivers is extremely influential politically. This is due to the ministry and goals of his Azusa Christian Community, a Pentecostal (COCIG) church in Dorchester, Massachusetts. Rivers has used his position and large congregation to take on the black political establishment, claiming that it has sold out black Americans who should pursue a new black political agenda.[39] To this end, his congregants are committed to implement Rivers's "Ten Point Plan for a National Christian Mobilization to Combat Black on Black Violence."

The minister, who works with the Boston police and lectures on gang violence around the country, was one of the clergymen invited to the White House by President Bush for the launch of his Faith-Based Initiative in 2001.

More importantly, Rivers has been a significant recipient of federal funds for his faith-community and law enforcement partnership. He is also a member of the Advisory Board of the Roundtable on Religion and Social Welfare Policy of the Pew Charitable Trust, and as such plays a role in engaging and informing the government about the role of faith-based organizations in such endeavors. In short, Rivers is well-connected within his church, the broader religious community, the government, and influential foundations.

While federal funds may tie some major religious leaders and their churches to the Republican Party, in actuality it is the support for moral issues that provide the crucial link between the two. Abortion, traditional family values, and opposition to homosexuality still trump other, broader moral issues such as poverty, immigration, and environmental reform, although the latter issues are gaining in importance, as will be shown in the next chapter.

Jesus Goes to the Movies and into Books

The Passion of the Christ by Mel Gibson opened the door for Christian film-makers in Hollywood. Reportedly, it took in $370 million[40] at the domestic box office in 2004, a profit that does not include revenues from the international market or from potential home video sales.

Attempting to capitalize on the faith-based market, Twentieth Century Fox and Lions Gate both vied for *Diary of a Mad Black Woman* by Tyler Perry. Lions Gate was successful, pulling in $21.8 million in its opening weekend, and Perry has reportedly made another $30 million himself through sales of the movie to small distributors.

That was when Twentieth Century Fox realized it had to jump into such a potentially viable economic market to be competitive and now has an "in-house special markets group,"[41] which is essentially a faith-based division. At its DVD screening center in Nashville, Tennessee, Fox allows Christian ministers and the Christian retail community to discuss its offerings while also soliciting feedback from the public through focus groups. Behind the project was the Christian Booksellers Association, which also represents thousands of retail stores nationwide supporting the effort to provide input on movies and publications in the nation.

Perhaps even more phenomenal has been the release of the apocalyptic book series *Left Behind* by Reverend Tim LaHaye and Jerry B. Jenkins. LaHaye has a Doctor of Ministry degree from Western Theological Seminary and an honorary Doctorate of Literature from Liberty (Baptist) University. He has written over fifty books, founded two accredited Christian high schools, founded the Christian Heritage College, and assisted in the creation of the Institute of Creation Research. He was instrumental in the development of the Moral Majority in the 1980s, and his wife Beverly LaHaye founded and served as the president of the Christian conservative organization Concerned Women for America.

LaHaye's coauthor and partner, Jerry Jenkins, has published over 150 books and has been a *New York Times* bestselling author sixteen times. He is an "as told to" author who wrote the autobiographies of Walter Payton, Nolan Ryan, Orel Hershiser, and many others. He is a "writer at large" for the previously mentioned Moody Bible Institute in Chicago.

The brainchild of LaHaye and Jenkins, *Left Behind* was published by Tyndale Publishing, which is now one of the top Christian publishers of fiction in the United States. Tyndale was founded in 1962 by Kenneth N. Taylor, whose original purpose was to publish a Bible paraphrased into everyday English for children and the general public to understand. As the company emerged, its purpose became clearer: to minister to people primarily through literature that is consistent with biblical principles. To that end, Tyndale announces clearly on its website that its corporate goal is to "Honor God. Excel in Business. Sustain controlled economic growth. Operate Profitably. And, Help employees grow."

Since the apocalyptic series appeared, Tyndale has, depending on whose statistics you use, sold between 60 to 75 million copies of *Left Behind*,[42] a total that translates into about $650 million in revenue for the publisher. Add to this another $10 million in related items such as games, music, apparel, collectibles, and a kids' series that purportedly rivals *Harry Potter.*

The vast appeal and financial success of the Christian last-days books appear as a definite religious phenomena and major moneymaker. Since the *Left Behind* series, Tyndale has put out three prequels to its apocalyptic series and continues to grow with each publication.

The *Left Behind* series has already been turned into three movies entitled *Left Behind, Left Behind II: Tribulation Force,* and *Left Behind: World at War.* The movies chronicle the end of the world in the context of modern geopolitics through the biblical prophecies in the apocalypse.

The first two DVDs have already been released and have sold 3 and 2 million copies[43] respectively—representing about another $100 million in consumer spending.[44] Just as interesting is the fact that attendance at the first movie was reported to have hit the 700,000 mark, and the second was said to have brought in 1.1 million people.[45] Although these numbers are significantly lower than the amount of people who attend mainstream movies, the *Left Behind* series provided a conservative, Christian alternative for evangelicals and others who are increasingly using the media as a means of religious witness, as well as a way to influence political thinking. In the *Left Behind* series, for example, the anti-Christ is portrayed as a political figure, "Nicolae," who was able to gain control of the United Nations. The series tied the end of times to immoral political domination and the vulnerability of international institutions to uncommitted leaders.

In a marketing coup, Cloud Ten Pictures, which distributed *Left Behind,* decided to show the LaHaye-Jenkins movies only in churches, rather than in movie theatres. The distributors, Peter and Paul Lalonde, believed that a network of churches could become "an alternative to the mainstream studio and theatre system."[46]

In the Christian-movie world, the licensing fee for *Left Behind* depends on the size of a church congregation, ranging from $69 to $199. Universities and schools are being charged as little as $49. Accompanying the charge is a marketing package that contains a specially created EVITE, promotional materials, a video message from the star, trailers, posters, and a church link to the official movie website. The entire deal is designed to bring in more congregants to those churches showing the movie, to raise awareness about the work of each participating church, and to highlight each church's commitment to sharing the gospel. In many cases (if not most) the movie is being paired with a homily or religious lesson afterwards.

The third movie in the series, *Left Behind: World at War,* was sold by the Lalondes to Sony. With a $1.2 million marketing budget, Sony has started its move into the spiritual market, having shipped 600,000 DVDs to WalMart in November 2005, with early sales that were reported as "strong."[47]

This previously untapped religious market represents a significant challenge to the values of the movie industry. Not only does it provide a new source of revenue but it has also opened a distinctive avenue for evangelization, involvement, reaction, and rejection to the secular world of Hollywood. A small case in point: the Traverse City Film Festival organized by Michael Moore in 2005 was challenged by a group of conservatives from Texas. They founded the Traverse Bay Freedom Film Festival and showed independent, politically oriented, conservative movies during Moore's festival. Their aim, of course, was to give the public a choice of ideologically diverse features at the movies.

Publishing is another obvious area of Christian media growth. Recently, major bestsellers with religious themes besides *Left Behind* have included *The Purpose-Driven Life* by Rick Warren, *The Da Vinci Code* by Dan Brown, and *The Five People You Meet in Heaven* by Mitch Albom. All of them represent and reflect the increasing American interest in spirituality, the meaning of life, the relevance of religion, and the quest for the afterlife—*values* that Hollywood and Washington have overlooked and marginalized, in their view.

The Christian Booksellers Association (CBA) reported that at its convention in 2003, retail representatives from over 2,600 stores attended its meeting. The purpose of CBA is to work with the 600-plus book publishers, record companies, gift companies, and Christian product suppliers to provide resources and impact lives for Christ.

This gives some indication of the number of stores selling books with evangelical themes, religious self-help messages, and Christian views on just about everything. And, it points out how the special influence of religious evangelism in popular literature and culture reinforces its relevance and explains its continuing influence on every aspect of American life.

Put Jesus into the World of Sports

Sports are influenced by conservative Christians as well. NBA players are calling for their teams to "PFJ," that is to "play for Jesus." And, moves like "the end-zone knee," "the sky point," and "the post-game kneel" are now part of NFL behavior. These are the actions of some football players who have discovered a way to overcome sin—by accepting the gift of Jesus's salvation and confessing to it. *The Christian Sports Magazine* will give the average sports fan a trial issue to find out more about it and how to do the same thing. Athletes, like Michael Chang, the retired tennis player, have grasped "every opportunity" to point people to "the one thing that has had the greatest impact on his life: having a personal relationship with Jesus Christ."

These new approaches augment a longtime organizational outreach to various players as well. The Fellowship of Christian Athletes (FCA) is a fifty-year-old organization founded by Don McClanen, Paul Benedum, Branch Rickey, and other Pittsburgh businessmen to "present to athletes and coaches and all whom they influence the challenge and adventure of receiving Jesus Christ as Savior and Lord, serving Him in their relationships and in the fellowship of the church."[48] Coaches and athletes are encouraged to "Compete for Christ," and the organization is based on the belief that Jesus was the greatest competitor of all time, fighting for the souls of men; a champion who was able to hang on the cross, the greatest teammate because he was able to lift up those around him, and the greatest captain, able to build a lasting team.[49]

Individuals become members of FCA by first submitting to the Competitor's Creed[50] and then living the life of a Christian. The Creed, which begins that "I am a Christian first and last," hung in the Air Force Academy locker room but was finally removed in the fall of 2007 when questions of religious intolerance were being investigated at the school.

At the basis of FCA are fundamentalist beliefs. Opponents of bringing religion into football claim that the First Amendment right to free religious exercise is being denied to non-Christians and atheists by the FCA and similar sports organizations to which many coaches belong. But, peer pressure and the fear of alienating a coach are among the reasons why no college athlete has yet to bring a legal challenge in court, according to the Reverend Barry W. Lynn of the Americans United for Separation of Church and State.[51]

This may change soon, however, as a case is wending its way through the courts in New Jersey regarding player-initiated pregame prayer. In the Garden State, the coach of the East Brunswick High School football team has always called his players together in the locker room and said a prayer for courage and to escape game injuries. Although it was essentially nondenominational, Marcus Borden was ordered to avoid participating in the prayer by the board of education. The case was brought before the U.S. District Court, with Judge Dennis Cavanaugh ruling that the coach can bow his head and bend his knee when the team captains lead the prayers. It remains to be seen if the ruling will stand and what impact it might have on college sports as well.

Another way that religion is entering the world of sport is through the Friday night minor league football game. In Birmingham, Alabama; Spokane, Washington; and Bridgewater, New Jersey, football and religion are now intertwined like horse and carriage; love and marriage. At specific games, promoters give away Bibles and bobbleheads of biblical figures such as Daniel, Noah, and Moses. In Birmingham, the hometown team wore jerseys with biblical verses on them before and after the game, and early numbers indicate that attendance is up at this new type of athletic event known as a "faith night."[52]

Organizers of these kinds of evenings insist that they are family-friendly activities in addition to providing spiritual messages. Churches get discounted tickets, and the teams play before filled stands. They believe that everybody wins all around.

What is most interesting is that Third Coast Sports, a Nashville marketing company, has established a new business venture that specializes in planning and selling church events, an entrepreneurial innovation that is moving into major league baseball soon. It is expanding by putting on faith nights with the Atlanta Braves, the Arizona Diamondbacks, and the Florida Marlins.

Put Jesus in the Public Arena

What the religious right, specifically the evangelicals, have been able to do in the last twenty-five years has been to create an alternative culture to the one that they envision as excessive, materialistic, and hedonistic. They have developed, instead, an American values-oriented culture that is infused with biblical teachings and the Christian message at all levels of living.

It is also an assertive type of witnessing to Jesus. It influences young people through Christian education and sports as well as others though a new type of media that produces movies and music with a biblical message. Individuals who have been looking for ways to live their lives in a more spiritually directed way now have a plethora of social alternatives and opportunities due to the saturation of the current culture by evangelicals and other religious conservatives.

It should come as no surprise then that acting in such biblical ways in so many facets of American life is simply part of a consistent pattern of evangelical behavior within the context of U.S. culture. What makes this so critical from a political point of view, however, is their leap to instill conservative moral values in American culture and their attempts to inculcate individual and institutional commitments to Jesus in the political arena. Evangelicals have been working steadily since the 1980s to advance their Christian ideas *politically* and to legitimize them through public policies, legislation, and the American judicial process.

How this involvement in the public arena occurred and grew is complex, and yet it is the natural consequence of a confluence of events that had been evolving since the Reagan administration. What was simply ephemeral before that time finally coalesced into a conservative, religious political movement, and then into the reality of providing significant support to gain political power that continues to play a critical part in the American political process today. The next chapter will look at this transition and show how the Republican-evangelical symbiosis evolved, how difficult it will be to challenge this *politically consistent* relationship in the future, and how it will continue to play a critical role in reasserting the politics of values in 2008 and beyond.

Notes

1. Kevin Phillips, *American Theocracy* (New York: Viking Press, 2006), ix. He also mentions the other pillars as being the oil-national security complex and the debt-dealing financial sector.

2. Jason De Parle, "Passing Down the Legacy of Conservatism," *New York Times,* July 31, 2006, A13.

3. De Parle, "Pasing Down the Legacy of Conservatism."

4. Laurie Goodstein, "Fearing the Loss of Teenagers, Evangelicals Turn Up the Fire," *New York Times,* October 6, 2006, l.

5. Goodstein, "Fearing the Loss of Teenagers," 20. The statistic was reported in

The Bridger Generation by Thom S. Rainer, a former professor of ministry, who said that he took the poll but that he did not follow up on it. The poll was 10 years old.

6. Goodstein, "Fearing the Loss of Teenagers."

7. Jesse McKinley, "A Youth Ministry Some Call Antigay Tests Tolerance," *New York Times*, September 9, 2007, A12.

8. www.silverringthing.com.

9. *It's Time*, SRT Newsletters, Fall 2004, Spring 2004, May 2004, and April 2004.

10. *ACLU of Massachusetts v. Leavitt*, No. 1:05-cv-11000-JLT, February 23, 2006.

11. The ACLU contended that federal funds for sexual abstinence programs had reached $206 million in 2006 and that funding organizations such as SRT was a type of religious indoctrination. SRT had held events in Alabama, Connecticut, Florida, Michigan, Minnesota, Pennsylvania, South Carolina, Tennessee, Texas, West Virginia, and Wisconsin. It also was slated to hold a number of other events across the South and Midwest in the future. See "ACLU Challenges Misuse of Taxpayer Dollars to Fund Religion in Nationwide Abstinence-Only-Until-Marriage Program," www.aclu.prg/reproductiverights/gen/12602prs200050516.html

12. Silver Ring Thing new release, February 26, 2006, www.silverringthing.com.

13. Ceci Connolly, "Teen Pledges Barely Cut STD Rates, Study Says," *Washington Post*, March 19, 2005, A3.

14. Connolly, "Teen Pledges Barely Cut STD Rates."

15. Connolly, "Teen Pledges Barely Cut STD Rates."

16. Rob Walker, "Consumed," *New York Times Magazine*, March 6, 2005, sec. 6, 28.

17. www.extremeclothing.com.

18. John Leland, "'Christian Diets' Fewer Loaves, Lots of Fishes," *New York Times*, April 28, 2005, G2.

19. www.goldstars.com/speakers/display.

20. Naomi Schaefer Riley, *God on the Quad* (New York: St. Martin's Press, 2005).

21. Riley, *God on the Quad*, 258–260.

22. Alan Finder, "Matters of Faith Find a New Prominence on Campus," *New York Times*, May 2, 2007, A16.

23. Russell Shorto, "With God at Our Desks," *New York Times Magazine*, October 31, 2004, 42.

24. www.reliancebankltd.com.

25. John Leland, "The Word in Bubbles," *New York Times*, August 26, 2006, 5.

26. Leland, "The Word in Bubbles."

27. www.christianradio.com/network.asp.

28. Stephen Winzenburg, "National Religious Broadcasters," in *Museum of Broadcast Communications Encyclopedia of Radio: 2004*, vol. 2, 1007–8.

29. www.gospelmusicchannel.com.

30. "Rocking for Jesus," December 8, 2004, www.cbsnews.com/stories2004/12/01/60II/printable658590.shtml.

31. See for example Bob Larson, *Larson's Book of Rock* (Wheaton, Illinois: Tyndale Publishers, 1987).

32. See http://hirr.hartsem.edu.

33. Joel Osteen, *Your Best Life Now: Seven Steps to Living at Your Full Potential* (Waynesboro, Georgia: Faithworks, 2004).

34. Joel Osteen, *Becoming a Better You: 7 Keys to Improving Your Life* (Simon and Schuster: New York, 2006).

35. Ralph Blumenthal "A Preacher's Credo: Eliminate the Negative, Accentuate the Prosperity," *New York Times*, March 30, 2006.

36. Hubert Morken, "Bishop T. D. Jakes: A Ministry for Empowerment," in Jo Renee Formicola and Hubert Morken, eds., *Religious Leaders and Faith-Based Politics* (Lanham, Maryland: Rowman & Littlefield, 2001), 28.

37. For a fuller discussion, see Hubert Morken, "Bishop T. D. Jakes: A Ministry for Empowerment," in Jo Renee Formicola and Hubert Morken, eds., *Religious Leaders and Faith-Based Politics* (Lanham, Maryland: Rowman & Littlefield, 2001), chap. 2.

38. Libby Copeland, "With Gifts from God," *Washington Post*, March 25, 2001, F1.

39. Cathy J. Cohen, "The Church?" A response to "Beyond the Civil Rights Industry," in *Boston Review*, April/May 2001, www.bostonreview.com.

40. Sharon Waxman, "The Passion of the Marketers," *New York Times*, July 18, 2005, C1.

41. See www.leftbehind-worldatwar.com/churchtheatricalrelease/howitworks.php.

42. Jerry Jenkins reports sales of 63 million on this website www.jerryjenkins.com, while www.rapidnet.com, which has consolidated statistics from a variety of sources, claims that 65 million is more likely with another 10 million for graphic novels and children's versions.

43. Sharon Waxman, "Sony Effort to Reach Christians Is Disputed," *New York Times*, November 2, 2005, E1.

44. Rob Walker, "God Is in the Distribution," *New York Times Magazine*, November 13, 2005, 38.

45. Walker, "God Is in the Distribution."

46. Walker, "God Is in the Distribution."

47. Waxman, "Sony Effort to Reach Christians Is Disputed."

48. www.fca.org.

49. www.fca.org.

50. See Appendix I for the Creed.

51. See Appendix I, 24.

52. Warren St. John, "Sports, Songs and Salvation on Faith Night at the Ballpark," *New York Times*, June 2, 2006, A1.

4

Extending Values:
Impacting the Political Process
and Public Policy

Introduction

EVERYTHING WITHIN THE RELIGIOUS RIGHT, from its social alternatives to
countercultural views, supports the same religious message: that the current American way of life mitigates traditional family values, is mired in
moral relativism, and assaults Christianity.

Spiritually, evangelicals see the answer to these problems in the message of
the good news of the gospel of Jesus Christ. It is His ethics, His philosophy,
and His teachings that must be the norms for personal behavior and salvation. They must be the clear, uniform, and unquestioned guides for living,
the values that stand on their own because of their intrinsic truth and justice.

Increasingly, evangelicals and other religious conservatives also believe
that the way to bring about a more humane society based on Christian religious values is through the active participation of members of faith communities in the American political process. At a seminal level, then, evangelical
political activity is predicted on the need for *consistency* in one's personal
beliefs and public actions. The move from literal, biblical rules for personal
conduct into decisions on public policy is simply a logical extension of the
coherent thinking of evangelicals. The political process is viewed as part of a
larger totality, as a way to enable individuals and society to witness to Jesus,
to be transformed by His salvation, and to implement His teachings within a
temporal, societal context.

A Short History of Values in Politics

While the notion of personal and political consistency is clear to evangelicals and continues to be spelled out more pragmatically among its leaders, the possibility of such coherence has been a source of debate throughout the course of political philosophy. The Greeks were the first to consider it. Plato believed that values such as wisdom, courage, moderation, and justice could be known, observed by the practices of the leaders of the state, and used as a means to provide the source of harmony within society. Aristotle maintained that similar virtues inhered in individuals as well as the state, leading him to go one step further than Plato and claim that politics was simply the public extension of personal ethics. Aristotle saw virtues as a means to provide both personal and political happiness—the latter being the ultimate end of the state.

St. Augustine, an early Christian priest-philosopher, advanced the idea that government was the protector of values. He argued in *The City of God* that man had to move to a higher, spiritual place beyond the "Earthly City." That is, from a place where life is characterized by love of self and imperfect virtues to the "Heavenly City," a metaphorical place that served as the repository of perfect values where one could enjoy the ultimate source of God's justice, compassion, and happiness.

It was not until the Renaissance and the questioning of all things religious that the practice of personal and political values were separated and justified both philosophically and empirically. In *The Prince*, Machiavelli pointed out that state unity and the maintenance of its power required that one must use virtue if he can, but resort to vice if necessary. He argued that the appearance of morality is as important as morality itself and that the pursuit of power for the unity of the state exempts the ruler from having to obey the same rules that he would have to follow in his personal life.

And so the battle was joined in the political world: to pursue one kind of values in one's personal life, but to practice a different set of principles in order to gain power for the political ruler and the unity of the state. Amoral political behavior was thus publicly sanctioned in the midst of rising humanism and the development of the nation-state.

History has furnished examples of rulers who have attempted to reconcile the notion of a dual ethical code with social and political obligations. For the most part, however, anything that advances the power position of the state, which political scientists call "realism," has become the standard for the practice of politics throughout the globe.

Americans like to believe that their political leaders have acted out of moral as well as pragmatic concerns and that their values reflect a higher order of behavior than those of autocratic, dictatorial, or collective power-hungry governments. In the Declaration of Independence, the founding fathers recognized the inalienable rights of all, the need for the consent of the governed, and the accountability of the state's leaders. They based the Constitution on these principles and added the Bill of Rights to further elaborate and protect the freedoms of individuals against a potentially overreaching federal government.

Within half a century of the ratification of the Constitution, John Quincy Adams, who was secretary of state at the time, wrote a document in 1853 known as the Monroe Doctrine. Named after the sitting president, James Monroe, it advanced the principle of Manifest Destiny, maintaining that America had the responsibility to bring freedom to the Western Hemisphere. This missionary notion was enhanced by the claim that territories within the American sphere of influence were no longer open to colonization by Europeans.

It was President Woodrow Wilson, an idealist, who attempted to bring a greater moral sense to American foreign policy. His belief in a League of Nations and a universal body to discuss world problems arose from his fundamental belief in reason and tolerance as evidenced in his Fourteen Points. Presented before a joint session of the Congress in 1918, Wilson's proposal called for freedom of the seas, the removal of trade barriers, the reduction of armaments, an end to secret diplomacy, and other ideas to shore up peace in the world.

After World War I and II, however, as "realists" came to control American foreign policy, their rationale for defeating Nazism and Communism gave greater credence to notions of power politics. One of the chief elements of realist ideology was the belief that the national interest must be defined in terms of power. Concomitantly, realists also argued that the national interest is fluid rather than static, and that the moral values of one state are not necessarily absolute or binding on other states. This type of foreign policy was the basis of the U.S. containment of Communism during the Cold War and carried the U.S. forward through its various conflicts with the Soviet Union in the latter part of the twentieth century.

It was only after the war in Vietnam and the abuse of political power by President Richard Nixon that Americans became seriously aroused about ethics in politics and began to demand greater accountability and personal moral values from their political leaders. President Jimmy Carter, a born-again Christian elected in 1976, believed that morality could be extended through politics and made a commitment to support human rights as the cornerstone of his foreign policy. His resolve was tested when the U.S.S.R. invaded Afghanistan and he refused to do business as usual with the Soviets.

Carter subsequently refused to allow American athletes to participate in the
Olympics in 1980.

President Ronald Reagan will be remembered for being the first president
to attempt to instill conservative values into modern American politics, particularly through his economic and foreign policy actions after his sweeping
defeat of Carter. By changing from the demand-side economic philosophy of
President Franklin Roosevelt and the Keynsians, Reagan adopted a supply-
side approach, which basically took the government out of playing the leading role in creating jobs and priming the pump with regard to the economy.
Instead, he called for tax incentives, the end of subsidies, and private rather
than public methods to move the American economy forward.

Attempting to create the "shining city on the Hill," Reagan also gave
emphasis to his conservative ideology by his political agenda designed to
defeat the "evil empire" of the Soviet Union. To that end, he updated the
U.S. military machine and gave impetus to the "Star Wars" defense system.
However, the Iran-Contra scandal scarred Reagan's presidency, even though
he has been credited by some with the downfall of Communism in Eastern
Europe.

President George W. Bush has brought the debate between personal and
political values to another level. As a Methodist, but not necessarily an evangelical, Bush is personally committed to advance the biblical message of
Christ through the political process. His is a consistent religious and political
message: be compassionate, respect life, support traditional family values,
advance democracy, and foster capitalism.

In Bush's mind, all of these principles are about morality at their core.
And, more importantly, he believes that they deserve to be given political
meaning, commitments that he has attempted to bring about though his own
Christian ideology—"compassionate" conservatism—and its attendant
political program, the Faith-Based and Community Initiative (FBCI).

By its establishment, Bush has effectively made a major domestic policy
shift by turning the public financing of social services upside down. And, by
his political determination to implement "charitable choice," a little-known
provision of the 1996 Welfare Reform Act, he promised to bring about a new
government policy that would equalize the funding of charitable programs
as part of his campaign platform. This had been part of the values agenda
pushed by the evangelicals and one of a myriad of promises that brought
Bush to the White House during his first, contested race for the presidency.

Compassionate, Yet Faith-Based, Conservatism

True to his word, George W. Bush unveiled the original Faith-Based Initiative
on January 29, 2001, only nine days into his administration. Its purpose was

to increase government concern for social services and to encourage religious organizations to compete for, and receive, federal funding for providing them.

Bush authorized the FBCI by signing two executive orders. The first created a new office within the White House known as the Office of Faith-Based and Community Initiatives, while the second extended such centers to five other cabinet agencies—Justice, Housing and Urban Development, Labor, Education, and Health and Human Services. Each agency was given, by its very establishment, the right to create specific regulations to end discrimination against religious groups within the purview of their areas of responsibility. In 2002, for example, the Department of Housing and Urban Development proposed to use federal funds to "acquire, rehabilitate or build centers"[1] used for nonreligious activities within religious buildings. These suggested policies gave pause to many on Capitol Hill.

The White House had attempted to support legislation that would assure the continued establishment, growth, and maintenance of the Faith-Based and Community Initiative long after the president would leave office. But a variety of bills, which showed promise in the House, met resistance and died in the Senate. Undeterred, the executive branch moved forward with its agenda.

In 2002, the White House simply reorganized all federal and state voluntary services. The president announced at the State of the Union Address that they would all become part of the new USA Freedom Corps. Thus, the Peace Corps, the Senior Corps, AmeriCorps, and the FBCI were repackaged as a new, complementary, voluntary, minority, social, and charitable agency.

The reorganization created a centralized administration of both secular and religious services headed by the director of the Domestic Policy Council in the White House, John Bridgeland. He was given the title of assistant to the president and director of the USA Freedom Corps and soon after, the programs were expanded and introduced on the local level in every state.

The FBCI office was headed early on by Jim Towey, whose major claim to fame was that he was formerly Mother Teresa's lawyer. He was charged with holding conferences across the country with religious and charitable providers—and keeping a solid relationship with them and the White House. Towey's deputy was David Kuo, who subsequently charged in his book, *Tempting Faith*, that many members of the Bush administration gave only "meager support" to the FBCI and exploited it politically.[2] He also maintained that many Christian allies were simply looked upon in White House circles as "boorish" and "nuts."[3] Towey denied such claims, and the White House commented that the program was "near and dear to the president's heart."[4]

The FBCI has grown significantly since its inception. By 2002, the president signed additional executive orders establishing faith-based offices in the

Agriculture Department, the Agency for International Development, the Environmental Protection Agency, and the Federal Emergency Management Agency. And it has been reported in *USA Today* that "faith based communities now receive more that 2.1 billion dollars a year from the federal government; making up about 11% of the 19.7 billion dollars awarded [in 2005] to community groups."[5]

To no one's surprise, this domestic program that has been most criticized by the political left is the most likely to be the first to get the ax should the Republicans lose the White House in 2008. Already, programs slated to provide special benefits and exemptions for religious groups that were brought up in the House are dead in the water. These include a series of bills that would allow religious groups to make partisan political endorsements, allow religious employers more freedom with regard to their hiring practices, and would change Bush's FBCI executive order into legislation—thus assuring that federal grants and contracts would continue to be available to religious organizations. Further, religious groups have entered the world of "hard lobbying," winning many grants by earmarking rather than by competing with government agencies for public funding. Their ability to gain such earmarks has tripled since the Bush presidency, leading skeptics to question whether or not many faith-based programs are truly worthwhile projects or the result of White House favoritism toward religious charitable and social institutions.[6]

The main opposition to the FBCI revolves around questions of employment, discrimination, and exemptions, as well as the principle of separation of church and state. Among the chief complaints from various segments of the secular left with the FBCI and the Bush affinity with religious, charitable organizations has been the growth of tax exemptions. The problem is fairly clear: as religious and charitable organizations have expanded their spiritual missions, their traditional tax exemptions have expanded as well.

On a personal level, clergy are exempt from income tax, housing costs, and can decline involvement in Social Security. In a significant case, Reverend Rick Warren, the author of *The Purpose-Driven Life*, which has purportedly sold over 25 million copies, was able to take on the IRS and expand the notion of the housing or "parsonage exemption." Warren, who pastors the 22,000 member Saddleback Church in Lake Forest, California, argued that the exemption based on a "fair market rental value" should be expanded to include actual housing expenses after he was denied the larger deduction in a tax audit. In 2000, the United States Tax Court ruled in Warren's favor.

But, the extension of tax exemptions went beyond the personal. As the FBCI came into effect, so did the growth of the phenomenon of the megachurch, the building of huge religious houses of worship, "cathedrals," on large tracts of land. Often attached to denominational shopping malls with restaurants, movies, coffee houses, fitness centers, and bookstores, some megachurches have even established music and video production companies—all tax exempt. Other large congregations, such as the AME Church of the Reverend Floyd Flake in Jamaica, Queens, is estimated to have about 10,000 parishioners and owns and operates a senior citizen facility, day care center, and a New York City block of retail stores.

In order to maintain such facilities in the inner city as well as in rural areas, tax exemptions have been allowed by the Bush administration through the FBCI, impacting property tax, personal income, payroll taxes, and even construction loans.[7] A new and growing practice has developed as well: issuing church building bonds, secured by local banks. These provide tax-free interest income and pay for the construction of a variety of church-related buildings. But these are not the only kinds of exemptions that have filtered down to the states. For example, Holy Land Experience, a biblical theme park in Florida, received a tax exemption from the Republican-controlled state legislature. In that state, the Bible, the Torah, the Koran, and other religious books are also exempt from the Florida sales tax.

But exemptions go beyond direct financial exemptions. In the book, *Faith-Based Initiatives and the Bush Administration: The Good, the Bad and the Ugly*,[8] Paul Weber, one of the co-authors, argues that a danger of using public monies for construction costs could result in redirecting federal building funds for other religious projects. And, he also cautions against religious affinity fraud, schemes that could be linked to people's desires to help with religious/charitable causes.

There have also been challenges to religious practices with regard to employment policies that have been developed to protect the management of religious organizations from government interference. Referred to as the "religious autonomy doctrine," such policies allow religious organizations to choose their own spiritual leaders, manage their own affairs, and to give preference to employees who adhere to their religious beliefs. This exemption was protected and written into the Civil Rights Acts of 1964 and 1972. Thus, gender, religious, and age bias are without merit in suits against religious organizations. In essence then, those religious/charitable organizations that receive federal funding through the FBCI and who are supposed to adhere to federal guidelines on such matters often do not in matters of employee rights.

Diana Henriques, a reporter for the *New York Times*, wrote a series of investigative reports on the proliferation of faith-based initiatives and also reported on a new way that religious groups have leveled the playing field to provide health care beyond the reach of regulators.[9] She revealed a new

ministry—one that is based on medical bill sharing. In essence, church members write a monthly check to an organization known as Christian Care Ministry, based in Melbourne, Florida, with offices in over 30 states. In turn,
Christian Care feeds checks to the American Evangelistic Association, its
parent organization, which then writes checks to health care providers.

Approximately 19,000 households participate in this type of insurance
coverage, a system that is essentially exempt from state insurance laws
because it is protected by historical, government limits on religious organizations. As a result, because the Internal Revenue Service cannot require public
financial statements or audits of internal religious congregations, the ministry that shares medical bill payments is without any real oversight. Participants are, therefore, vulnerable to the potential diversion of funds, fraud, and
other mismanagement.

As such religious exemptions continue, it might be expected that courts
will come under increasing pressure to deal with the web of financial and
workplace changes that have occurred under the faith-based initiatives. Many
see these exceptions as having gone beyond the traditional tradeoff of tax
exemptions for free social services. But, judicial challenges are becoming a
more remote possibility now with the legacy of a Republican-appointed conservative Supreme Court.

In June of 2007, the justices refused to hear a lawsuit disputing the use of
public monies to support the various faith-based programs that have been
funded through the FBCI. In a five to four vote, the Supreme Court ruled in
Hein v. Freedom From Religion Foundation, Inc., that taxpayers cannot sue
the government for expenditures with which they disagree, even though an
exemption exists allowing legal challenges for programs that promote religion.[10]

Based on the precedent established in *Flast v. Cohen* in 1968, the plaintiffs
were rebuffed recently when the Court insisted that the precedent was "an
inkblot"[11] on its jurisprudence and essentially illogical. As a result, individual
cases at the state level might survive some specific legal challenges, but a
national ruling that could enjoin the funding of all faith-based programs
seems highly unlikely, considering the make up of the current Supreme
Court.

If indeed the FBCI does end up on the political chopping block after the
2008 election, there are still long-term policy implications to consider. How
long will it really take to dismantle the infrastructure of religious/charitable
organizations and *the intermediary groups* that have been put in place by the
symbiotic relationship of the religious right and the Bush administration?
And, if faith-based programs were left unfunded, would the Supreme Court
allow such a reversal of policy to occur?

The implementation of President Bush's major domestic policy shift has been a feat that religious conservatives have been trying to accomplish throughout much of American history. Now they can see the reality of these policies and enjoy the rewards of the *programs* that have emerged, having been given new importance and meaning by George W. Bush.

The FBCI is only one program that has been instituted by the president and his party; it has whetted the appetite of the evangelicals and other Christian conservatives. Therefore, there is no reason to expect that evangelicals will curtail their political support of polices, programs, or candidates who reflect their religious ideas in the political arena. They have just begun to flex their political muscle.

Evangelical Religious and Political Consistency

Christian conservatives, particularly evangelicals, have reinforced their social, economic, and religious subculture by calling for personal and religious consistency in politics. Their political success in the last decade is, in a way, sweet vindication.

The history of evangelicals in America is characterized as being the step-child of mainline Protestantism. Poorer and less educated than Episcopalians and Presbyterians, evangelicals like Southern Baptists, Pentecostals, and others were often dismissed by mainstream Protestants as Bible-thumping fundamentalists who evangelized and functioned outside of established cultural, educational, and religious structures in a liberal, progressive America.

Being on the fringes of society and falling into cultural disrepute, particularly with the loss of their creationist views at the Scopes Trial in 1925, evangelicals spent the better part of the 1930s developing their own Christian infrastructure and looking inwardly. By building mission agencies, Bible institutes, revival grounds, and publishing houses to preach the word of Jesus, they created their own religious world within the more acceptable mainstream one of their Protestant stepbrothers. Individual ministers took on such organizational tasks and operated within their own spheres of influence and theology.

The most significant organizational advancement of the disparate religious conservatives was the establishment of the National Association of Evangelicals (NAE) in 1942. Its formation facilitated the National Religious Broadcasters (NRB) in 1944 after the major radio networks announced that religious broadcasting time would be distributed by the Federal Council of Churches, part of the mainline Protestant establishment. The NAE brought together fundamentalists and other conservative religious denominations, and as a result, the embryonic NAE encompassed about 500,000 members within a relatively short period of time.

In 1951, the NAE went international and established the World Evangelical Fellowship. Representatives of the NAE were invited to the White House by President Dwight Eisenhower, and by 1960, the religious organization had grown to thirty-two denominations representing nearly 1.5 million members.

It was President Ronald Reagan who received the blessings of the evangelicals' first major foray into elections. With the help of Dr. Billy A. Melvin, the executive director of the NAE, the evangelicals had constructed the Evangelical Center in Wheaton, Illinois, and expanded its Office of Public Affairs. The NAE enlarged its government operations, and with individuals like Richard Viguerie and direct mailings, prepared "report cards" on candidates seeking public office. The ability to register new voters and to educate them changed the entire social and political focus of the National Association of Evangelicals. It changed their power, too.

Reagan, who came to power with evangelical support, spoke at the NAE's national meeting in 1983, giving the organization greater political visibility, legitimacy, and clout. Garnering support for their mutual agendas, Reagan noted in his speech that the "prevailing attitude" of many who turned to "modern day secularism" was "discarding the tried and time-tested values upon which . . . our civilization is based."[12] Signaling a return to traditional values, Reagan began to lay the groundwork for a future Republican-evangelical political symbiosis.

At that same meeting, Reagan denounced the collectivist ideology of the Soviet Union and its aggressive impulses in the arms race. He made international headlines when he called the Soviet government "the focus of evil in the modern world," before the evangelical gathering. To ignore such facts, he maintained, was "tantamount to removing the U.S. from the struggle between right and wrong, good and evil."[13]

Reagan, who equated ideology with theology, reiterated the same message the following year at the National Prayer Breakfast. He said,

> I believe that faith and religion play a critical role in the political life of our nation, and always has, and that the church—and by that I mean all churches, all denominations—has had a strong influence on the state and this has worked to our benefit as a nation.[14]

The conservative president invited and consulted with many evangelical leaders such as Jerry Falwell during his tenure in the White House. According to Linda Chavez, head of the White House Office of Public Liaison during the Reagan presidency, evangelical influence was so significant and clear because evangelicals could—and did—register hundreds of thousands of new voters each year—many of whom eventually would vote Republican.[15]

One can also say that evangelical political power also came from the fact that the Catholic bishops during Reagan's administration opposed the president's economic policy and his willingness to use American nuclear power if attacked by the Soviet Union. Coupled with the fact that Catholics did not vote as a bloc or pose any kind of united opposition to Reagan's foreign policy, evangelicals were able to flourish politically. They emerged as the most influential religious group within the Republican, conservative, Reagan administration and remembered where their bread was buttered for the future.

Since the 1980s, the NAE has grown exponentially and significantly. Point in fact: the 2004 election garnered about 80 percent of the evangelical vote for George W. Bush because it was an overwhelming referendum on his character and political *values* (read religious values) and a way to reward his support for the unified, evangelical call for consistency in private and public life.

In return, the White House showed its appreciation as well. President Bush or one of his key advisors spoke *weekly* with the Reverend Ted Haggard, the former head of the NAE and later his successor during the course of the Bush administration. In this way, evangelicals had an open line to the White House to comment on appointments and proposed policies. Their access was significant, their views considered, and their support virtually unconditional.

This solidifying religious-political symbiosis was a result of evangelical spiritual consistency, its attempts to advance Christian political values, and its cohesive political organization. To the general public, this appeared to be a pragmatic coalition, but in reality it was part of a larger strategy by the evangelicals to impact the U.S. political process.

In 2001, at their annual convention, the NAE had commissioned nearly two dozen of its leading scholars to look at the role and potential strategies that its organization could pursue to significantly influence public policy on social issues such as abortion and gay marriage, as well as broader problems such as poverty, justice, and human rights. Their findings and recommendations were critical to their political success with the Republican Party and the Bush administration.

A document entitled *For the Health of the Nation: An Evangelical Call to Civil Responsibility*[16] emerged in October 2004 and was endorsed by 90 of the NAE's most prominent ministers in March 2005. The document was recognized as one that could carry "substantial weight in the evangelical community," a number that some now say represents "30 million people in 45,000 churches and 52 denominations in the U.S."[17]

For the Health of the Nation gives an insight into the way that evangelicals see themselves within American culture and society. The document also articulates their religious beliefs—a literal acceptance of the Bible and the gospel message of Jesus; a commitment to personal transformation and the rejection of sin; a witness to the salvation of Christ; and an attempt to bring His teachings and example into every aspect of one's life. Further, *For the Health of the Nation* is a blueprint that shows how those religious beliefs can, and should, impel the evangelical participation in the American political process and serves the basis for action to influence U.S. public policy.

Originally concerned with the fact that only half of all evangelicals vote, the authors of the document cited with alarm that religion's involvement in public issues is being continually attacked; that there is a rise in assertive secularism; that 9/11 has polarized global conflict; and that evangelicals must do more globally on issues such as AIDS and human rights. Most critically, the NAE recognized that American political actors are beginning to see their roles in moral terms.[18]

The preamble to *For the Health of the Nation* clearly shows that the NAE knows that this time and their position in America society are an historic opportunity "to shape public policy in ways that could contribute to the well-being of the entire world." For them, "Disengagement is not an option."

The principles that the NAE is committed to are sevenfold:

- the maintenance of religious freedom and liberty of conscience;
- the support of the family and protection of children;
- the sanctity of human life and the safeguarding of its nature;
- the quest for justice and compassion for the poor and vulnerable;
- the respect for human rights;
- the commitment to peace;
- and the protection of the environment.

To this end, *For the Health of the Nation* states that "A good government preserves the God-ordained responsibilities of society's other institutions, such as churches, other faith-centered organizations, schools, families, labor unions, and businesses."

The NAE principles are turned into concrete concerns by the organization's involvement and activism as well as its belief that the First Amendment allows "gospel pluralism," or equal access for all religious groups to voice their spiritual tenets and practices, along with juridical standards to protect them. With regard to issues then, the NAE is committed to work for laws that protect the traditional family and oppose those that compromise its integrity, such as gay marriage. It supports human dignity and therefore opposes abortion, euthanasia, and human experimentation. It believes in economic justice and therefore supports governmental social welfare programs that provide opportunity and self-sufficiency. It believes that government should support agencies that empower the poor, including those that are faith-based. On foreign policy, the NAE is on record supporting democracy in former colonial lands, Muslims nations, and emergent post-Communist ones.

The means for evangelical political engagement are also set up clearly in *For the Health of the Nation.* The NAE specifically states that it is "committed to support Christians who engage in political and social action in a manner *consistent* with biblical teachings." And the organization urges all Christians to become informed, to vote, to communicate their biblical values to their representatives, and to encourage vocations to public service.

It is no surprise then that the evangelicals would support President George W. Bush in the 2004 election, were counted on to be working for those seeking public office in the midterm election of 2006, and are expected to be committed to their avowed religious principles for the presidential election in 2008. With a blueprint in place, and with the clout that they now have with the Republican Party, the NAE is potentially in a position to influence American elections for years to come.

Catholics, Political Consistency, and Moral Coherence

Catholics, too, have tried to reconcile their religious beliefs with the various political ideologies that characterize their adherents, but they have not been as successful as the evangelicals in the American political arena. This is due to the sociological make up of the diverse membership of the Catholic Church; its broad social justice agenda, its political opposition to both major parties in the name of morality, and its sporadic political efforts to advance dogmatic concerns in the public arena.

Originally, Catholics who immigrated to the United States faced great difficulty in finding a place within its social, economic, and political mainstream. Derided and victimized until after World War II, this was a result of their emigration into a country that was essentially a white, Anglo-Saxon bastion from its inception. Catholic newcomers were poor, uneducated, and segregated by choice. They moved into neighborhoods, or ghettoes, that reflected their ethnic and religious mores. Their religious leaders served as more than spiritual teachers; they were surrogate political and cultural mentors as well. Catholic churches provided social services, found jobs for their adherents, and educated the children of the immigrants in parochial schools until they were integrated into the mainstream.

Due to the soaring increase in their numbers, the patriotism that they showed in World War I and II, and the educated class that they developed, economic doors opened to them in the 1940s. Catholics slowly acquired credibility and legitimacy within the political arena, and the election of John F. Kennedy in 1960 seemed to assure their ability to attain the American dream. Good times seemed to be ahead for the hard-working, patriotic, college-educated Catholics of the new generation.

Therefore, in 1973, when the Supreme Court decided to hear the case of *Roe v. Wade,* the American bishops believed that their moral position was secure enough within the nation's consciousness and that they did not have to involve themselves judicially in the case that has polarized the country for the last 25 years. However, after the Court's decision was handed down, the bishops realized that they had lost a crucial moral battle within the public arena, that their leadership role among their adherents had been damaged, and that they would have to begin to play a much more active political role in the United States to have any kind of future moral clout in the development of public policy America.

The Vatican, which has a history of speaking out on questions regarding the social and political order,[19] has supported political activism during the last quarter of a century and urged coherent religious and political behavior. A variety of statements and documents were issued from Rome in 2002, when Joseph Cardinal Ratzinger, the current Pope Benedict XVI, discussed the participation of Catholics in political life.

At the time, Ratzinger pointed out that Christians have had a 2,000-year history of involvement in the political life of their communities. Even though they fulfilled their civic duties in the past, he contended that there was still a great need for a fuller participation in the future in terms of voting, developing political solutions, and providing legislative choices for the common good.

This was due, according to Ratzinger, to the rise of cultural relativism, a phenomenon that served as a defense for something more insidious: ethical pluralism. The Vatican viewed this trend as the reason for a tolerance of decadence in society as it manifested itself in a lack of understanding and respect for the dignity of the human person.

In order to counter this disregard and ignorance, the Vatican asked Catholics to be guided by their Christian consciences. This meant that they were expected to infuse politics with Christian values, to respect the nature and autonomy of the political process itself, and to cooperate with other citizens.[20]

Theologically concerned and centered on the importance of human life, the Vatican reiterated that lawmaking bodies have a "grave and clear obligation to oppose"[21] any law that attacks it. While the church tried to make clear that it did not intend to exercise political power in any particular state, it was clear that it did hope to play an instructive role in forming the consciences of its adherents, particularly those who were involved in political life.

Their actions and those of all Catholics were expected to be "morally coherent," that is, motivated by their united and indivisible consciences. "There cannot be two parallel lives in their existence; on the one hand, the so-called 'spiritual life,' with its values and demands, and on the other, the so-called 'secular life,' that is life in a family, at work, in social responsibilities, in the responsibilities of public life and in culture."[22] All Catholics, therefore, either as citizens or as elected officials in authentic democracies, would be expected to oppose laws that compromised human life and dignity. To do less, the Vatican felt, would be to accept intolerant secularism and could potentially lead to a Catholic "cultural diaspora," or to indifference and a society without truth.

These ideas were reinforced by the American Catholic hierarchy, acting in concert as a canonical organization known as the United States Conference of Catholic Bishops. As a group, they had been issuing reflections on faithful citizenship in advance of each presidential election since 1976, an attempt, perhaps, to regain a teaching role by discussing three specific moral dimensions of politics. These included aspects of values that dealt with (1) the Catholic responsibility to participate actively in faith-filled citizenship; (2) to be properly informed about matters of conscience; and (3) to publicly support human life and dignity especially as it applies to the poor and the vulnerable.[23]

These values and their attendant obligations were reiterated in the election of 2004. The bishops intended to provide moral and political guidelines for Catholic voters as well as for the Catholic presidential candidate, Senator John Kerry.

In essence, the bishops called for a politics focused on moral principles, viewed though the eyes of faith, and based on a consistent concern for human life and dignity. They saw it as their responsibility to "measure all candidates, policies, parties, and platforms by how they protect[ed] or undermine[d] the life, dignity, and rights of the human person, [and] whether they protect[ed] the poor and vulnerable and advance[d] the common good."[24]

Interestingly, the bishops believed that the most important assets that Catholics brought to the public square were their consistent moral framework, their experience in serving those in need, and their large and diverse community of believers. As to the notion of moral consistency, they continued to stress that political polices must serve human life and dignity. As Catholics, they said, "we are not free to abandon unborn children because they are seen as unwanted or inconvenient" or "to create and then destroy human lives in a quest for medical advances or profit."[25]

As a church, the bishops maintained that Catholic adherents must enrich the political process with their moral beliefs and work to make them the moral priorities of public life. Specifically, they called on Catholics to reject abortion, euthanasia, assisted suicide, the death penalty, and the preemptive use of force. They "welcomed" government efforts to work with faith-based groups as a partner. They believed that Catholics should support marriage as a lifelong commitment between a man and a woman, and called for U.S. law to reflect this principle. Other matters such as social justice, welfare and social security reform, the reduction of poverty, and affordable and accessible health care were clearly among their concerns as well, but all revolved around the one basic, consistent principle: the right to human dignity and development.

When Kerry rejected these ideas, he shattered the notion of moral coherence within the Catholic political psyche. His personal beliefs were held to be private and internal, more importantly, *separate* from his political stands.

Kerry's inability to bring his Catholicism more forcefully into the public arena led many of the bishops to simply be totally "objective" in the 2004 presidential race and to treat the presidential candidate with ambivalence. Some, however, wanted Kerry to be punished for his lack of moral coherence, and so, there were some among the Catholic hierarchy who wanted to refuse him the right to take the Sacrament of Communion.

Behind the scenes, the bishops were grappling with how to handle Kerry and his fragmented morality politics. A Task Force on Catholic Politicians had been set up in 2003 and was to make general suggestions after the election of 2004. However, at an interim meeting before the election, a group of disaffected bishops emphasized their right to deny communion within their dioceses based on canon law. As a result, Kerry became anathema within certain Catholic hierarchical circles, and suspect in others.

In the end, Kerry's inability to be morally coherent about his religious and political convictions did not serve him well as Catholics were concerned. Indeed, only 47 percent of Catholics voted for Kerry in 2004, while 52 percent supported President Bush. Thus, while the Catholic candidate could not win the vote of his own religious community, his morally consistent Methodist opponent could.

Kerry, instead, managed to split the Catholic vote, again relegating Catholics to a swing position rather than one of significant political clout. Representing about 25 percent of the population, a number similar to that of the evangelicals, Catholics remained fragmented by Kerry's inconsistent positions and splintered by a variety of values that he held. In the end, Catholics again lost the opportunity to have a larger moral and political voice in America, being ostensibly sidelined by a candidate unable to be morally coherent.

The Black Church: Another Source of Consistency and American Politics

Historically, the black church in America has always been committed to more than religious worship. All of its denominations have served variously as sanctuaries, social organizations, sources of charitable help, and training grounds for political activism.[26] And, according to Fredrick C. Harris, the author of *Something Within: Religion in African American Political Activism*, black religion still continues to assist African Americans with becoming a part of the political process today.[27]

There are a number of theories about the role of the black church throughout American history. Some scholars argue that religion simply served as an opiate, as a means of oppression and social control, as a way to subvert black resistance to slavery. They see the black church as an institution of political quietism. Others claim that religion played a central role in black culture and liberation, serving as a catalyst for collective involvement in critical moral and political issues such as civil rights.

The earliest black churches, however, were founded by white Christians for their slaves and were a blend of African and Protestant worship rituals. By 1816, Bishop Richard Allen of Philadelphia founded the African Methodist Episcopal Church (AME) out of sociological, rather than theological, grounds—that is, as a way to end discrimination against blacks within Christian houses of worship. Today, the AME is a member of the National Council of Churches and the World Council of Churches and the sponsor of a number of independent, historical black colleges. Other black denominations flourished as well: the National Baptist Convention, which was founded in 1894, and the Church of God in Christ (COGIC), established in 1907, the latter being based on Pentecostalism and Holism.

After the Civil War, black churches served in charitable capacities and helped to resettle freed slaves in both the North and the South. Additionally, the black church in America has been historically political. Black ministers were for the most part the best-educated members of their congregations and often the links between white politicians and the majority parties and districts that they controlled. The religious leaders were courted for their influence and the votes they could deliver from their congregants for specific candidates.

Black ministers became an important resource in the white political infrastructure. They provided access and introductions to important members of the black community; they could encourage voter registration, campaign contributions, and political rallies—or not. They controlled social networks and meeting places and could be formidable in presenting political grievances to those in power. In appreciation, they were often plied with minor patronage positions and given a certain amount of social status within segregated societies across the United States. Some ministers even got loans and gifts in exchange for allowing candidates to speak to their congregations.[28] There were also those ministers who got "street money"—such as those in New Jersey in the not too distant past who were paid for the busses and cabs that were supposed to take the clerics and their congregants to the polls to vote for Republican Christine Todd Whitman in her first gubernatorial race.

In 1955, when Martin Luther King called on his congregation to take up the cause of Rosa Parks and civil rights, first in Alabama and then in the rest of the United States, the black church, with its various denominations, became united as one. Its ministers became the leaders of demonstrations, marches, and political activity for civil rights, creating a moral force with *political* power to effect change in the culture, mores, and way of life in America. The Reverend Ralph David Abernathy, the Reverend Jesse Jackson, and many others took the lead economically and politically to implement the principles of the Civil Rights Act in 1965 and the Voting Rights Act in 1974 to bring meaningful political change for the future. But, today there are some fissures within its ranks.

The black church continues to be a major force in the lives of black Americans, and statistics show that 85 percent of blacks consider religion "very important" to them.[29] However, some of their traditional values and methods are beginning to be questioned by church leaders. Concerns about discrimination and oppression are being challenged by issues of personal morality. A *New York Times* headline recently revealed that "Black Churches Struggle over Their Role in Politics."[30] Ministers such as Bishop Harry Jackson, Jr., of the Hope Christian Church in Maryland are promoting a "Black Contract with America on Moral Values," a call for a commitment from members of faith communities to oppose same-sex marriage and abortion. And many others, such as the well-connected Reverend Eugene Rivers, continue to take money from the federal government for the president's faith-based initiative.

Some black intellectuals, who make no value judgments about such views or actions, claim that this should come as no surprise. They argue that the black church provides a moral dimension to politics, that it sets out an alternative worldview, a sacred assurance or confidence of guidance and protection—as well as a sense of personal self-worth and competence.[31]

Others have challenged and continue to question the credibility of the black religious establishment, specifically ministers such as Reverend Al Sharpton who have been able to have a major political impact across the United States. In 2001 when this author interviewed him, Sharpton was ahead of the religious-political curve.[32] He understood that blacks needed to be empowered through united pressure on the media and business organizations. He encouraged black political participation and worked tirelessly in New York, where he ran for local and statewide office.

Even with its natural internal debates, the black church still continues to provide a sense of religious and political consistency in the United States. It continues to infuse the political process with an historical sense of the value of individual equality and freedom. It has fostered social and charitable priorities in the political arena, bringing special attention to those who are marginalized within society. And, in some cases, it has also pragmatically participated in federal programs to gain monies for the work of its faith communities to help those who are disadvantaged among them.

The Nexus of Evangelical Saturation, Christian Consistency, and Politics

So what does all this mean? First, it clearly shows that evangelicals are in ascendancy in American politics, and that such dominance will help them to continue to control public policy and the political leadership in the United States in the future. They are better organized than Catholics politically, much larger in numbers than black Christian adherents, and more clearly focused and united on specific conservative religious issues. The reason for their increasing ability to have a major social and political influence in America is based on the naturally evolved, evangelical commitment to infuse and saturate American society with biblical principles that consistently adhere to the message of Jesus.

Politically, evangelicals are engaged in public life because they believe theologically that people are made in the image and likeness of God, were given dominion over the earth, and are responsible for its just governance. They believe that such governance is a way to witness to the fact that Jesus is Lord—that to opt out of this responsibility would be tantamount to rejecting the stewardship of the world as commanded by God and abandoning it to the forces of evil. They believe they must act prophetically and work for the renewal and reform of the structures of the world that have developed between Jesus' first and predicted second coming.

This apocalyptic belief plays into every political judgment that Christian civic engagement requires. Evangelicals hold that social problems must be corrected by personal decisions and structural changes, by personal conversions, and by the transformation of unjust institutions. Even though they accede to humility and civility, evangelicals are clear and say "When we as Christians engage in political activity, we must maintain our integrity and keep our biblical values intact . . . we must never compromise principles . . . we must be clear that biblical faith is vastly larger and richer than every limited, inevitable imperfect political agenda . . ."[33]

Thus, the politics of evangelicals are essentially based on biblical teachings in the Old and New Testament, literally understood. It will be difficult to argue or change such beliefs, especially as they are taken up in the name of God.

Second, evangelicals are not the only conservative Christians who can be counted on to join in their values-oriented politics. Catholics have the potential to be strong allies in such battles. While Catholics have a broader ideological constituency, they do hold many values in common with evangelicals, for example, the belief in "imago dei," that is the notion that the person is made in the image and likeness of God and is therefore worthy of respect and dignity before birth, during life, and at the end of life. Life issues unite both religious constituencies. Support for the family, marriage as an institution between a man and a woman, cautious scientific approaches to stem cell research, opposition to euthanasia, and death with dignity are further issues and forces to unite them at election time, if values again take center stage in the presidential election of 2008.

Third, religious conservatives, especially black Christians, have one message on which they all agree: that Jesus died for them, saved them, and freed them and that they must use that reality in their daily lives and their political behavior. Even though the black church may choose to enlarge its moral agenda in the future and increasingly consider matters of personal morality, it will continue to unify its members politically. Regardless of what its detractors may say about how the black church should proceed within the political process, its prophetic history cannot be denied: It has always spoken truth to power, and will continue to do so in the future.

The leading religious conservatives have clear blueprints to follow in the political arena. But, evangelicals, more specifically, have reconciled their religious and ideological beliefs and staked out a relationship with a political party that is willing to accept them with open arms. With other religious groups being less organized and more diverse, how can they possibly fail to continue to impact the American political process in the future? Or are there other religious groups who might be able to mount a challenge to their political influence? The next chapter takes up this question and looks at the competing agenda and new role of religious progressives and centrists in America. More importantly, it explores the possibility of a new relationship between the spiritual left and center with political liberals—and the potential for a new twist on what the values vote may come to mean in the United States.

Notes

1. Eric Lichtblau, "Bush Plans to Let Religious Groups Get Building Aid," *New York Times*, February 23, 2002, A1.

2. David D. Kirkpatrick, "Book Says Bush Aides Ridiculed Christian Allies," *New York Times*, October 13, 2006.

3. Kirkpatrick, "Book Says Bush Aides Ridiculed Christian Allies."

4. Kirkpatrick, "Book Says Bush Aides Ridiculed Christian Allies."

5. Richard Benedetto, "Faith-Based Programs Flourishing, Bush Says," *USA Today*, March 10, 2006, 5A.

6. Diana B. Henriques and Andrew W. Lehren, "Religious Groups Reaping Share of Federal Aid for Pet Projects," *New York Times*, May 13. 2007, A1.

7. For a fuller description of such exemptions, see the series by Diana B. Henriques, "As Religious Programs Expand, Disputes Rise Over Tax Breaks," October 10 and October 1–20, 2006, *New York Times*.

8. Jo Renee Formicola, Mary Segers, and Paul Weber, *Faith-Based Initiatives and the Bush Administration: The Good, the Bad and the Ugly* (Lanham, Maryland: Rowman & Littlefield, 2003).

9. Diana B. Henriques, "Sharing the Health Bills," *New York Times*, October 20, 2006, C1.

10. 127 S. Ct. 2553.

11. Linda Greenhouse, "Justices Reject Suit on Federal Money for Faith-Based Office," *New York Times*, June 26, 2007, A8.

12. "Excerpts of the President's Speech to National Association of Evangelicals," *New York Times*, March 9, 1983, A18.

13. "Excerpts of the President's Speech to National Association of Evangelicals."

14. Phil Gailey, "Reagan, at Prayer Breakfast, Calls Politics and Religion Inseparable," *New York Times*, August 24, l984, A2.

15. Interview with Linda Chavez, head of the White House Office of Public Liaison, January 14, 1986.

16. National Association of Evangelicals, *For the Health of the Nation: An Evangeli-*

cal Call to Civil Responsibility, www.nae.net/images/civic-responsibility2pdf. Herein referred to as *For the Health of the Nation*.

17. American Family Association Journal, "Evangelical Strategy Statement Gains Approval," May 2005, www.afajournal.org/2005/may/5.05evangelicals.asp.

18. *For the Health of the Nation*.

19. See the following Papal Encyclicals: by Leo XIII—*Rerum Novarum*; by Pius XI—*Quadragesimo Anno*; by John XXIII—*Mater et Magistra* and *Pacem in Terris*; Paul VI—*Populorum Progressio* and *Octagesima Adveniens*; and John Paul II—*Centesimus Annus* and *Sollicitudo Rei Socialis*.

20. Congregation for the Doctrine of the Faith, "Doctrinal Note on Some Questions Regarding *The Participation of Catholics in Political Life*," sec. l, para. 2. This is in keeping with the Catholic Catechism, letters of Pope John Paul II, and the documents of the Second Vatican Council. Accessed via www.vatican.va/roman_curia// congregations/cfaith/documents/re_con/cfaith.doc_2000.

21. Congregation for the Doctrine of the Faith, "Doctrinal Note," sec. 2, para. 4. The statement also says quite clearly that ". . . a well-formed Christian conscience does not permit one to vote for a political program or an individual law which contradicts the fundamental content of faith and morals . . ." See also John Paul II, *Evangelium Vitae*, on the subject.

22. Congregation for the Doctrine of the Faith, "Doctrinal Notes" sec. 3, para. 6.

23. The Administrative Board of the United States Catholic Conference, *Faithful Citizenship: A Catholic Call to Political Responsibility*, www.usccb.org/faithfulcitizen ship/bishopStatement.html.

24. The Administrative Board of the United States Catholic Conference, *Faithful Citizenship*, part 3.

25. The Administrative Board of the United States Catholic Conference, *Faithful Citizenship*, part 4.

26. For a comprehensive history see Reverend Michael Battle, *The Black Church in America* (Malden, Massachusetts: Blackwell, 2006).

27. Fredrick C. Harris, *Something Within: Religion in African American Political Activism* (New York: Oxford University Press, 1999).

28. Harris, *Something Within*, 92.

29. Pew Forum, *Religion in Public Life*. Section IV. www.people-press.org/reports/ display.php3?pageID = 115.

30. Neela Banerjee, "Black Churches Struggle over Their Role in Politics," *New York Times*, March 6, 2005, A23.

31. Harris, *Something Within*, 69–72.

32. Jo Renee Formicola, "The Reverend Al Sharpton: Pentecostal for Racial Justice," in Jo Renee Formicola and Hubert Morken eds., *Religious Leaders and Faith-Based Politics* (Lanham, Maryland: Rowman & Littlefield, 200l).

33. *For the Health of the Nation*.

5

The Democrats Respond:
Let's Talk Values

Introduction

CAN THE RELIGIOUS RIGHT continue to play a consistent, coherent, and pivotal role in the politics of values? Or can it be replaced by more formidable opponents—specifically, spiritual progressives?

American politics creates strange connections. Take, for example, the emerging courtship between the growing religious left and center with its like-minded ideological, political counterparts. During the 2008 presidential primaries, these spiritually progressive groups showed just how keenly they were interested in getting to know, and working with, political candidates. For example, religious organizations like Sojourners, Catholics in Alliance, The One Campaign, OXFAM America, and the Christian Eastern University held a Faith Forum in the spring of 2007 at George Washington University in the nation's capital. Its purpose was to get specific answers from the presidential contenders about their spirituality, personal attitudes about moral issues that impinged on politics, and their views on faith-related public policies. With a carefully screened audience, they were questioned by Soledad O'Brien of CNN, the Reverend Jim Wallis (founder of the Sojourners), and other religious leaders about how they would deal with moral questions such as abortion, poverty, and war.

Beyond those policy-related issues, Senator Hillary Clinton was unabashedly asked about the role that her religion played in dealing with her unfaithful husband. Senator John Edwards was questioned about the worst sin he had ever committed. And, Senator Barak Obama, who was asked whether or not God was on the side of U.S. troops in Iraq, was clever enough to spend most his time discussing the plight of the poor thus using up the time that had been set aside for his personal religious scrutiny. All of the candidates, however, were willing to discuss their own sense of religiosity[1] and personally appeared to know most of the members of the clergy panel who questioned them.

What the forum was able to do, besides informing the public about the religious values of the Democratic candidates, was to show how the religious left and center are uniting and emerging as a formidable constituent base for the upcoming presidential race. The improving political clout of these religious groups, who can potentially counter the influence of the evangelical right, represent a possible political alternative to, and for, the "values voter."

Just as importantly, the religious left and center are beginning to flex their political muscle—witness their very ability to bring together the major players in the Democratic race for the presidency. Nothing like this has happened before.

Can the growing relationship between the religious left and center with the Democratic Party lead them to an authentic partisan political marriage? Or are the religious left and center simply pursuing a marriage of convenience? Can they just be satisfied with living together for the time being?

Democrats, however, have been historically conflicted about getting into a marriage that could spawn a religious "bridezilla"—a spiritual force that will feel empowered and deserving of political attention based on its own religious principles. Since 2004, and especially in the 2006 midterm elections, Democratic candidates have been more forthcoming about their religious views and willing to do outreach to large segments of the religious left and center, but remain unsure as to where to proceed from there.

Although spiritual progressives have been marginalized ideologically by the Republicans, they are similarly concerned with many of the same broad public policy issues that motivate the Democrats. Health care, jobs, domestic violence, peace, economic reform, and environmental justice are some of their shared interests. It would be hard to deny that a symbiotic relationship of some kind might be a possibility in both their futures.

The Democrats: Looking for Values in New Places

The Democratic Party has a long history of many proud successes and social progress. It led the fight for civil rights, gender equality, and reproductive freedom in the not too distant past, going against the tide of popular opinion and winning greater liberties for all Americans. It has worked to raise the standard of living for the less advantaged during periods characterized by economic scarcity. The Democratic Party has always taken, and held, the high road.

What has happened, though, since the turn of the twenty-first century? Everyone seems to be asking if the economic and social values that brought the Democratic Party so much success in the past are still valid today.

The answer is really quite simple: The Democratic Party is having a hard time defining itself, its values, and its goals in the millennium. This is because of its own seminal dedication to pluralism and multiculturalism, its historical commitment to so many diverse ideas and beliefs, and its strong sense of tolerance. Many see these values as strengths and a means of constituent inclusion, while others see changing principles on issues such as abortion and gay marriage as signs of a lack of clarity about absolutes—in culture, religion, ethics, and politics. Indeed, Obama says the party is "confused," that it has become the party of "reaction," and that increasingly there is a "need to match the Republican right in stridency and hardball tactics."[2] In short, it is possible to say that the Democratic Party today lacks the same unified, coherent, optimistic, God-given message that has been advanced so forcefully and symbiotically by the partisan relationship of the religious right and the Republican Party.

So what does the Democratic Party have to do to find greater success with the values voter, specifically, in the political arena today? Should it embrace the growing moral agenda of the politically emerging, progressive religious constituency in the United States, or should it simply try to function in a values-free zone? Can the Democratic Party afford to avoid the growing political voice of the religious left and center?

The answer is essentially predicated on how the Democratic Party wants to identify itself in the future, how it is perceived by the media, defined by its opponents, and accepted by the public. There is no clear answer; there are only proximate solutions within the complex organization that is the Democratic Party.

Conservatives claim that the Democratic Party is the captive of the Hollywood power brokers, the limousine liberals, and the political wannabes. They contend that the Democratic Party is made up of status-seeking donors who want to sleep in the Lincoln bedroom and that it is still the platform for the big labor unions—the AFL-CIO, the Teamsters, and the NEA. Many think it is manipulated by minorities, the disaffected, leftover pot-smoking hippies, and chronic complainers and protestors. Some say it is the safe haven of the godless, the elite, the effete, Northeast intellectual snobs, and the media.

Liberals reject this characterization and insist that the Democratic Party has always reflected the values of average Americans who champion the sensible, pragmatic principles of the middle class. They believe that it is the embodiment of the work ethic, the sense of fair play, and commitment to the belief that everyone should, and can, have a piece of the American pie.

These opposing images of the Democratic Party are a major concern for those within its leadership circles. They know full well what the party is *not*, but many lament that Democrats have lost sight of what they are about— their priorities and what they want the party to be in the future. Worse yet, if the Democratic Party did know the answers to these deep-seated philosophical questions, would it be lacking the innovative techniques and policy know-how to achieve positive goals in the current political climate? In short, many within, and in opposition to, the Democratic Party believe that it is looking for its contemporary identity—seeking relevance in a world that many argue has passed it by, much like the call for flower power and the tie-dyed shirts of the 1960s.

What is most frustrating to many is that the Democratic Party is ideologically flummoxed as to how to respond to the clearer conservative vision of the Republicans and the religious right today. Take for example the huge moral and political dilemma of how to deal with life and death. Matt Bai of the *New York Times* said recently that the Democratic Party became a seeming "bystander,"[3] in the context of contemporary morality, as could be seen in the Terri Schiavo case. He questioned whether or not it was it the Democrats' abdication of dealing with critical values that gave the Republicans a clear path to fight the emotional and political battles to save her life.

Bai commented that even though the Republicans lost the Schiavo fight, they still won the values war—emerging publicly as the positive "party of life."[4] He reported, however, that Democratic inaction, on the other hand, left some operatives within the party concerned and fearful that it might subconsciously be viewed as uncaring and still worse—as the party of death.

It is apparent that on many levels and issues the Democratic Party is ideologically and morally fragmented within itself. It is split in a number of different ways by a commitment to classical liberal values, a la Governor Howard Dean, Senator John Kerry, and Vice President Al Gore; by a more spiritual, communal approach to social issues as advanced by Obama and Edwards; by a pragmatic policy approach as advanced by Speaker of the House Nancy Pelosi, and by a centrist vision of a moral, caring America as articulated by Senator Hillary Clinton.

While each of these Democratic leaders has the most principled of intentions, it shows the fragmentation within the party, specifically on how to prioritize as well as deal with issues such as poverty, health care, education, and other social problems. While Democratic politicians are currently united in their opposition to the war in Iraq, this issue will soon be resolved, leaving the party still without a clear vision of what values to pursue afterwards.

The Democratic Party Searches for Common Values

Howard Dean, as the original front-runner for the Democratic presidential primary in 2003, was able to use technology effectively, create a volunteer base, raise huge amounts of money, and get his ideas across to the public as he stumped the country. Although he also spent a lot of money, he lost the Iowa caucus to Kerry and gave his "I have a scream" speech. In it, the media and the public got a glimpse of another side of the man who would potentially have been President and rejected him.

However, even in his defeat, Dean would not and did not go away. Instead, he ran for party chair in order to still be able to articulate and implement his views. The conventional wisdom is that Dean has been true to his liberal beliefs—consistently arguing that Democrats have moral values, as evidenced by their continuous support of health care reforms, minority rights, and numerous other programs and policies to secure social and economic advances for all Americans.

In order to implement such moral and social values, Dean brought the notion of the "fifty state strategy" to his tenure as chairman. Broadly, it meant that under him, the Democratic National Committee (DNC) would begin to pay the salaries of "hundreds" of new organizers and needed personnel for the state Democratic parties in order to alleviate the financial stress of the local partisan units.[5]

Matt Bai, who reported on Dean's management changes, chronicled how he also applied management principles to the functioning of the party. One of his most significant projects had been to put assessment teams in place and send them to every single state. In that way, Dean could get an objective evaluation of the effectiveness of the party on the state level, build up the party infrastructure, and make it competitive throughout the country.

Dean's major problem in leading the party has been in the area of fundraising. Bai contends that while he has done an adequate job, the Democratic congressional campaign committees, headed by Senator Chuck Schumer (NY) and Rep. Rahm Emanuel (IL), wanted Dean to provide them with resources (about $10 million) to target campaigns in specific states where they believed Democratic candidates would have the best chance of winning during the 2006 midterm elections. Dean refused, holding on to the money that the DNC had been given, intending to use it for building the party infra-structure.

Dean's disagreement with Schumer and Emanuel was a difference of opin-ion over long-term versus short-term strategy. However, after pressure from party leaders, Dean did turn over about $2.6 million to the congressional campaign committee, while still refusing to use any of the money that had been earmarked for the fifty state long-term plan.

In the end, the Democratic congressional candidates won in many tight races for a variety of reasons—Dean's organizational prowess, Republican scandals, the war, and even taking a moderate approach to some wedge issues that also reflected Howard Dean's moral, social vision for America. Indeed, after the election Dean said on National Public Radio that candidates should talk about their faith, and if they were uncomfortable doing that then they should talk about their moral values.[6]

Obama recognizes the criticality of progressive religious outreach for the Democratic Party and for his own presidential bid. At the most basic level, he understands why the religious right has been successful in the political arena and in creating a working relationship with the Republican Party.

He maintains that the growth of the evangelicals is about more than its ability to market religion and the charisma of its leadership. He believes that the religious right has tapped a hunger for "the product they are selling," that is, "a sense of purpose," and a feeling that "somebody out there cares about them, is listening to them—that they are not just destined to travel down a long highway toward nothingness."[7]

Obama has been very open about the importance of religion in politics to him. In a speech before his own denomination, the United Church of Christ, he admitted that he had been raised as a "spiritual skeptic" but that he found religion when he became a spiritual organizer in Chicago. Now he recognizes that the religious right has "hijacked" faith and divided the country by emphasizing wedge issues.[8]

At another event, Obama gave the keynote address before a major religious conference on "Building a Covenant for a New America." Sponsored by the Reverend Rick Warren, author of the now famous *The Purpose-Driven Life*, the Illinois senator told the "Call to Renewal" audience that

> for some time now, there has been plenty of talk among pundits and pollsters that the political divide in this country has fallen sharply along religious lines. Indeed, the single biggest gap in party affiliation among white Americans today is not between men and women, or those who reside in so-called red states and those who reside in blue, but between those who attend church regularly and those who don't.
>
> Conservative leaders, from Falwell and Robertson to Karl Rove and Ralph

Reed, have been all too happy to exploit this gap, consistently reminding evangelical Christians that Democrats disrespect their values and dislike their church, while suggesting to the rest of the country that religious Americans care only about issues like abortion and gay marriage; school prayer and intelligent design.

Democrats for the most part have taken the bait. At best we may try to avoid the conversation about religious values altogether, fearful of offending anyone and claiming that—regardless of our personal beliefs—constitutional principles tie our hands. At worst some liberals dismiss religion in the public square as inherently irrational or intolerant, insisting on a caricature of religious Americans that paints them as fanatical, or thinking that the very word "Christian" describes one's political opponents, not people of faith.[9]

A few Democrats like Obama are willing to profess their personal values. In fact, he has even been willing to repudiate Republican attempts to grab the high road and to join in a religious conversation about public policy in America.

Senator John Edwards, as well, has an interesting point of view about values, religion, and politics. He has essentially disavowed the position of his running mate, John Kerry in 2004, who maintained that he would not allow his faith to affect his decision-making. Edwards now openly contends that separation of church and state does not mean that politicians have to be free from their faith. He proudly says that "My faith informs everything I think and do. It's part of my value system."[10]

In a recent interview,[11] Edwards admitted that a gap exists between people of faith and the Democratic Party, and that one of his responsibilities as a presidential hopeful is to bridge that gap. To him, restoring America's moral leadership abroad must begin with the removal of U.S. troops from Iraq; while at home, his definition of morality must equate to overcoming poverty.

Edwards is most concerned about the growing disparity between the wealthiest Americans and the working poor. This worsening inequality is morally and politically unacceptable to him, a stance that could ultimately test the financial resolve of liberals, centrists, and others who would have to endure higher taxes to pay for his health care plan and other poverty-fighting programs. He understands that this is something that all segments of society will have to work on together if strategic social change is to occur. Edwards even goes so far as to say that the poor "would not survive" without the existence of good, effective faith-based charitable organizations, and that after fixing potential problems in the current program there could possibly be room for continued government-religious work on behalf of the poor.[12]

This approach to a values-based politics is in total contrast to John Kerry, as mentioned previously, who virtually spent the campaign for the 2004 presidency denying his personal, Catholic religious beliefs and supporting instead pro-choice policies, gay marriage, and stem cell research in the political arena. Unfortunately, it was his choice of those more politically liberal social values coupled with his inability to communicate his own personal beliefs about moral issues that helped to lead him to defeat in the election.

The Kerry loss in 2004 brought other changes within the Democratic Party infrastructure and political psyche, as well. Nancy Pelosi, the House minority leader at the time, astutely recognized the importance of communications with religious leaders and values voters and established the House Democrats' Faith Working Group in February 2005. She appointed James E. Clyburn (D-SC) to head up the organization designed to coordinate dialogue between Democrats and various faith communities. Clyburn was quick to point out that the Democrats were "less than effective in communicating" how their moral values guide their policies, and that he was interested in leading the House Democrats' efforts to communicate the party's values, "which are fundamentally American values."[13]

In setting up the Faith Working Group, Pelosi recognized the need to find a way to link the members of Congress to America's religious leaders and their congregants—a way to create some type of "political fellowship with the faithful."[14]

A developing alternative to the existent Bush White House religious relationships, the Faith Working Group also represents a challenge to continued Republican attempts at further denominational outreach. Pelosi has signed a Catholic Statement on Principles with fifty-five other Democrats, essentially agreeing to support the church's view on a variety of critical moral issues while also ascribing to the undesirability of abortion. She has also urged her fellow Democrats to infuse their political arguments in biblical terms and to talk about a "consistent moral framework for life." Pundits are wondering if the Democrat-controlled Congress under Pelosi has finally found religion.

Although it is difficult at this time to assess how much progress the Faith Working Group has made from an electoral perspective, in terms of outreach it is working to create better relationships with Catholics and other religious groups. It is also appears to be trying to understand how to use the politics of values, as the Faith Working Group has been discussing moral issues at the Democratic Issues Caucuses since its inception. Further, it has provided new opportunities for religious dialogue on potential legislation, as it has done recently with the Evangelical Lutheran Church in America and the 2007 Farm Reform Bill.

The various strategies put forward by different individuals within the Democratic Party are serious approaches to domestic problems, but they do not begin to deal morally with the other critical issue in the upcoming presidential race: the war in Iraq. While evangelicals can view the war in a values context, Democrats cannot or will not. The religious right sees all politics on a moral continuum and raises serious questions about the philosophical, ideological, and political thinking of potential leaders on matters of both domestic *and* foreign policy.

Some political analysts, such as Michael Ignatieff of *Newsweek*, have been asking if defending democracy is really "God's work" as President Bush has been claiming. Ignatieff terms this kind of thinking as "democratic providentialism," that is, a way of organizing the foreign policy vision of the current White House within a moral context. While he maintains that this approach beat the prudent realism of the Democrats in the 2004 election, "hands down,"[15] the turn in the midterm election leads pundits to wonder if a serious change toward current Democratic values about war and peace is occurring.

Why has the Republican approach to foreign policy been so much more formidable than the Democratic one in the past? Clearly the notion of spreading democracy has existed throughout American history and has been part of its drive toward Manifest Destiny, as practiced by James Monroe. It has been one of the goals of Woodrow Wilson, the case for the Four Freedoms of Franklin Roosevelt, and the dream behind creating the "Shining City on the Hill" of Ronald Reagan. All were about a higher order of politics: prophetic, transcendental, universal. The Bush approach to foreign policy adds a new, moral dimension to carrying out democratic providentialism according to Ignatieff: the missionary zeal of doing God's work, as exhibited in Iraq.

Understanding this approach to foreign policy has still left the Democratic Party fragmented on how to deal with the war in Iraq. Its response has been a more specific, short-term, pragmatic one: opposing the war on prudential and financial grounds. And while there have been unsuccessful calls to cut funding and to bring the troops home, there has been no consensus on how, and when, to end the war.

This lack of a clear position based on unified moral and political principles continues to reflect the lack of a consistent Democratic approach to international relations, one predicated, for instance, on peace and cooperation as a moral goal for the future. Instead, while the Democratic Party has been raising a greater political voice, it has been unable to communicate a clear, simple *moral* message in a coherent way about its solution to the war.

Senator Byron Dorgan (D-ND) who is in charge of the Democratic Policy Committee in the Senate, says that "I can describe, and have always been able to describe, what Republicans stand for in eight words . . . lower taxes, less government, strong defense and family values . . . Democrats [on the other hand] . . . can meander for 5 or 10 minutes in order to describe who we are and what we stand for."[16]

In essence, communications critics contend that the party is unable to frame the current foreign and domestic political debate. They argue that it is unable to take charge of issues, interpret the values conflict that surrounds them, and place events within an overall policy structure that reflects Democratic social and political values.

Some Democratic strategists have argued that in order to be truly competitive with the Republicans, Democrats need a new focus—one that reflects more meaningful language to reach voters who identify moral values as a top issue for them."[17] George Lakoff, author of *Don't Think of an Elephant!* has become an advocate for better political communication.

A professor at UCLA, Lakoff contends that voters respond to "grand metaphors."[18] Thus, rhetoric like "culture of life" and "flip-flopper" resonate with voters, while terms like social security reform and raising the minimum wage do not.

This is part of what the Republicans do so well—create terms and positive images to define the morality of every issue. "Creationism vs. evolution" has been neatly folded into questions of "intelligent design." "Tax cuts" have become "tax relief," "drilling for oil" has become the positive experience of "exploring for energy," while "social security reform" has come under the rubric of "privatization" in the Republican vocabulary.

At the same time, Republicans have given new, negative connotations to the language of their opponents. Being "pro-choice" has been turned into "favoring abortion." "Late term" abortion has been referred to as "partial birth" abortion. "Emergency contraception" has been dubbed "the morning-after pill." "Death with dignity" and "physician-assisted suicide" have simply been recast as "euthanasia." And, in the most blatant of all Republican word-grabs, "stem cell research" was characterized at one point as "murder" by Tony Snow, the president's former press secretary. Even though Snow recanted the use of the word later, President Bush still contended that it is immoral to take an "innocent human life in the hope of finding medical benefits for others." Such an authorization, he said, "crosses a moral boundary that our decent society needs to respect, so I vetoed it."[19]

Thus, anything to do with the quality or quantity of one's existence has become part of the "culture of life." It is the Republican moral umbrella, a way to portray the "high road" and by inference, a way to characterize the Democrats as supporting the "culture of death." With a reinterpretation of a very few words, the Democrats have become, in the minds of some, the equivalent of the dark side of Darth Vader.

Republicans are also able to create narratives to explain their message.

Such stories make their values concrete and take them from the realm of pie-in-the-sky to everyman. When President Bush vetoed the stem cell bill for the first time, he was flanked by parents and their children—babies who were born from existent stem cells. His veto became more meaningful, the children became special, and their stories became the reality of the Republican culture of life.

The Democrats are still looking for a meaningful, relevant, moral message and a way to advance it. For example, Virginia's Governor Timothy M. Kaine campaigned on religious themes on evangelical radio stations—and Democratic Party leaders eventually understood the strategic change in this type of campaigning. Some even called it a national model. It should not come as a surprise if Democrats adopt this kind of campaigning in the 2008 election and in the future.

Thus, the importance of a moral agenda, outreach to the religious left and center, and other changes in campaigning are being increasingly recognized by the Democratic leadership and its presidential hopefuls as an important way to gain greater credibility and the support of the values voters. But, in order to challenge the symbiotic relationship of the religious right with the Republican Party, it will still be important for the Democrats to find a united and coherent moral message that speaks to more than the unacceptability of the war in Iraq. The war will end eventually, but the Democratic Party will still need an ideological base, part of which could be the religious left and center, that will appeal to a broad segment of Americans. Enter, Hillary Clinton!

The Democratic Center: Sensible Middle-Class Values That Can Win

Is it possible to be a Democrat, sensible, religious, pragmatic, and progressive all at the same time? Democrats in Georgia and Alabama and across the South are attempting to do just that. In Georgia, State Senator Kasim Reed has sponsored a "Bible curriculum bill" that would allow school districts to teach courses in conjunction with a new textbook entitled "The Bible and Its Influence." Developed as a result of a nonpartisan, ecumenical project, the text was developed by Chuck Stetson, a conservative New York banker who believes that people no longer know the stories of the Bible. His text is meant to recount the narratives while assessing the role of the Bible in influencing history, literature, and art. A similar bill, initiated by Assemblyman Ken Guin, the leader of the Democratic majority of the legislature in Alabama, has recently been introduced as well. The *New York Times* reports that Howard Dean now believes that teaching the Bible as literature is a good thing, and that the Democrats in "other states are moving in the same direction, jumping into a conversation about religion and values. . . ."[20]

Certain members of the Democratic Party have also been calling for the party to deemphasize one of its critical stands—its support of abortion. Immediately after the election of 2004, Donna Brazile, who managed Vice President Al Gore's earlier presidential campaign in 2000, recognized that the abortion question left the party vulnerable in the heartland. She said, "Even I have trouble explaining to my family that we are not about killing babies."[21]

Dean recognizes the need for some reassessment as well. He has said that "We ought not turn our back on pro-life people. . . ."[22] And, others in the party believe that this stance could create new opportunities for party growth.

There are also rumblings that the party should reconsider its stance on parental notification for an abortion. The leading Democratic presidential contender who epitomizes this shift in thinking on abortion is Senator Hillary Clinton. In a variety of stances on this issue and others, the senator from New York has moved herself to the ideological center and taken some of the party with her.

While Clinton says that she does not like to wear her religion on her sleeve, she has been greatly influenced by her Methodist upbringing in Illinois. As a teenager, she was first exposed to "faith in action" by her minister and learned about the responsibilities that individuals have to the common good. These lessons have followed her through life and have had an impact on her political ideology as well.

In a speech given at the Abyssinian Baptist Church in New York on the "Role of Religion in Public Life,"[23] Clinton made her position on values quite clear: Government should interact with the private and public sectors, including religion, for the common good and without promoting a particular business or religion. She supported streamlining a process by which nonprofits could receive tax breaks, making it possible for all to take tax deductions for charitable giving, and she opposed vouchers for religious education and government intrusion into confidential church affairs that might result from more federal funds being given to them.

Clinton is not afraid to talk about her religious beliefs or to deal with contentious values in her campaign. In the summer of 2007, in the midst of the Democratic primary battle, she gave an interview to the media about her religious convictions. Claiming that religion is "a huge part of who I am," Clinton talked about reading the Bible and books on other people's faith journeys. She even spoke of experiencing "the presence of the Holy Spirit on many occasions."[24]

Clinton has hired Burns Strider, an evangelical Christian who headed the religious outreach efforts of Nancy Pelosi for Democrats in the House. His new job is to interact with values voters, to explain her views, and to draw those disaffected religious constituents into her camp.

This is becoming more of a possibility. Speaking to a large gathering of pro-choice supporters early in 2005, Clinton stated her support for *Roe v. Wade* while simultaneously praising the influence of religious and moral values that discourage young girls from becoming sexually active. Calling for people of good faith to find common ground on the abortion debate, she maintained that everyone should work to assure that children are wanted, cherished, and loved.[25] Her emphasis has always been on the positive, on prevention, and on sex education that her senatorial website says should be "medically accurate" and that "encourages young people to abstain from sexual activity."[26] She supports family planning and the availability of morning-after contraception.

Clinton's shift and the discussion of the party about its stance on the abortion issue has caused a rift between The National Abortion and Reproductive Rights Action League (NARAL) and some of the party faithful. NARAL interprets any change on reproductive policy by the party as a capitulation to a "defensive role," while Planned Parenthood believes that the basic stance still represents the "high ground" since it is focused on "the prevention of unintended pregnancies."[27] Others within the party, in a more pragmatic stance, simply point to the loss of South Dakota's Senate Minority Leader Tom Daschle's seat in 2004 and claim that his defeat was a result of his support for abortion rights.

Clinton also defended her vote on approving the war in Iraq. While Edwards apologized for his support and Obama was not a senator at the time, Clinton alone was able to justify her continued support for the troops while calling for an end to the war. Blaming Iraq on the president, his misguided information, and the Republicans, Clinton reminded Democrats that although the candidates had differing views on how to end the war, they were united in the fact that the war must end.

Clinton's views reflect a shift in the thinking of mainstream Democrats and portend an ideological transformation within the party. A possible Hillary Clinton presidency could signal the return to the centrist policies of her husband and bring back what many Americans have been craving in politics: common sense for the common good. But the caveat remains: While the party may be able to make short-term gains based on its opposition to the Iraq war, as it did in the 2006 midterm elections, a negative or reactive agenda will not be able to carry either the party or the nation forward for a sustained period of time without a clear moral compass to lead the way.

After the 2006 midterm elections, Senator Charles Schumer, who led the Senate reelection committee, wrote a book entitled *Positively American: Winning Back the Middle-Class Majority One Family at a Time.* In an interview with the *New York Times* about his book, Schumer was asked about the inability of the party to clearly articulate Democratic values. His answer was shocking. Schumer said: "No one has a good answer. I felt anguish about that. I felt a burning need to have us thinking beyond the immediate."[28]

So, when even a major player in the party leadership continues to be concerned about the inability of the party to explain its values, the party still has problems. As a logical consequence, it still does not have a clear path to the White House. Defining its values remains a critical challenge for any Democrat who wants to be president, and outreach to a more spiritually progressive constituency might be one way to solve the philosophical quandary that the party faces in the 2008 presidential election.

The Religious Left Faces a Philosophical Quandary Too

While the religious right has been fighting for moral dominance in the United States, it has also battled for political clout to implement its values within the political process, most specifically during the Bush presidency. The religious left has not responded in kind, in intensity, or in unity. Instead it has been in out in the cold. In fact, it now finds itself in a philosophical quandary: What role should it be playing in the political process, if any, to advance its own progressive and prophetic values agenda?

Throughout American history, the religious left has served as the conscience of American politics. It has called its adherents to work for social justice, economic equality, and peace. It has a legacy of preaching and demonstrating on behalf of civil rights in the 1960s, supporting the program for the war on poverty, and playing a part in the protests of the Vietnam War. It has spoken truth to power, providing a values insight into the American political debate and supporting policies that helped to advance the well-being of all people. How could its prophetic message become so obscured and clouded by the traditional spiritual message of the religious right—one tied to personal conversion, financial success, and family values? How did the future become overtaken by the ideas of the past? How can the religious left become relevant again?

The religious left has two major interconnected philosophical problems. First, it has to figure out how to establish a coherent spiritual voice in America, particularly in light of the united, conservative, optimistic Christian message that has been interpreted and "hijacked," according to some. And second, it must decide how to recapture and recast the broader social message of Christianity within the context of religious pluralism and the diverse spiritual agenda that now exists within the United States.

Barbara A. McGraw and this author addressed part of this problem in the book *Taking Religious Pluralism Seriously*.[29] In it, McGraw articulated that there is a place between the secular left and the religious right, a place that can serve as an arena for a conversation among people of faith; a place that she calls "America's Sacred Ground." In that place, she argues, religious groups can work together to help create a better society from the ground up for the common good.

McGraw believes that there are two forums where religious dialogue can occur: the civic forum and the conscientious public forum. In the first, religions can have an impact on public policy by working within the confines of the law, its attendant responsibilities, and the strictures of the principle of separation of church and state. In the conscientious public forum, however, there is room for religious groups to try to impact public policy by teaching their values and respecting the values of others. What the book was able to illustrate is that the increasing number of religions in the United States has broadened the political priorities, agendas, and influence of a myriad of religious groups in the public arena—many of whom are ideologically at odds with the religious right.

The basic problem, however, on America's Sacred Ground, is how to identify and support everyone's religious priorities within the broader social and cultural milieu in the United States. And even further, once those priorities have been identified, how can they be implemented and become part of viable political policies?

Today, there is a slow but growing movement to resuscitate the religious left that had so much visibility and influence during the l960s. It was black ministers who fought for civil rights and who, by their protests, were able to turn their moral demands for freedom into significant legislation to secure voting, educational, work, and housing equity during the decade. As "inclusion" became the watchword of the time, women and others also protested for rights and were supported in their endeavors by Jewish rabbis, mainline Protestant ministers, and liberal Catholic priests.

However, the religious leaders of more progressive theologies began to lose their influence over issues of social justice as civil rights took on aspects of black power, women's liberation became further radicalized by feminism, and congregations became more wealthy and conservative. In many cases, the spiritually progressive clergy became nothing more than "generals without an army."[30]

In contrast, the message of more conservative evangelical ministers began to take hold in the 1970s. Their theology equated personal conversion with individual transformation, a commitment to God, and a dedication to infuse the institutions of society with the teaching and values of Jesus. It became a message that resonated with those who opposed the financial entitlements, sexual excesses, and the moral relativism of the Great Society. Individual responsibility, family stability, and moral values moved to the forefront of evangelical teachings and began to appear on public policy agendas as evangelicals became more politically active.

The religious right grew stronger and more vocal from the 1980s forward, and their religious clout brought political advances as well. While the secular left demanded that religion be kept out of politics, the Republican Party embraced conservative denominations and adopted the evangelicals' concern for, and definition of, the spiritual malaise in American society. As a result, the religious right has been able to articulate its Christian moral values and advance them within the public arena with Republican support.

One of the best ways that the Democrats can compete successfully with their political antagonists, the Republicans, is to recognize and accept a spiritual vision of the world. To do this, the party would have to be willing to develop a coherent, clear political agenda with a spiritual foundation.[31] The religious left could then challenge the critical role that the religious right has been playing in the political arena by starting to participate more actively in America's moral debate. Since religious progressives believe strongly that religions should be defined by more than just their stands on abortion and traditional family values, they argue that America's political agenda should be broadened to reflect its social needs. Consequently, the religious left is beginning to speak out, to develop organizational structures, and to create agendas that can serve as the basis for public policies to deal with pressing social problems such as poverty, racial justice, education, the environment, and immigration. The next chapter will explore the awakening of the new religious left and explain the ways that it is hoping to adapt its religious beliefs within the American political arena.

Notes

1. Aaron Krager, "Faith, Values, Poverty: Sojourner's Forum—Barak Obama," http://faithfullyliberal.com/?p = 45.

2. Barak Obama, *The Audacity of Hope* (New York: Crown Publishers, 2006), 38–9.

3. Matt Bai, "Democratic Moral Values?" *New York Times Magazine*, April 24, 2005, 25.

4. Bai, "Democratic Moral Values?"

5. See a more detailed account about Dean's leadership in Matt Bai, "The Inside Agitator," *New York Times Magazine*, October 1, 2006, 55–60.

6. Joseph Lindsley, "Finding Religion: Democrats Try to Talk Like God-fearing Folk," *Weekly Standard*, April 17, 2006, www.weeklystandard.com/Content/Public/Articles/000/000/012/070vzfcm.asp?pg = 2

7. Obama, *The Audacity of Hope*, 202.

8. Laurie Goodstein, "Faith Has Role in Politics, Obama Tells Church Convention," *New York Times*, June 24, 2007, A22.

9. Senator Barak Obama, "Barack Obama Speaks Out on Faith and Politics: 'Call to Renewal' Keynote Address," http://obama.senate.gov/podcast/060628-call.to.renewal.

10. David Kuo, "Interview with John Edwards," www.beliefnet.com/story/213/story_21312.html.

11. Kuo, "Interview with John Edwards."

12. Kuo, "Interview with John Edwards."

13. News release from Congressman James E. Clyburn, February 4, 2005, http://Clyburn.house.gov/press/050204faithgroup.html.

14. Joseph Lindsley, "Finding Religion: Democrats Try to Talk Like God-fearing Folk," *Weekly Standard*, April 17, 2006, www.weeklystandard.com.

15. Michael Ignatieff, "Democratic Providentialism," *New York Times Magazine*, December 12, 2004, 29.

16. Matt Bai, "The Framing Wars," *New York Times Magazine*, September 17, 2005, Sec. 6, 44.

17. Patrick D. Healy, "Clinton Seeking Shared Ground over Abortions," *New York Times*, January 25, 2005, B5.

18. Matt Bai, "The Framing Wars," *New York Times Magazine*, September 17, 2005, Sec. 6, 43.

19. Edward Epstein, "Stem Cell Bill Veto Is First by Bush," *San Francisco Chronicle*, July 20, 2006, A11.

20. David D. Kirkpatrick, "Democrats in 2 Southern States Push Bills on Bible Study," *New York Times*, January 27, 2006, A20.

21. Adam Nagourney, "Democrats Weigh De-emphasizing Abortion as an Issue," *New York Times*, December 24, 2004, A25.

22. Nagourney, "Democrats Weigh De-emphasizing Abortion."

23. Senator Hillary Clinton, Speech given at the conference on "The Role of Religion in Public Life," sponsored by the Brookings Institution and The Pew Forum on Religion and Public Life at the Abyssinian Baptist Church in New York City, December 11, 2001.

24. Michael Luo, "For Clinton, Faith Intertwines with Political Life," *New York Times*, July 7, 2007, A1.

25. Healy "Clinton Seeking Shared Ground over Abortions."

26. See her Senatorial webpage: http://ClintonSenate.gov/issues/women

27. Nagourney, "Democrats Weigh De-emphasizing Abortion."

28. Deborah Solomon, "You Listening to Me?" *New York Times Magazine*, January 28, 2007, 18.

29. Barbara A. McGraw and Jo Renee Formicola, eds., *Taking Religious Pluralism*

Seriously: Religious Pluralism on America's Sacred Ground (Waco: Baylor University, 2006).

30. Robert Booth Fowler, Allen D. Hertzke and Laura R. Olson, *Religion and Politics in America* (Boulder: Westview, 1999) 2nd ed., 43.

31. Lerner, 101.

6

The Religious Progressives Reply: Let's Get Involved

Introduction

IN JUNE 2006, THE EPISCOPAL CHURCH in the United States chose a woman, Bishop Katharine Jefferts Schori, to serve as its national leader. In a social and public policy context, Bishop Schori is calling for her church to focus on feeding people, providing better primary education, working to heal people with AIDS, addressing tuberculosis and malaria, and supporting sustainable development.[1] Her agenda reflects the social values of a larger, emerging, and growing religious left, one that, at the time, supported same-sex unions and approved of the consecration of openly gay bishops.

Bishop Schori is part of a larger and growing movement among religious progressives to redirect the moral values and political agenda of American society. Originally part of the Christian mainstream, Episcopalians, Presbyterians, Catholics, disaffected evangelicals, and now even certain Jewish leaders are joining together to impact U.S. public policy in a more socially conscious way.

One tactic within their arsenal is to articulate inclusive Christian values and responsibilities while raising awareness about the problem of using literal, rigid interpretations of Jesus's message to solve today's social, cultural, and political problems. In this way, they hope to provide an alternative interpretation of Christianity that counters the conservative one that has been advanced by evangelicals and their supporters in America.

At the basis of contemporary religious literature, today's progressive social and moral theology challenges the evangelical image and catechesis of Jesus. Publications such as *Stealing Jesus: How Fundamentalism Betrays Christianity* (1992) by Bruce Bawer; *Rescuing the Bible from Fundamentalism: A Bishop Rethinks the Meaning of Scripture* (1991) by John Shelby Spong; *The Heart is a Little to the Left: Essays on Public Morality* (1999) by William Sloane Coffin; and *God and the Other Famous Liberals: Reclaiming the Politics of America* (1992) by F. Forrester Church started the movement to bring the religious left back to life during the last decade.

More recently, Senator John Danforth (R-IN) published *Faith and Politics: How the "Moral Values" Debate Divides America and How to Move Forward Together* in 2006, calling for religiously committed people to articulate and investigate today's religious/political agendas. Danforth writes from the perspective of a former U.S. senator, a U.N. ambassador, and Episcopal priest. He contends that religion in America today is divisive and that conservative faith communities have convinced themselves and others that their political agenda is God's agenda.

Danforth argues that "the error of the Christian Right is that in its attempt to codify the requirements of faith in a legislative program, it crowds out the demands of the Love Commandment. The effect is that law takes precedence over love, rather than the other way around."[2] This religious certainty manifests itself in political certainty, a stance that Danforth rejects.

He makes a distinction between being a Christian in politics and having a Christian agenda for politics. Danforth's anthropology is the basis for his religious belief that there is continual struggle within each individual, an ongoing search to understand and do God's will that always leaves people uncertain as to what it really is. It is that uncertainty, he says, that makes the reconciling work, or compromise, of politics possible.[3] And, according to Danforth, it is the notion of reconciliation that holds out the hope that people of good will can move forward together in society and politics.

Danforth ends his book with a chapter entitled "Paul's Primer on Politics." His allusion to the missionary who carried the message of Jesus outside of Judea is relevant because he uses the letter of Paul to the Romans as a basis for his own approach to politics. Building on the responsibilities that Paul articulated for Christians who must function within the temporal world, Danforth stresses six major points to end the divisiveness among religious adherents in the American political process today. These include the need to keep politics in its proper place; to recognize that no one has total ownership of the truth; that people and institutions have limitations and must use compromise to advance the common good; to love and honor each other; to engage with adversaries; and to recognize that reconciliation begins with each person.

Leaders in the Religious Left: Seeking Prophetic Values

Among the leaders in the forefront of the religious left today are Reverend Jim Wallis and Rabbi Michael Lerner. Each represents a different faith community but seeks to infuse politics with transcendent values that can bring civility, honesty, justice, love, and charity to the public arena.

Wallis, an evangelical liberal and author of the bestselling book, *God's Politics: Why the Right Gets It Wrong and the Left Doesn't Get It* (2005),[4] is one of the primary challengers of the religious right. He has thrown down the liberal, spiritual gauntlet, contending that there has been a "takeover" of the Republican Party by conservatives and a "highjacking" of religion by the religious right.[5] His answer to this situation is to use a spiritual approach to politics that is termed "prophetic," that is, he supports political behavior typified by that of Moses and the prophets of old.

Historically, prophetic politics has its roots in antiquity, a time when religion, culture, and politics were deeply interconnected. Moses is the prototype of the prophetic leader: one who taught truth to power by articulating the plight of the oppressed Jews, condemning the pharaoh for his repression, demanding social justice in God's name, and calling for a new political reality. Christians later added to the prophetic tradition by claiming that social responsibility, political engagement, and public witness were an integral, necessary part of their religious faith. They saw these obligations as the way to move from the temporal world to a higher spiritual and perfected one. Most of these ideas were diluted after the rise of nation-states and later movements toward materialism, capitalism, nationalism, atheism, and Marxism. Ultimately as power politics based on nuclear weapons became the pervasive means of carrying out foreign policy in the second half of the twentieth century, all thoughts of a higher order of politics were lost.

The notion of prophetic politics was resuscitated by Neal Riemer in 1984 in his book *The Future of the Democratic Revolution: Toward a More Prophetic Politics*.[6] A political science professor who was deeply interested in the relationship between politics and ethics, Riemer argued that only a transcendent, universal politics could transform the struggle for power into a rational means to implement civilizing values such as peace, human rights, and economic well-being. According to him, there were essentially three ways to accomplish this: (1) by articulating a commitment to transcendent and constitutional values, (2) by fearlessly critiquing the existing political structures, and (3) by searching for creative breakthroughs to solve the problems of humankind.

Wallis's politics are a return to the prophetic model articulated earlier by Riemer and others.[7] He wants to be in the forefront of teaching truth to

power, of articulating the social injustices of the day, and of trying to find a
new, transcendent political approach to politics that will provide social justice. He says that the way to move forward together is through a dialogue
among people of faith working to find common ground—to recover a biblical agenda for peace and help for the poor. Then, he says, faith communities
can bring their moral concerns to policymakers.

Wallis recalled in an interview with Ron Suskind[8] how he has done this
personally and of his own experience with President Bush. In December
2000, Bush sat in the classroom of a Baptist church in Austin, Texas, with
thirty or so clergy members and asked, "How do I speak to the soul of the
nation?" . . . "I've never lived around poor people," Wallis remembers Bush
saying. "I don't know what they think. I'm a white Republican guy who
doesn't get it. How do I get it?" Wallis recalls replying, "You need to listen
to the poor and those who live and work with poor people." A month later,
an almost identical line—"many in our country do not know the pain of
poverty, but we can listen to those who do"—ended up in the president's
inaugural address, according to Suskind.

Wallis has established a reputation for trying to find solutions to social
problems and making others aware of them. He has created a voice to communicate such ideas, a magazine entitled *Sojourner*. It is a publication for
evangelicals and others who are concerned about peace and social justice. He
also founded a policy organization known as Call for Renewal, whose purpose it is to turn prophetic ideas into public practice. Thus, *Sojourner* and
Call for Renewal work together as a "faith-based movement to overcome
poverty."

Call for Renewal is a national network that has access to a quarter of a
million names, and it is an organization that is growing quickly and becoming mobilized.[9] In the area of public policy it is concerned with everything
from social security and welfare reform to help for low-income families and
children. And it has enough clout to meet with administration officials and
to discuss its efforts to do more to help alleviate poverty.

What Call to Renewal does on a daily basis is to encourage advocacy to
overcome poverty. It sees its role as one of building support and getting its
membership to communicate with legislators by letter writing as well as by
telephone calls and email. It encourages pastors/religious leaders to create
candidate forums and to educate their members.

Wallis believes that political advocacy has a religious dimension. He urges
ministers to be proactive, persistent, and willing to talk with individuals who
have different beliefs and agendas. Those kinds of activities, he maintains, are
part of advocacy and, in turn, part of religious stewardship. As a result, Wallis

contends that advocacy, taken to the prophetic, transcendent level, has the potential to lead others to a higher level of politics characterized by compassion.

Wallis recently launched a new religious organization to counter the religious right. Known as "Red Letter Christians," Wallis's organization takes its name from those Bibles that print Jesus's words in red print. The group has become politically assertive, establishing an organization that intends not only to challenge conservative evangelicals but also to broaden the religious agenda that it has set for those in evangelical faith communities by the religious right.

Rather than ask "What would Jesus do?" Wallis's organization asks "What did Jesus say?" Red Letter Christians are faith-based and non-partisan but will still carry out political activity in Jesus's name. They are committed to putting poverty in the forefront of the 2008 political agenda.

The organization has scheduled media appearances and debates and has promised to unveil the formation of "Faith and Justice Churches" soon. This is a congregational network that Wallis believed would include nearly 1,000 congregations by September 2007.[10] Further, it was expected to produce voter guides and speakers to implement its "voting our values" campaign.

Red Letter Christians as an organization was unveiled at about the same time that the Values Voter Summit (VVS) was being held in Washington, D.C. The VVS was a meeting sponsored in the fall of 2006 by the conservative Family Research Council (FRC) and intended to draw about 1,800 evangelical participants. Conservative Republican Party leaders spoke out on traditional family values and pro-life issues in order to keep such issues alive before the public, the media, and the government.

The meeting was prompted by Dr. James Dobson, founder of Focus on the Family, the parent organization of the FRC, who warned that he was "extremely disappointed with what the Republicans have done with the power they were given."[11] This disaffection within the ranks of the evangelical Christians provided an impetus, if not a possible opening, and an alternative to well-meaning progressive Christians in the future. Red Letter Christians is an organization to watch.

Another growing voice for the religious left is Rabbi Michael Lerner. The leader of Beyt Takkun synagogue in California, he is the editor of *Tikkun* magazine and the author of several significant books—one of the most important being *The Left Hand of God: Taking Back Our Country from The Religious Right.*[12] In that book, the Jewish religious leader claims that the "unholy alliance" of the political right and the religious right is on a self-destructive course, one that threatens to destroy America and to equate God with militarism. He charges that this political-religious symbiosis creates "ecological irresponsibility" and an antagonism toward science and rational thought, as well as "insensitivity to the needs of the poor and the powerless."[13]

As an antidote, Lerner challenges the religious left to do two things: to address the spiritual hunger of Americans, a condition that he believes has resulted in the alienation of many people from liberal politics, and to articulate this national spiritual crisis to the secular left so that it can deal with it politically. Lerner maintains that there is a desire among people to transcend the individualism and selfishness of the marketplace and to connect their personal lives to a higher order of being. So, he challenges the religious left to work with the secular left to advance a "politics of meaning" in the world of today.

The California rabbi sees this happening in a realistic way through the organization that he founded known as the Tikkun Community and his leadership position as its national chair. An interfaith organization that Lerner claims has over 100,000 members and supporters,[14] Tikkun is philosophically based on two principles. First, that spiritual consciousness must be wed to political consciousness in order to heal and transform the world. Second, that social change and inner change must go hand in hand to foster loving relationships and dispose people toward charity. All this can be accomplished, according to Lerner, through the principle of solidarity.

Concerned about the fact that the religious right has gained so much spiritual and political power, Lerner has expanded his vision of the Tikkun Community and established another, larger religious-left group known as the Network of Spiritual Progressives (NSP). In his book, he argues that NSP can do for the Democratic Party what the religious right has done for the Republican Party. Composed of over "1,500 religious leaders, scholars, academics, cultural leaders, poets, writers, philanthropists, social changes activists, and citizens of the world,"[15] the organization's purpose is to bring together diverse religious groups and to form an interfaith alliance.

What Lerner proposes, a la Newt Gingrich and the Republican Contract With America, is to establish The Spiritual Covenant with America. Criticizing the elitism and relativism of the current liberal political thinking in the United States, Lerner has called for the implementation of an eight-point plan that would clearly articulate spiritual values that would, in turn, lay the groundwork for political policies that could redefine the religious left and the Democratic Party.

First, the Covenant supports families, but does so by calling on the government to provide them with a living wage, full employment, access to childcare, health care, education, and flexible work schedules. Beyond that, families should be respected and honored. Second, the Covenant advocates personal responsibility, respects privacy and diversity, and is dedicated to alleviate suffering. Third, the Covenant is committed to social responsibility. It is concerned with the elimination of poverty, full employment, and public safety—the protection of the vulnerable in society and ethical business practices. Fourth, the Covenant calls for values-based education—the teaching of virtue and providing free college education for everyone who is capable of college work. Fifth, the Covenant supports affordable health care, a model that would ensure help for physical, mental, emotional, and spiritual well-being. Sixth, the Covenant stresses the importance of environmental stewardship and ties the preservation and protection of the earth to national and international commitments for ethical consumption of resources. Seventh, the Covenant calls for building a safer world through generosity rather than military might. It would support creating a Global Marshall Plan to eliminate homelessness, hunger, and poverty while advancing education and health care around the world. Finally, the Covenant would separate church, state, and science. It would "Keep religion out of government and government out of religion, and both out of science."[16] In an attempt to end the creationism debate, to find middle ground on life issues, to advance peace, and to provide a balance with regard to first- and third-world economic disparities, in Lerner's view, the Covenant can provide a vision of hope through morality; a spiritual plan with political relevance and purpose that can be implemented by the articulation of the religious left and the public policies of the Democratic Party in the future.

How these principles will be played out in the real world and implemented politically remains to be seen as the NSP must deal first with it own seminal problem: trying to define its mission. At the present, there are those within the nascent movement who are concerned with issues and policies, while others are concerned with simply establishing a "religious voice" that will build relationships and create an awareness of the views of the religious left.

In the spring of 2006, the NSP met in Washington, D.C., to "wrest the mantle of moral authority from conservative Christians"[17] and to figure out how to bring their concerns to those in power, according to the *New York Times*. But the task was daunting. The meeting ended with the NSP still trying to define its agenda: whether or not to pursue a discussion of spiritual values, to raise consciousness, or to simply try to get the attention of the president and Congress.

By the end of the summer, the NSP began to find its voice, attempting to challenge the "paranoid and cynical 'political realism' that generates endless wars."[18] It called for an end to the Israeli attacks on Lebanon and urged that Hezbollah and Hamas stop engaging in violence against Israel. While there are no serious expectations that NSP can actually influence such terrorist groups, there is the hope that raising awareness about violence and aggression is a role that social progressives can play in American society. They can urge the U.S. and other governments to support nonmilitary actions in conflicts. And they can support in more specific cases the pursuit of ceasefires, embargoes on all shipments of weapons, and international efforts to provide security during border conflicts. For example, with a full-page ad in the *New York Times* about the Israeli-Lebanese dispute, the NSP began to speak louder and with greater direction. Although the jury is still out on its potential for effectiveness, the NSP has strengthened the voice of the growing religious left while providing another platform for its point of view to be articulated.

Other groups are springing up as well. In Ohio prior to the 2006 midterm elections, Reverend Tim Ahrens, the senior minister of the First Congregational Church of Columbus, Ohio, founded "We Believe Ohio." A statewide organization of progressive clergymen, it is dedicated to making sure that the religious left is heard throughout the state.[19] What is significant about this organization is that it is challenging the political establishment. The religious leaders in Ohio realize the potential power that they have to affect public policy, their opportunity to help create a political agenda that reflects their aggregated spiritual concerns, and their ability to influence the values vote of their congregations.

We Believe Ohio started out with about fifty local pastors and now includes more than 400 diverse religious leaders, all of whom are focused on social justice issues that unite people of faith, rather than divide them. Challenged by building a diverse coalition, the organization claims to be positive and proactive by espousing a mission that works for justice, religious pluralism and expression, the common good, and recognizing that the voice of religious traditions should be used to inform public policy.[20] Among its concerns are human rights atrocities in Darfur, the death penalty, the environment, health care, HIV/AIDS, immigration reform, peace in Iraq, decent wages, help for Katrina victims, poverty, hunger and homelessness, taxes, and torture.

Besides taking a stance on such values, We Believe Ohio has also inaugurated action that will invariably also have political consequences. The organization is committed to informing and engaging its faith community about the electoral process. It has set a goal of reaching 80 percent of its membership for the next election.[21] Further, We Believe Ohio is attempting to get its message out through the media so that it will become a statewide, and a potentially nationwide, voice for the religious left in America.

Cooperation with We Believe Ohio could be the future model of a positive political relationship between Democrats and moderate, progressive organizations—a template that could impact new ways of doing business between religious and political groups in America. This is extremely significant electorally as well, because Ohio. a traditional Republican state, has seen in-roads by the Democrats since the midterm elections in 2006. It cannot be counted on as being in anyone's political pocket until the last vote is tallied. Therefore, contenders for political office, both Democrat and Republican, will have to pay attention to proliferating progressive religious organizations such as We Believe Ohio in order to have some influence on the values voters in that state. Democrats could have a significant opportunity to count Ohio as one of their own in the future and to possibly move Ohio to the blue state column if they would be willing to articulate how their party would infuse progressive religious values into their political agenda.

The Religious "Center"

Another long-standing voice in the religious progressive world has been that of Dr. Ronald Sider. A Mennonite layman, he is an academic who has a master's of divinity degree and a Ph.D. in Reformation History from Yale University. Sider is also the founder of Evangelicals for Social Action (ESA). An outgrowth of a 1973 Thanksgiving meeting with several evangelical leaders, ESA is now a national religious organization committed to social activism with a potential to carry out political action to advance social justice. Rejected at its inception by strident fundamentalists such as Bob Jones, the organization began to slowly but surely produce its own literature and put on workshops at evangelical colleges to advance its concerns about poverty in America.

Now, thirty years later, Sider is the author of twenty-two books and a progressive evangelical who, during the course of his career, has challenged many of the public policy stands of the religious right. In 1977, he wrote *Rich Christians in an Age of Hunger*,[22] a seminal work that questioned American materialism and economic excess. Calling for a biblical response to social injustice, his book has sold over 350,000 copies,[23] turning Sider into a national figure—a public intellectual—who has continued to fight against poverty while galvanizing the religious center.

In an interview with the author,[24] Sider was emphatic that he is not part of either the religious left or the religious right, but that he is conservative on matters such as the sanctity of life, euthanasia, and the fact that marriage is meant to be between a man and a woman. But, he claims that he is "progressive" on other issues such as poverty and the care of creation.

Sider is quite vocal about his opposition to the religious right. He opposes its use of moral values within political discussion and characterizes as "nonsense" its claims that only conservatives have concern for moral values. He believes instead in a religious/philosophical commitment to a fundamental normative framework, one that deals with an understanding of the person and justice. Sider maintains that there cannot simply be a sexual starting point on this. Religion, he believes, provides a set of norms; norms that everyone in politics has but that the religious right thinks that only it has.

Sider's basic approach to public policy issues is one that is biblically based and biblically engaged. This means that his approach starts with the question What are God's concerns as articulated in the Bible? His answer is quite clear. He believes that God's concerns are tied to the needs of the poor and to peacemaking. Therefore, Sider argues that the religious right needs to be more biblical, more inquisitive, and less impacted by politics. Indeed, the situation should be the other way around, according to him: Religion should impact politics.

With the public and academic recognition of Sider's book, *Rich Christians in an Age of Hunger,* has come advocacy for the poor and, over the last two decades, a growing concern for the responsible treatment of nature. As a result, Sider founded the Evangelical Environmental Network (EEN) in 1993 to educate evangelicals about creation and man's role in the stewardship of the environment. Among its political successes was the EEN's tireless work to influence the passage of the Endangered Species Act in 1996. Most recently, the Reverend Jim Ball, executive director of EEN, and his wife Kara were profiled in the *New York Times* for their efforts to inform evangelical churches about the threat of global warming. They even allowed Laurie Goodstein, a *Times* reporter, to see how they lived the "Gospel of Green,"[25] driving a Prius, using environmentally friendly cleaning products, buying used, and recycling.

Recently Sider branched out again, this time establishing the National Religious Policy Partnership for the Environment. It is a clear example of one of his greatest strengths: the ability to espouse progressive, prophetic policies while still maintaining a significant working relationship with others of different ideologies within the Christian community.

Most recently, he was invited to co-chair the writing of the seminal, collaborative document, "For the Health of the Nation: An Evangelical Call to Civic Responsibility." A blueprint for evangelical involvement in the political process, the statement crystallized evangelical Christian concerns that much of its leadership felt should have been addressed in the 2004 election. It was signed by Charles Colson, James Dobson, Richard Land, and Rick Warren among others, while containing "public policy proposals . . . strikingly similar to those that emerge from official Catholic social teaching."[26] Sider believes that "For the Health of the Nation . . ." rejects the past one- or two-dimensional religious, political agenda and calls for a biblically balanced one aimed at helping the poor, protecting the sanctity of life, providing ecological stewardship, peacemaking, and civic engagement.

Sider contends that his role in producing the "Evangelical Call to Civic Responsibility" was important because it brought progressive concerns to the evangelical table, challenged the religious right, and assured its signers that the Bible would be used to set the future political agenda of 25 percent of the nation's population. He contends that this was something that the religious right did not allow to happen until then. As a result, Sider has now become a recognized force within a variety of religious circles and has managed to be able to bring the issue of poverty to the traditional evangelical public discussion.

The "centrist" religious leader recognizes that evangelicals have a larger voice in the public arena than ever before in American history. Sider understands that it is possible to squander the current opportunity that exists to speak out for social justice. He has therefore attempted to create a theological framework to deal with pressing public policy issues in the United States. This consists of developing a biblical perspective of the world and its people while attempting to relate both to concrete concerns.[27] He maintains that this requires study, understanding the complexity of the task, and a willingness to cooperate ecumenically.

Sider has been calling for an enlightened approach to social problems since his days as a graduate student. Now, having reached the pinnacle of his career, he continues his work on behalf of the poor and the environment by lecturing and heading up the Sider Center on Ministry and Public Policy at the Eastern Seminary in Pennsylvania.

In sum, Sider believes that an evangelical center "is emerging" and characterizes it as a movement toward greater civic engagement based on a biblical agenda. Interestingly, he credits other individuals like Reverend Rick Warren, the author of *The Purpose-Driven Life*,[28] for playing a major role in making it happen.

Warren, a Southern Baptist minister, is the founding pastor of Saddleback Church in Lake Forest, California, a faith community that consists of about 22,000 people. Holding a Doctor of Ministry degree from Fuller Theological Seminary, along with several honorary doctorates, his book *The Purpose-Driven Life* sports a sticker that tells each potential buyer that over 25 million copies have already been sold. Why not? It attempts to explore the eternal question of "Why am I here on earth?"

Warren has been invited to speak at national and international forums and named to all kinds of top leadership lists by *Time*, *Newsweek*, and *U.S. News and World Report*. His acclaim is far reaching, his influence profound, and his personal life inspiring. It has been widely reported that Warren and his wife, Kay, have donated 90 percent of their income into three foundations to serve those affected by AIDS, to train church leaders in developing countries, and to fight poverty, disease, and illiteracy.

In *The Purpose-Driven Life*, Warren attempts to articulate life's purpose and explain how an individual can fulfill his/her spiritual destiny. His book, by the way, was the book that Ashley Smith[29] read to the convicted Atlanta courthouse killer, Brian Nichols, when he held her hostage in March 2005.

Warren's message is clear: Individuals were planned for God's pleasure, to be part of God's family, to become like Christ, to serve God, and to fulfill His mission. Within this understanding of what drives the life of a Christian, Warren is concerned with Christ's followers becoming *servants*; indeed, he says that service is the pathway to a significant life and that individuals serve God by serving others.

This type of service, according to Warren, is characterized by personal willingness, by paying attention to the needs of others, by individual dedication, by pragmatism, and by humility. He sees Christian servants as stewards, as people who identify with Christ and see service as an opportunity rather than an obligation.

Warren does not seem to have a political agenda like many of his Southern Baptist compatriots, but he does understand that activists essentially see doing Christ's work as a way to confront evil and bring about social justice. While he is not in the political mainstream, his focus is on transforming the lives of people, one at a time, and showing their spiritual leaders how to do the same. Popular press estimates report that he has reached over 400,000 pastors and church leaders though his seminars and conferences and that over 189,000 church leaders subscribe to *Ministry Toolbox*, his weekly newsletter. Warren, then, is one of a growing number of religious leaders who head up megachurches and have the potential to make a religious and a political difference with regard to public policy on social issues—if they want to.

One way to do this is by hiring Christian public relations experts like Larry Ross, whose client list has included the likes of Billy Graham, Bishop T. D. Jakes, and the Promise Keepers. He has promoted films like the *Left Behind* series as well, thus making Ross a man that has the contacts and the know-how to sell Warren, his church, his books, and his message to the public.

Ross tries to balance Warren's image, using an approach that appeals to participants in faith communities who may or may not want to be politically involved.[30] For example, in February of 2006, Warren was among eighty-six evangelical leaders who backed a safe, broad, nonpartisan values issue: global warming. The first stage of a larger "Evangelical Climate Initiative" that would include television and radio advertising and educational campaigns in churches and some Christian colleges, he was among a number of prominent ministers who have supported nonpartisan public policies such as the Reverend Jim Ball of EEN, the Reverend Floyd Flake (himself a former congressman) of the Greater Allen AMC Cathedral in Queens, New York, and others.

Thus, Warren and other ministers like him represent a progressive religious component and a possible constituency for Democratic political hopefuls. Warren has already provided a platform known as Pentecost 2006 for Democrats by including presenters such as Hillary Clinton, Howard Dean, and Barack Obama. It was the senator from Illinois who described his own spirituality and distrust of those denominations who would claim to have a corner on the truth. Articulating that he was "tired of seeing faith used as a tactic,"[31] Obama understood how spirituality, rather than denominationalism, holds the key for Democratic political candidates in the future.

It is important to consider, then, as the politics of values continues to play out, that left and center religious leaders could use its tactics more positively in the next election and become important consultants on social justice policy initiatives. They are a patriotic as well as a pastoral bloc; a group who deserve the outreach and support of the party.

Can the Politics of Values Be Turned Around?

While most of the next presidential campaign will likely revolve around the war in Iraq, the moral values agenda—now firmly established by the religious right, left, and center—will not go away after 2008. Andrew Kohut, president of the Pew Research Center, which studies religion in public life, admits that as of yet, there is no "sea change"[32] in the political clout of the progressive religious groups. Essentially, this means that currently there are no identifiable voting blocs or clear values constituencies that can be associated with such organizations.

However, liberal/progressive religious groups in America are beginning to recognize their own potential and special power that conservative groups already understand: By forming coalitions or interfaith alliances and working to advance progressive values-based agendas they can possibly influence a huge voting constituency in the future. In fact, this is beginning to happen exponentially within socially progressive religious circles.

In April of 2006, a self-described "broadest-ever Christian unity organization in American history,"[33] was launched to fight poverty. Known as Christian Churches Together in the USA, it encompasses five significant Christian denominations. They are Roman Catholics, various mainline Protestants churches, some evangelicals and Pentecostals, as well as the two most important historically black Baptist churches (the National Baptist Convention USA and the National Baptist Convention of America) and the Orthodox Church in America. Their purpose is to provide Christian witness to the problem of poverty in the U.S. and to complete an ongoing five-year effort to "dismantle decades of political, doctrinal, and historical animosity among U.S. churches."[34]

Through the leadership of Dr. Ron Sider, Catholic Bishop Stephen Blaire of Stockton, California, and Reverend William Shaw of the National Baptist Convention, organizers have committed themselves to work along with groups such as Bread for the World, Call to Renewal, and the Salvation Army. *They claim to represent more than 100,000 million American Christians.*[35]

It is as if a religious sleeping giant has awoken, is rubbing its eyes and looking for a hand to pull it up on its feet. If the Democratic Party would be willing to do this metaphorically, particularly with a candidate such as John Edwards, who says that poverty is the central moral and political issue of his campaign, a new moral/political symbiosis could possibly emerge—one that could challenge the conservative relationship of their counterparts. But, if the Democratic Party cannot or will not reconsider, persuasively reinvent, and better articulate a clear set of values, it will lose its opportunity to be a beneficiary of the support that progressive religious constituencies represent.

In order to gain a long-term position of political power in America, the Democratic Party must create its own version of the politics of values. It must create new meaningful linkages with the progressive values voters and clearly articulate their middle-class, moderate, religious and social beliefs. Democrats, themselves, must be willing to identify and support candidates who are unafraid to discuss their personal values and tie them to their political agendas. And they must be concerned with finding innovative ways to deal with an America obsessed with the drive for super-wealth and security.

The next chapter deals with the implosion of the Republicans in 2006 who blindly pursued such financial and military policies and who abused their political power. It analyzes the resulting political disaffection of the religious right and posits the possibility of a values void for the future. Might wedge issues, then, be able to be turned into broader magnet ones, and could outreach to the religious left and center become a new way to implement the politics of values and to gain a long-term political advantage in the United States?

Notes

1. "Interview with Katharine Jefferts Schori," *Time Magazine*, July 17, 2006, vol. 168, no. 3, 6.

2. John Danforth, *Faith and Politics: How the "Moral Values" Debate Divides America and How to Move Forward Together* (New York: Penguin Books, 2006), 29.

3. Danforth, *Faith and Politics*, 52.

4. Jim Wallis, *God's Politics: Why the Right Gets It Wrong and the Left Doesn't Get It* (San Francisco: HarperCollins, 2005).

5. Lisa Anderson, "Christian Middle Seeking a Turn at Bully Pulpit," *Chicago Tribune*, September 21, 2006, www.chicagotribune.com.

6. Neal Riemer, *The Future of the Democratic Revolution: Toward a More Prophetic Politics* (New York: Praeger, l984).

7. Some of their other critical works include: James E. Wood, Jr., "Public Religion vis-à-vis Religion's Public Role," *Journal of Church and State* 41 (Winter l999): 51–79; Robin Lovin, ed., *Religion and American Public Life: Interpretations and Explorations* (New York: Paulist Press, l986) and James Darsey, *The Prophetic Tradition and Radical Rhetoric in America* (New York: New York University, l997).

8. Ron Suskind, "Faith Certainty and the Presidency of George W. Bush," *New York Times Magazine*, October 17, 2004, www.nytimes.com/2004/10/17/magazine/17Bush.

9. Suskind, "Faith Certainty and the Presidency of George W. Bush."

10. *Sojourner* Media Advisory, September 18, 2006, www.sojo.net.

11. M. E. Sprenglemeyer, "Dobson: Rallying Family Values Voters," *Rocky Mountain News*, September 23, 2006, www.rockymountainnews.com.

12. Rabbi Michael Lerner, *The Left Hand of God: Taking Back Our Country from the Religious Right* (San Francisco: HarperCollins, 2006). See also *Spirit Matters: Global Healing and the Wisdom of the Soul* (Hampton Roads, 2000).

13. Lerner, *The Left Hand of God*; Michael Lerner, ed., *Tikkun Reader: Twentieth Anniversary* (Lanham, Maryland: Rowman & Littlefield, 2006).

14. www.tikkun.com.

15. See their ad to "Stop the Slaughter in Lebanon, Israel and the Occupied Territories!" in the *New York Times*, July 31, 2006, A9.

16. Lerner, 238.

17. Neela Banerjee, "Religious Left Struggles to Find Unifying Message," *New York Times*, May 10, 2006, A17.

18. Banerjee, "Religious Left Struggles to Find Unifying Message."

19. Eric Gorski and Karen E. Crummy, "Democrat's Goal: Demonstrate Values," *Denver Post*, August 6, 2006.

20. See the organization's webpage, www.webelieveohio.org.

21. See www.webelieveohio.org.

22. Ronald J. Sider, *Rich Christians in an Age of Hunger: A Biblical Study* (Dallas: Word Publishing, l977).

23. Jo Renee Formicola and Hubert Morken, eds., *Religious Leaders and Faith-Based Politics: Ten Profiles* (Lanham, Maryland: Rowman & Littlefield, 200l), chap. 8, "Dr. Ron Sider: Mennonite Environmentalist on the Evangelical Left," by Joel Fetzer and Gretchen Kearns, 163.

24. Phone Interview with Dr. Ron Sider, October 23, 2006.

25. Laurie Goodstein, "Living Day to Day by a Gospel of Green," *New York Times*, March 8, 2007, F1 and 10.

26. Ronald J.Sider, "The Radical Religious Middle," *The Review of Faith and International Affairs*, vol. 4, no. 3, Winter 2006, p. 44.

27. David P. Gushee, ed., *Christians and Politics Beyond the Culture Wars: An Agenda for Engagement* (Grand Rapids, Michigan: Baker Books, 2000). See Chapter 6, "Toward an Evangelical Political Philosophy," by Ronald J. Sider, 79–96.

28. Rev. Rick Warren, *The Purpose-Driven Life: Reflections on What on Earth Am I Here For* (Grand Rapids, Michigan: Zondervan, 2002).

29. See her account in Ashley Smith and Stacy Mattingly, *Unlikely Angel: The Untold Story of the Atlanta Hostage Hero* (Zondervan/HarperCollins, 2005).

30. Strawberry Saroyan, "Christianity, the Brand," *New York Times Magazine*, April 16, 2006, 48–51.

31. Lois K. Solomon, "Political Voices of Religious Left," *South Florida Sun-Sentinel*. July 24, 2006.

32. Solomon, "Political Voices of Religious Left," A15.

33. Kevin Eckstrom, "Broadest-Ever U.S. Church Unity Group Launched," *The Roundtable on Religion and Social Welfare Policy*, April 5, 2006, www.socialpolicyand religion.org/news/article.cfm?id = 4017.

34. Eckstrom, "Broadest-Ever U.S. Church Unity Group Launched."

35. Erkstrom, "Broadest-Ever U.S. Church Unity Group Launched."

7

The Right Implodes: Scandals, Corruption, and Rejection

Introduction

THE STORY COULDN'T HAVE PLAYED OUT any better if it were a soap opera. In one scene, a religious leader with major political ties to the White House is accused of a sordid affair with a male prostitute and of using drugs—a week before a crucial election. In another somber scene the president of the United States is standing before the White House press corps capitulating his party's "thumping," while congratulating his opponents on their election victory and accepting the resignation of the Secretary of Defense for a failed war policy. In a back lot, the feisty political strategist is contemplating his party's eroding power, which is now becoming a bad dream. The leader of the Senate, who gave up his seat ostensibly to run for the presidency, drops out of the future race and says that his political career is at an end—at least for now. Other aspiring politicians litter the landscape. The House is lost. The Senate is lost. Governorships are lost. There is weeping and wailing and gnashing of teeth. Election Day comes to be known as "Bloody Tuesday." But wait—bring in the professional mourners, a.k.a. spin doctors! And—there emerges from the ashes of defeat the promise of religious restoration and political cooperation. A female Speaker emerges! A conciliatory president appears! Tune in next week to see if there really can be peace in the valley.

Clearly the ongoing scenario could have described the midterm elections and the political fallout of 2006. And, any resemblance to persons living or dead is definitely coincidental! The facts bear this out, and nationwide exit polls give a demographic picture of what really happened to the Republican Party, its evangelical allies, and their formerly dominant conservative ideology in the November election.

In broad terms, 54 percent of the total vote of the electorate went to the Democrats and 46 percent to the Republicans. In breaking down the numbers, whites made up 79 percent of the electorate and voted 48 percent for the Democrats and 52 percent for the Republicans. That 4 percent Republican lead was eaten up by the Democratic surge of minority voters. Among blacks, who represented 10 percent of the electorate, 89 percent voted Democratic and 11 percent voted Republican. Hispanics (8 percent of the total) and Asians (2 percent of the total) overwhelmingly also voted Democratic. The gender, age, and education numbers represented similar support for the Democrats.

The only constituency where the Republicans had success was among Christian, conservative, religious groups. They garnered 55 percent of all Protestants, of which they won 62 percent of white Protestants. They also took 71 percent of the votes of those describing themselves as white, evangelical, born-again Christians. The total Catholic vote (which represented 26 percent of the electorate) was split—56 percent to 44 percent for the Democrats. White Catholics voted 51 percent to 49 percent for the Democrats and represented 19 percent of the electorate.[1]

In electoral terms, what do these numbers tell us? Empirically, they clearly and briefly say that the Republicans appealed to whites, and the Democrats held their own traditional constituencies. Democrats were also able to attract the largest number of minority voters to their party. Politically, the numbers say that the minority vote rallied behind the Democrats for a change in party politics, ideology, and policy. It was, in part, a political call for new leadership, fresh ideas, and innovative thinking on how to solve the nation's problems, specifically President Bush's approach to, and conduct of, the war in Iraq. It was also, however, a referendum on the politics of values as well as questions of integrity and character.

Looking back, the most interesting part of the whole political tale is how that message was sent, the "back story"—the story behind the story. What happened to the Republican revolution this time around? What happened to the Republican/evangelical values agenda? Is the intense love affair between the two of them over? Possibly! Can the Republican Party save itself by continuing to play the politics of values and pull out a presidential or congressional victory in 2008? Minimally, can it retain the seats that it has or maybe win a few more? The story is writing itself now, and as they say, only time will tell. But, there are some significant points to be made and lessons to be learned from the most recent past.

The Republican Party Commits Suicide: Scandals

The day of the midterm election, CNN did an exit poll measuring the intensity of voters' feelings on four significant issues. Although it was expected that Iraq would lead their list of concerns, it was actually distress over corruption and crime that came out first on the list of voter priorities. At 42 percent, values were still the issue that meant the most to the average American, with the war coming in a close second at 40 percent. What was even more surprising was that the values that most concerned the public were different from those that the Republicans had touted. The politics of values in 2006 was really *not* about the wedge issues—gay marriage, abortion, or stem cell research—instead, it reflected genuine concern about the most important, prevailing, and unifying American value of all—the character of its leaders.

In June of 2005, the ethical expectations that Americans had of their leaders were tested in California, opening the door to an issue that the Republican reelection infrastructure wanted to avoid. At that time, a defense contractor named Mitchell Wade purchased a home from Randall "Duke" Cunningham, a Republican representative from California. Located in an upscale section of idyllic San Diego, Cunningham's southern California home netted him $1,675,000 from Wade. A month later, however, Wade sold the expensive real estate at the "reduced" price of $975,000. Why did he take almost $700,000 less than he had paid for it? Did he just make a business mistake? Or did he knowingly overpay the congressman for his house? The deal smelled.

Cunningham, who had been in Congress since 1991, was a retired officer in the Navy, a former flying ace in Vietnam, and on the House Defense Appropriations Subcommittee. He was in a key power position.

After having paid so much more than the actual worth of the house, however, Wade suddenly found himself receiving millions of dollars worth of new defense and intelligence contracts. Furthermore, while Cunningham performed his legislative "duties" in Washington, D.C., the congressman lived on a yacht, and its maintenance was paid by none other than Mitchell Wade. Cunningham referred to the yacht as his "bouy toy," and had also been given the use of a Rolls-Royce and gifts such as Persian rugs, antiques, and jewelry by Wade and others.

But this was just the tip of the iceberg. Cunningham had also been involved in other questionable property real estate loans with others too, and had participated in shady deals with diverse defense companies. One of these was ADCS Inc., owned by Brent Wilkes. In return for $630,000 in cash and favors from Wilkes, Cunningham used his influence to try to get the Pentagon to buy a document-digitization system manufactured by Wilkes's company. A subsequent investigation showed that Cunningham had traded influence for money and favors, forcing him to plead guilty to tax evasion, conspiracy to commit bribery, mail fraud, and wire fraud. He resigned his position in the House, and in a plea deal Cunningham forfeited his new $2.55 million home and more than $1.8 million in cash and other items.

The gravity of the situation reverberated throughout the halls of Congress and the Republican Party. The Chair of the Intelligence Committee, Pete Hoekstra (R-MI), immediately announced that his committee would investigate to see if there had been any improper influence on the Intelligence Committee's work since Cunningham was a member. The chair of the Defense Appropriations Subcommittee, Bill Young (R-FL), planned to review Cunningham's requests for defense projects.

Wilkes was investigated for his ties with the majority leader's PAC, and it soon became public that he did business with the wife of Tom DeLay, the majority whip's wife. Wade pleaded guilty to paying Cunningham $1 million in bribes.

In June 2006, in a special congressional election, Brian Bilbray, the Republican candidate, barely won Cunningham's seat by a thin margin in the heavily GOP district in California. It was an omen of other corruption that was going to be investigated and a foreshadowing of some of the other critical election challenges that were going to be front and center in the midterm election.

The most serious corruption challenges grew out of the scandalous behavior of Jack Abramoff, a Republican activist and lobbyist, as well as a number of key Republican House members, including Mark Foley (R-FL), Tom DeLay (R-TX), Richard Pombo (R-CA), John Doolittle (R-CA), and Robert Ney (R-OH). The investigations of their activities reflected voter concern about character and corruption and were as acutely important an issue as the war in Iraq.

This fact either eluded the Republican reelection leadership during the midterm congressional campaign, or Karl Rove et al. believed that wedge issues could, and would, continue to dominate the political agenda. Whatever the case, concern over character was in great part the fact that led to the demise of the Republican Party's values agenda and the loss of the loyal constituency that came to be known as "the values voter."

These were the people who had supported the party and President Bush during the hard times: the contested election of 2000, the entrance into the

Iraq war and staying the course, the Kerry challenge in 2004, and the appointment of conservative Supreme Court justices. But most importantly, the values voters stood behind the president and the party during those times because they saw their political loyalty as a critical way to garner government support for their values agenda—overturning *Roe v. Wade*, limiting gay marriage and stem cell research, returning school prayer to the classroom, and continuing federal funding for faith-based social services. As the corruption began to unfold, the most loyal constituency within the Republican Party, the values voter, began to become more and more disappointed and less and less interested in the midterm elections. Many felt betrayed by the party and questioned its commitment to the values agenda. And, as the corruption continued, their support eroded.

The Jack Abramoff scandal is different from the Duke Cunningham debacle. Cunningham was greedy and got caught; Jack Abramoff was interested in power, abused it, and covered it up for a long time before the truth came out.

Abramoff, a New Jersey native, grew up in California, went to college in New York, and became National Committee Chairman of the College Republicans from 1981 to 1985. His was an accomplishment that mirrored the early political rise of political strategists like Karl Rove and Lee Atwater, President George H. W. Bush's campaign manager.

Abramoff was mentored by Grover Norquist, a man who never held national political office but who became one of the most powerful people within the right wing of the Republican Party because he headed up Americans for Tax Reform. Norquist served on the boards of the National Rifle Association and the American Conservative Union. Wednesdays were usually put aside for the Norquist "meeting," a salon of sorts for Hill and White House staffers and others within the Beltway. It was the place where tax-reform ideas from people at conservative think tanks and lobbyists would come together.

Norquist's ideas interested Karl Rove early on and were the reason why "the Architect" had invited him to meet George W. Bush twenty years earlier. A relationship between the future president and Norquist eventually became the link between Norquist's friend, Jack Abramoff, and influential Washington people like Ralph Reed, former campaign manager for Pat Robertson and subsequent head of the Christian Coalition.

With Norquist, Reed, and other influential friends and connections, Abramoff was able to create a comfortable place for himself in conservative circles. He established the Freedom Foundation, an anti-Communist think tank, and rose to become the top lobbyist in Preston Gates Ellis Greensberg and Taurig, a major "K Street" lobbying firm. He headed up the National Center for

Public Policy Research, another conservative think tank, and played a crucial role in Toward Tradition, a religious, right-wing Jewish organization.

Abramoff became a major power broker, the kind of person who could make things happen. By 1995, he was representing a number of Native American tribes with gambling interests. He also became involved in a variety of political ways to influence policy that affected Tyco, Inc. (the firm of CEO Dennis Kozlowski who was convicted of security fraud), the government of Malaysia, the government of the Sudan, Channel One News, and some Israeli telecommunications firms. He and his lobbying company reportedly made $82 million from Native American tribes, and later, he admitted to defrauding four of them out of millions of dollars.[2] What is so astounding is that his client list was so formidable.

Public records show that the Abramoff "team" had about 200 contacts with the new Bush administration in 2001, including individuals in the White House, the Congress, their assistants, and others. These relationships enabled Abramoff to approach and, eventually, to influence public officials and government policies. He entertained, wined, dined, and took a number of them on trips, until the Senate Indian Affairs Committee began to investigate Abramoff's practices in 2004.

One such high government contact was J. Steven Griles, the second highest official at the Interior Department, the agency that oversees Indian Affairs—including those tribes with gambling interests that Abramoff represented on the Hill. On March 23, 2007, Griles pled guilty to lying to the Senate Indian Affairs committee about having a special relationship with Abramoff.[3] Prosecutors said that Abramoff "sought and received" advice and help from Griles for his Indian tribe clients.[4]

Abramoff had taken the Fifth and refused to testify. But, after a wide-ranging series of investigations by the IRS and the FBI, he finally pled guilty to fraud, tax evasion, and conspiracy to bribe public officials in 2006. Part of his plea bargain required that he provide evidence about members of Congress.

The fallout was devastating. First, the little fish were hooked. Then, the big ones were caught, stuffed, and hung on the wall. In November 2005, Michael Scanlon, the former press secretary to House Majority Leader Tom DeLay, pled guilty to receiving illegal gifts and favors from Abramoff. Then Tony Rudy, a former top aide to DeLay, was found to have been a secret partner in Abramoff's scheme to defraud the Native American tribes. Rudy was implicated in attempting to use his influence to kill certain bills before the House and of having taken a job in Abramoff's firm without waiting the mandatory year required before lobbying former bosses. Rudy pled guilty in January 2006. Just three days later, the majority leader, Tom DeLay, resigned as well.

The Tom DeLay story was about abused ambition. He was brought up in Venezuela where his father worked in the gas and oil industry. He returned to the United States during his teens and married his first love, Christine, in 1967 and later graduated from the University of Houston. After running a successful pest extermination business, he entered politics and was elected to the Texas State House in 1978 and to the U.S. Congress in 1984.

DeLay was only 37 years old when he went to Washington D.C., but at that time, according to his own account, he was a hard-drinking man with a wandering eye for the ladies. He became a born-again Christian in 1985 though, and turned his life around, claiming that his newfound faith not only transformed his soul and his ethics but also his vision of the nation as well.[5]

During his time in state office, DeLay had used his influence to raise large amounts of corporate money to outspend Democrats and win control of the legislature. Winning the party plurality meant that the Republicans could re-draw the congressional district lines within the state, and as a result of his efforts, DeLay and the Republicans did just that to reflect the large concentration of Republicans in former Democratic strongholds. He had helped to turn the state around from a blue one to a red one. Only seven years later, when DeLay was elected to the U.S. House of Representatives, he was already considered a living and formidable political legend—one who knew the system, one who could manipulate it, and one who could make it work for the party.

DeLay's partisan expertise served him well on the national level. He rose quickly within the leadership ranks of the House. Elected deputy minority whip in 1988, he served under the minority whip, Dick Cheney, for six years until he was elected the majority whip in 1994. He was well connected in the House and after the retirement of his fellow Texan, Dick Armey, DeLay became majority leader in the House during the Republican revolution that had been engineered by Newt Gingrich.

DeLay's nickname in the Congress was "the Hammer" because he was a strict party disciplinarian, a leader who demanded political loyalty and one who would pay back those who opposed him. He was a formidable fund-raiser, and his movement up the party ladder brought him into contact with many people seeking access to those in high office and those who wanted to influence public policy through legislation. DeLay was one of a very few people in the House who could either stop a bill or make it happen.

Along the way, DeLay used his power in a number of aggressive—often negative and questionable—ways. He admits in his autobiography the he was part of a group that wanted Newt Gingrich to vacate his leadership position in the House. He was accused of threatening judges, of blatant gerrymandering, and of accepting excessive amounts of corporate money for his PAC,

Americans for a Republican Majority. He was challenged for these ethical violations in the House by congressman Chris Bell of Texas, and in 2004 he was investigated by the House Ethics Committee. DeLay was subsequently admonished for behavior that was "objectionable" and for taking gifts that allowed individuals to have "special access" to him.[6] The charge that did him in however, was Bell's complaint that DeLay improperly raised funds from corporations that were used to finance local Texas legislative campaigns through his PAC. This was illegal in the Lone Star State. DeLay resigned in April 2006, claiming that he would have to spend his time defending his good name in the Texas courts, a task that preoccupies him now.

In the process, however, he contributed to the discrediting of the Republican Party. Other allegations and investigations have now also surfaced—their trails leading back to Jack Abramoff. DeLay has admitted to having had a friendship with Abramoff and to receiving over $70,000 in political donations, expensive overseas junkets to Scotland, the Mariana Islands, and Russia—all of which were tracked back to Abramoff. It did not take long before it all became public. Taken together, the gifts represented the tip of the iceberg, part of a visible relationship with the influential lobbyist who was now a convicted pariah in Washington power circles. DeLay contends that he did nothing illegal, that all of the allegations against him are simply "liberal lies" perpetuated by the press.

The DeLay story has more tentacles too, some still in the process of being discovered. There are questions about the connection between Edwin Buckham, a close political and spiritual adviser to DeLay, and his payments of nearly $4,000 a month to DeLay's wife, Christine. There is the investigation of U.S. Family Network—considered a nonprofit front for Buckham and others who received one million dollars from Abramoff's Russian clients. There is the fact that Michael Scanlon, DeLay's communications director, went to work for Abramoff after his employment with the congressman. There is the fact that Tony Rudy admitted to accepting money to work for a specific policy while he was on DeLay's staff. He has been convicted. Do birds of a feather really flock together?

What is surprising, but not unusual, to those who know "the Hammer" is that DeLay has attributed the party's loss of power after the 2006 midterm election to others rather than himself. In a new book entitled *No Retreat, No Surrender*, DeLay contends that voter frustration with President Bush, the war, and a "general perception of Republican incompetence and lack of principles"[7] was responsible for the sweeping Democratic victory in 2006. He maintains that poor communications and the inability to deal with issues raised by the media were also central to the loss of the House and the Senate.

As for DeLay's role in the midterm debacle, he contends that he has been subject to ten years of political persecution. He admits to the fact that he is flawed like all individuals, that he "can sometimes be aggressive, even mean," and that sometimes he even worked from anger in his soul.[8]

Representative Robert W. Ney was the one congressman who was named by prosecutors in the court papers that were filed against Abramoff. Formerly the chair of the House Administration Committee, Ney worked with DeLay and the Republican leadership. He was accused of meeting with one of Abramoff's clients in Russia in 2003 to expedite a visa, of agreeing to help a California Indian tribe on tax and post office issues, of backing Abramoff's efforts to gain control of a Florida gambling company, and of using his influence to advance a contract to wire the House of Representatives for a telecommunications client of Abramoff's.

Ney's relationship with Jack Abramoff and the Justice Department's subsequent investigation of the congressman resulted in Ney's resignation from the House in October of 2006, only days before the midterm elections. It was another blow to the Republican Party, as Ney pleaded guilty to two counts of conspiracy to commit multiple offenses including fraud, false statements, and violating the one-year lobbying ban. He also admitted to soliciting and accepting valuable items from Abramoff and his lobbyists including trips, meals, drinks, tickets, and campaign contributions. In a final admission, Ney confessed that he used tens of thousands of dollars worth of gambling chips from a foreign businessman who was hoping to do business with the American airplane industry.[9] He is now serving a thirty-month prison sentence at the federal prison in Morgantown, West Virginia. Ney's chief of staff, William Heaton, also subsequently pleaded to a federal conspiracy charge regarding the acceptance of favors from Jack Abramoff and/or his associates in return for helping the lobbyists' clients.

A relationship with Abramoff was the political glue (or slime) that was used in a number of races to tie Republican candidates to the convicted lobbyist. For example, in California, Richard Pombo and John Doolittle were smeared because Abramoff and his clients purportedly gave "tens of thousands of dollars in campaign contributions to their past campaigns."[10] Neither was named by the Justice Department in the Abramoff probe, but Pombo was also attacked on his environmental record by the Sierra Club and Doolittle faced Democratic opposition because his wife, as his chief fundraiser, took a 15 percent commission on the political events that she organized. As a result, "safe" Republican seats suddenly morphed into unsafe seats, and then into potential seats for the Democratic taking.

In order to save their candidacies, President Bush campaigned for the two California congressmen, Pombo and Doolittle, both of whom were forced to spend a significant amount of money on phone banks and mailings, expenditures that they never had to make in their other, safe campaigns.

Pombo returned $7,500 he got from Abramoff as a campaign donation, claiming that he and the lobbyist had met only two or three times. Doolittle was forced to participate in his first debate since having won his congressional seat.

In the end, Pombo lost his election to his Democratic challenger. Four months later, in February 2007, the former congressman joined PAC/West Communications, a lobbying and public relations firm in Washington, D.C. His new job is to advise grassroots activists how to maneuver within the congressional political infrastructure. He was, after all, a former member of the House Natural Resources Committee while he was in office.

Such cozy relationships between lobbying firms and former government officials have long been part of the way of doing postelection business for losers in the nation's capital. Republican legislation to stop the abuse of moving from Congress to lobbying firms had attempted to establish a one-year cooling off period in response to the Abramoff scandal. But it really changed nothing. In fact, the "time-out" was considered essentially "ineffectual" according to Public Citizen, an interest group that follows the government afterlife of congresspersons. It reported that of eighteen people who left Congress in 2004, all had jobs with lobbying firms by 2005.[11]

Former congressional attempts to end the legislative exodus to lobbying firms have again surfaced in the Democratically controlled Senate. In 2007, Senator Russ Feingold (D-WI) and Senator Barak Obama (D-IL) introduced legislation that would build on Feingold's earlier lobbying disclosure bill, S. 2349. It would require a two-year period of time before congresspersons could take lobbying jobs, and it instituted a variety of other reforms. As of this writing, however, the bill is still awaiting consideration.

John T. Doolittle, in hot water with Pombo, managed to squeak by with a congressional win. But recently, the politician's home in Washington D.C. was the object of an FBI search in connection with the activities of Sierra Dominion Financial Solutions, Inc., a fundraising company run by his wife, Julie Doolittle.

Other information has also emerged about the sitting congressman, who is serving his ninth term in the House. It appears that as a member of the House Appropriations Committee, Doolittle directed about $37 million in earmarks to Brent Wilkes, the same San Diego contractor who was involved in the Duke Cunningham scandal.[12] Can an FBI investigation be far behind?

While all these stories were about ego, money, and power, the Mark Foley story was about the pathetic, sick congressman who represented the Palm Beach, Florida district. A handsome bachelor, Foley loved the limelight and the media attention that his position afforded him. In Washington, D.C., he was part of the glitterati, but behind the scenes, he was a dark enigma. While Foley was the spokesman for legislation to protect children, he was secretly emailing House pages with suggestive and pornographic messages.

Within a few days of the revelations, however, the shocking and complex Foley story began to unravel. Foley had sent the emails. Foley had a drinking problem. Foley himself was allegedly abused by a Catholic priest. Foley was going into rehab. Foley would not run for reelection. Further, the perception among the public was that the old boy's political network had protected Foley, that those in power had looked the other way. The winks and nods, the pretense that the innuendoes in his emails were simply misunderstood messages of genuine interest in the pages, all seemed to find credibility too, when the House Ethics Committee, made up of an equal number of Democrats and Republicans, eventually censured no one after investigating the allegations against Foley.

Nevertheless, the scandal, according to Tony Perkins, president of the Family Research Council, took the "air out of the tires" of most conservative evangelicals.[13] And, to add insult to injury, the election rules in Florida made it virtually impossible to remove Foley from the ballot. Instead, a complicated write-in situation came into play with the new Republican candidate, Joe Negron, trying to explain it to the District 16 constituents. The whole charade was to no avail. In the end, Tim Mahoney, the Democratic candidate, narrowly defeated the incumbent 50 percent to 48 percent in a tried-and-true Republican safe district, a win that was essentially based on the complexities in the voting rules, the loss of evangelical support, and the debacle that was the Republican scandal of Mark Foley.

The number, variations, and gravity of the scandals were a major contributing factor to the Republican midterm losses, no matter what party functionaries or conservative pundits might contend. But, even more importantly, the concern for the scandals reflected the average American's insistence on what might be called the character imperative. Sophisticated policy nuances aside, the individual who goes into a voting booth wants an honest person to represent him or her—it's that simple. Character was not just a critical part of the values voters' agenda, but everyone's agenda. The Democrats understood the importance of character after the scathing repudiation of John Kerry in the 2004 election, but the Republicans either forgot or tried to continue to play the politics of values and push wedge issues in 2006. They did not pay enough attention to those values that unite people—like honesty and integrity. And, their misuse of values for political expediency, rather than for their intrinsic worth and for the common good, resulted, in great part, in the Republican loss in the midterm election.

There is a lesson in here for the Democratic Party as well. If it intends to participate in a positive use of the politics of values in the future—to de-emphasize wedge issues, to pursue those values that unify the electorate and to stress the character of its leaders—it will have to be vigilant and consider how it will handle local and national abuses of power. Current scandals such as those affecting conflicts of interest—including those involving Democratic Governor John Corzine of New Jersey, allegations of abuses of power by Democratic Governor Elliot Spitzer in New York, and problems of honesty with other high-ranking Democrats—will make them as vulnerable to political losses as the Republicans. Democratic values voters are as concerned about integrity as Republicans.

The Evangelical Right Goes into a Tailspin

Evangelicals had their own issues to deal with before the midterm election. Some within the Christian right had become increasingly disaffected with the Republican Party and its agenda, particularly James Dobson and his religious conservative organization, Focus on the Family. Dobson complained mightily about the fact that Focus on the Family had worked hard to turn out the vote for Republicans in 2004, but that since then he had "been extremely disappointed with what the Republicans [had] done with the power they were given."[14] Dobson wanted to see a greater policy emphasis by the White House and a more significant congressional push for legislation to deal with issues like abortion and same-sex marriage. Instead, he thought that dealing with issues like tax cuts and social security reform would risk the support of values voters. As mentioned previously, Dobson held his own summit in Washington, D.C., in the fall of 2006 to try to rally values voters and to bring their concerns to the Republican agendas of those who were running for office.

Dobson's opposition began to fragment the tenuous alliance between religious and social conservatives. Dick Armey, the former majority leader in the House and an economic traditionalist, accused Republican legislators of "pandering" to Dobson and his "thugs," and worse, of abandoning their need for budget cutting.[15] Within the context of this conservative fracturing, the religious right began to come apart as well. On October 27, a week before the vote, the president-elect of the Christian Coalition of America, the activist, political arm of Pat Robertson's ministries, resigned before officially taking office.

Reverend Joel C. Hunter, pastor of the Northland Church, a Florida mega-congregation, gave up his future leadership role in the Christian Coalition because the organization refused to support his concern for poverty and global warming and make it part of the Coalition's political agenda. Author of *Right Wing, Wrong Bird: Why the Tactics of the Religious Right Won't Fly with Most Conservative Christians*,[16] Hunter reflected the views of a growing number of conservative Christians, some of whom were moving more toward the ideological center and becoming increasingly intent on broadening the agenda of the policy arm of their denominational coalition.

Officially, the administrative leadership of the Christian Coalition accused Hunter of neither consulting nor representing the organization's base, thus giving the appearance that his resignation was the result of a process breach rather than a substantive disagreement. Left without a leader, the Christian Coalition was abruptly forced to find a new head before it could be considered politically credible and effective in the future.

While the Christian Coalition leadership crisis did little or nothing to help conservative Republican candidates at the midterm election, the evangelical community suffered a second and more disastrous loss of a policy leader just a few days later. That scandal was the one that would take the values voter movement into total disarray.

The chaos grew out of the preaching of the pastor who was able to hold thousands in the palm of his hand with his message and his charisma. He was good-looking, articulate, and even godly—an example for all to follow. In fact, Ted Haggard had started his Colorado Springs megachurch, The New Life Ministry, himself in 1985. As an outgrowth of the Bethany World Prayer Center in Baton Rouge where he had served as youth pastor, the church had been nurtured in his family's basement and grown into a congregation of 14,000. Reportedly, Haggard, his wife Gayle, and their five children represented what was the best in evangelical Christianity: a personal commitment to Jesus Christ and traditional family values, an abiding sense of citizenship, and an unshakable loyalty to America.

Haggard's dedication and exemplary life soon became the stuff of legends, advancing his reputation within evangelical circles, being named by *Time* magazine as one of the nation's 25 most influential evangelicals, and culminating in 2003 with his election as president of the National Association of Evangelicals. An umbrella organization of over thirty different denominations, the NAE represented over 25 million evangelicals in America.

Haggard led the organization brilliantly and even stepped into the political world. Flexing the muscle of the NAE, Haggard was able to use the growing number of registered Republican voters within the evangelical organization, and the potential to provide more, to get the full attention of the Bush White House. Haggard and several other religious leaders spoke weekly with officials at the White House on matters of importance to their religious and political agendas. His access was envied. His position was secure. His life was exemplary. What could possibly be wrong with this picture?

On Halloween 2006, a Tuesday and one week before the midterm elections, the story broke that Ted Haggard had been paying a male prostitute for sex over a three-year period. Further, it was alleged that he had also been buying drugs from the same man, his accuser, Mike Jones.

Haggard originally denied the charges, even saying that he did not know Jones. Then he admitted to getting a massage from Jones and buying methamphetamines from him once. Haggard claimed that he bought the drugs but threw them away. He said he "was tempted"[17] but never used them. However, within two days the full story was out: Haggard had contacted Jones either through an ad that the male "escort" had placed in a gay newspaper or possibly through a gay website.

The gory details are that Haggard used an alias, "Art," and would go into Denver once a month to carry out his illicit affair with Jones. His accuser claimed that Haggard used meth before their sexual encounters to "heighten his experience."[18]

Haggard was investigated immediately after Jones's accusations by a religious, independent board of overseers, resigned on a Thursday, and was fired on Saturday for sexually immoral conduct. On Sunday, two days before the election, Pastor Larry Stockstill of the Bethany World Prayer Center in Baker, Louisiana, head of the investigative board that looked into the allegations against Haggard, read a letter from the disgraced pastor to the congregants of the New Life Church. In part it said

> I am a deceiver and a liar. There is a part of my life that is so repulsive and dark that I've been warring against it all of my adult life . . . The public person I was wasn't a lie; it was just incomplete. When I stopped communicating about my problems, the darkness increased and finally dominated me. As a result, I did things that were contrary to everything I believe . . . I created this entire situation. The things that I did opened the door for additional allegations. But I am responsible: I alone need to be disciplined and corrected. An example must be set.[19]

While Haggard called on his former flock to remain faithful to God through service and giving, the evangelical world stood still as it tried to internalize the loss of a beloved pastor, a powerful leader, and the voice of their values agenda.

Haggard had in fact been a key member of the coalition that drafted Amendment 43, the Colorado defense of marriage legislation. It legally defined marriage as a union between one man and one woman and was a critical part of the evangelical political cause. Indeed, it was Haggard's signature political stance that had reportedly motivated Mike Jones to disclose his relationship with the religious leader. Jones maintained that he found Haggard's stance on gay marriage hypocritical and that, as a matter of conscience, he had to divulge their affair to the public.

So, two days before the midterm elections, evangelicals found themselves in disarray. With no moral leader and no real credibility, no one was quite sure what impact the Haggard scandal would have on Colorado or national politics.

The White House immediately distanced itself from Haggard, claiming that the disgraced minister had had some conversations with the president by phone but that his access had been exaggerated by Haggard and the press. Some pundits thought Haggard's dismissal would further alienate values voters who were already disaffected with the scandals within the Republican Party and keep them away from the polls. But, an analysis of the issues and numbers shows a complex picture of how they actually responded.

Professors Mark Silk and John C. Green, two experts on religion and politics, have scrutinized a variety of election statistics from 2002 forward.[20] They contend that there has been an increasing polarization of the electorate along religious lines, but that white evangelicals are still committed to, and are a critical part of, the GOP base.

Legislation banning gay marriage bore this out. The issue was on the ballot in eight states: Idaho, South Carolina, Tennessee, Virginia, Wisconsin, Colorado, South Dakota, and Arizona. At the end of October, the Republicans desperately tried to resuscitate the issue when the war was taking center stage and every other issue was falling apart around them. The New Jersey Supreme Court had decided a week before the election that gay couples were entitled to the same legal rights and financial benefits as heterosexual couples, a holding that President Bush highlighted while he was campaigning in Iowa. In the end, the only state that approved gay marriage was Arizona. Amendments to ban it passed in all of the other states that considered gay marriage. Thus, it does not appear that the evangelicals lost any significant ground on the issue of gay marriage, the policy that was central to Ted Haggard in his home state of Colorado.

What is most curious, however, is the fact that the Haggard scandal has given rise to the voice of another constituency: gay evangelicals. Stories about gay evangelicals in the press have revealed the theological confusion within the ranks of what had appeared to be a monolithic, conservative theological doctrine on human sexuality. In December, a month after the midterm election, Reverend Paul Barnes of the Grace Chapel megachurch in Englewood, Colorado, resigned his pastor's position after being confronted with allegations of homosexuality and confessing to infidelity.

Although his outing may be unique among evangelical clergy, it could foreshadow other revelations. There are reportedly thousands of gay evangelicals who are attempting to sort out their lives and their religious beliefs and who are caught in the crosshairs of the values debates over traditional family values. Justin Lee, the founder of gaychistian.net, is one of those individuals. Lee has claimed that in 2006 alone more than 4,700 registered users had visited his website seeking to cope with same-sex attractions.[21] What this might mean for the presidential election in 2008 is just beginning to emerge. It could represent the fact that wedge issues, such as gay marriage, will have to be reconsidered and reprioritized by the Christian right.

Currently, at least, there is an attempt to keep evangelical thinking on message—on conservative message, that is. In general, evangelical priorities remain committed to the sanctity of life, human rights, caring for the vulnerable, family integrity, environmental stewardship, and peacemaking. Entering into the political world to implement such a biblical agenda, however, is beginning to be recognized as a more complicated task than previously understood. It is about more than numbers, and it is about more than having a connection with the White House—it is about a long-term strategy to implement Christian values within a political context that can, and might, change radically in the coming election. Evangelicals realize now that they must view political activity in a much more realistic and sophisticated context.

Major evangelical thinkers/academics see three basic facts that need to be acknowledged, understood, and used as a starting point for meaningful political action within the U.S. public arena. For example, according to Professors Stephen Monsma and Mark Rogers, the first is to recognize "the sinful, broken nature of the political world," the fact that "something terrible has gone wrong in the political world."[22] The second is that evangelicals bring "a burden of biased perspectives, incomplete knowledge, and their own sinfulness"[23] to the policy table. Third, they posit that politics has been dominated by a cultural and media elite that control attitudes as well as public opinion. This situation, according to them, requires that Christians train their own cadre of teachers, reporters, and political actors who can counter liberal relativism and simplistic explanations of traditional values as simply "homophobic" or "intolerant." Thus, some critical evangelical thinkers understand that their gains may be modest in the political arena at best, but effective if they vote, educate others about issues, work in affiliation with like-minded groups, and are willing to compromise for the partial achievement of biblical goals.

And Ted Haggard? After three weeks of intensive therapy, newspapers were reporting that he is now 100 percent heterosexual. The status of his New Life

Church in Colorado Springs is questionable, though. Donations are down, and forty-four of its 350 workers have been laid off. Nevertheless, sources close to Haggard report that "he is authentically repentant and humble."[24] What that means for his personal future and the political agenda of the National Association of Evangelicals is certainly up for speculation. But for a more informed understanding, the public can now buy a copy of *I Had to Say Something* by Mike Jones, who wants to get a job at Sea World.[25]

They Huffed and Puffed and
Blew the Architect's House Down

After the success of the presidential election of 2000, the midterm elections of 2002, and the reelection of George Bush in 2004, Karl Rove had built himself a house of power, a structure that was held together by his personal relationship with the president. The *New York Times* characterized it as one in which Rove was "both mastermind and supplicant," and the president was "both leader and follower."[26] In short, theirs was a very special political bond.

"The Architect" had received accolades from the president, grudging admiration from some of his opponents, and derision from much of the liberal press and the media. But what did he care? What did he have to worry about? After effecting Bush's second presidential victory, his professional reputation and personal power were the stuff of legends. The *Washington Post* even reported that Rove had acquired "something close to cult status" among conservatives, and that he was the "most powerful draw on the GOP fundraising circuit"[27] after the president, Laura Bush, and the vice president. It was no surprise then that Rove "headlined more than 100 fundraisers during the 2004–6 election cycle and that he was able to raise close to $13 million for Republican candidates and causes."[28] How could anyone dismiss his ability to be all things to all members of the party?

Rove was rewarded for his strategic political savvy and financial acumen by being appointed Deputy Chief of Staff for Policy in 2006 by his long-time friend, the president. It was a position that was expected to bring together his expertise on winning political races and creating viable and relevant public policy. Rove's detractors were waiting to see what the relationship between the two would be. Would he use his astute knowledge of political practices to drive policy decisions? Would he let policy needs take the lead in forging the agenda of partisan politics? Or would he bring politics and policy together somehow to create a winning strategy for the president's reelection and the party's success in the midterm election?

The power that Rove could, and did, wield was formidable. He reportedly met with the president everyday, in fact sometimes several times a day, on politics and policy issues. The *New York Times* reported that the president gave him "clearance to run the White House midterm elections plan according to his standard playbook, even as other Republicans began to question Mr. Rove's reputation for strategic brilliance and detach themselves from Mr. Bush and the Iraq war."[29]

Rove also worked closely with Ken Mehlman, head of the Republican National Committee, but some aides reported that Rove "was controlling strategic planning, day-to-day policy management, politics and often communications . . ."[30] Other insiders complained that Rove was not able to manage the White House policy machine. Some said he was disorganized, while staffers maintained that the new White House chief of staff, Josh Bolten, was "bothered" by his policy "stumbles."[31]

Rove's appointment as Deputy Chief of Staff for Policy reflected the president's dependence on his campaign architect for strategic policy and political thinking. It also foreshadowed the need for a strong individual to shore up the increasingly insular White House bureaucracy. Within the media, it was portrayed as a stumbling organization, one that desperately needed to create confidence and find policy issues that would underscore the ability of George W. Bush to lead the country in the right direction.

This problem was even more daunting in policy circles. Rove was expected to formulate a way to deal with the corruption within the party in order to hold Republican seats at the midterm; to identify and present domestic policy solutions that would bring the sagging presidential approval numbers up; as well as to be able to reunite the party now coming apart at the seams over the war in Iraq. There was a lot riding on Rove's shoulders.

During the course of his first year as Deputy Chief of Staff for Policy though, Rove had participated in some policy missteps and been identified with others. Among them were his support of social security savings accounts, comprehensive immigration reform, a complicated Medicare prescription drug benefit program, the debacle of Katrina relief, and the nomination of Harriet Miers for a seat on the Supreme Court. In the process, some thought he had alienated Hispanic voters; angered blacks, the elderly, and other minorities; and antagonized the crucial, religious conservative base.

By April 2006, Rove's effectiveness was being reconsidered within the inner circles of White House power. Some were beginning to ask if he was part of the administration's policy problem or the iconic strategist who could find solutions to the critical issues that were proliferating. In a swift internal move, Rove was either replaced or demoted in the summer before the midterm elections—at least that was how a variety of pundits explained it.

The White House spin machine, however, reported that Rove was no longer going to work on policy issues because he was needed to focus solely on the congressional elections. Moved from his corner office in the West Wing to a windowless one across the hall, Rove was still expected to work his magic—to play the politics of values, to motivate grassroots activists to support Republican candidates, and to get the party behind the president's domestic and foreign policies.

In the midst of all these internal machinations and rising expectations, however, a frightening specter haunted Rove while he served as deputy chief of staff for policy and later in his "more focused" political role. It was the fact that he was implicated in the CIA outing of Valerie Plame in 2003. The fear of possibly being indicted and prosecuted hung over his head for three long years.

The wife of former Ambassador Joseph E. Wilson, Plame's identity was disclosed a few days after her husband wrote an op-ed piece in the *New York Times*. In it, he claimed that the Bush administration had distorted intelligence about Iraqi efforts to obtain uranium in Africa. Wilson maintained that the president's rationale for going to war was incorrect and that someone in the White House had revealed his wife's covert role at the CIA as a means of getting back at him. A special prosecutor was appointed to look into the matter, and Rove was among those called to testify before the grand jury about the outing of Plame.

He acknowledged having been a verifying source for a July 2003 column by Robert Novak in which the journalist disclosed her identity, but he was not indicted. Instead, the investigation centered on I. Lewis "Scooter" Libby, Vice President Dick Cheney's chief of staff, who was eventually charged with obstruction of justice, lying to the grand jury, and perjury.

With such ominous clouds, in January 2006 Rove spoke in his best campaign strategist mode before the winter meeting of the Republican National Committee, putting the potential felony behind him and introducing a clear, but difficult, campaign strategy for beating the Democrats at the midterm. While the Democrats had plenty of ammunition and were going to focus on corruption, Rove intended to stress terrorism instead; while the Democrats would challenge the necessity and effectiveness of the war, the Republicans would emphasize the imperative for national security. Was Rove in a time-warp or in the Rose Garden? Was he out of touch with the average voter and the values voter? Had he adopted a bunker mentality? Had he lost his edge? Had the hardball game of Valerie Plame's outing become too hot to handle? Who's to say? A week before the midterm election, Rove was still confident as he was interviewed on National Public Radio.

I think Iraq and the economy play a role in virtually every race. But there are also local considerations in the local contests between two individuals that at the end of the day matters for a great deal of the contest . . . Politics is a complex equation [in] which voters are going to be examining a variety of characteristics as they arrive at their decision[s].[32]

But clearly, those other "characteristics" had escaped the Rove radar: character, scandals, and supporting rigid religious agendas. His misreading of them showed how out of touch the Republican strategy of using the politics of values was with its base as well as the average centrist voter. A week before the midterm election, Josh Bolten told a reporter for the *Washington Post* that he believed in Rove's optimism about Republican success. "I believe Karl Rove," he said, claiming that "somewhere inside that massive brain of his, [he] has figured out the political landscape more clearly than the entire collection of conventional-wisdom pundits and pollsters in the entire city of Washington."[33]

Unfortunately, Bolten's trust was misplaced and rejected by the public. The day after the election, when the senior White House staff met in the Roosevelt Room, Josh Bolten thanked Rove for his work. There was spontaneous applause for his efforts, but, underneath it all were questions about Rove's insistence on playing the politics of values: pushing wedge issues, his party's general discontent and malaise, the values voter's underlying dissatisfaction with the Bush domestic agenda, and the social conservative opposition to rising deficits. Clearly, "the Architect" had misread the realities of the campaign and its outcome.

In a postelection interview with *Time* magazine, Rove admitted, "The profile of corruption in the exit polls was bigger than I'd expected . . . Abramoff, lobbying, Foley and Haggard added to the general distaste that people have for all things Washington, and it just reached critical mass."[34] Although Rove understood that Iraq played a central role in the election, he did not think that it was the critical issue that tipped the Republican loss of the House and the Senate. Instead, Rove saw the midterm debacle as a "transient, passing thing,"[35] maintaining that Republican core values and the president's foreign agenda would ultimately achieve a long-term majority for the party in the future. He specifically alluded to issues such as fighting the war on terror and bringing democracy to the Middle East, domestic reforms on entitlements, energy, taxes, immigration, and education.

Rove had gone from being the president's friend, mentor, and campaign manager to the Republican Party's chief strategist and fundraiser. He was dubbed "the Architect," and appointed Deputy Chief of Staff for Policy in the White House. His rise to the top ended with a quiet thud, as he became increasingly irrelevant playing the politics of values and losing the midterm elections in 2006; the man who somehow got out of the Valerie Plame scandal; and the person who could not, or would not, see debacle on the horizon.

So much was expected of Rove, maybe too much, and so many outside factors played a role in his inability to deliver a Republican Senate and House. He even had to step aside from trying to orchestrate the governor's races in 2006. He was not able to hold Republican candidates in line, was forced to hear them criticizing the president and his policies, and even to suffer the ignominy of being avoided at public events.

But Rove would not be finished with either the White House or the party after the midterm election. A few months later, into the New Year, the trial of Scooter Libby began for obstruction of justice, lying to the grand jury, and perjury. Rove was again being implicated in the Plame outing. This time, however, there was a surprising defense—that the vice president's former chief of staff was being used as a scapegoat to protect Karl Rove.

Libby's defense attorney, Theodore Wells, argued that this occurred "because he [Karl Rove] was Mr. Bush's right-hand man" and "was most responsible for seeing [that] the Republican Party stayed in office."[36] The assertion, of course, was meant to show that Libby had been set up and sacrificed to save Karl Rove. The details read like a spy novel: Libby was the only White House official authorized to speak to reporters in 2003 about the conflicting intelligence reports that Iraq was purchasing uranium from Africa to produce weapons of mass destruction. Those CIA accounts were proven false by former Ambassador Joseph Wilson who had been sent to Niger to investigate the claims. Someone wanted Wilson to pay for challenging the administration. Libby was the only member of the White House staff who was indicted.

Libby was essentially left on his own. His defense attorney tried to prove that Libby did not reveal Plame's identity to reporters from the *Washington Post*, the *New York Times*, or *Newsweek*. The timeline, which became increasingly blurred, was critical to the matter of who said what and to whom and when. During the Libby trial, Robert Novak, who wrote the article that revealed Plame's undercover status in the CIA, testified that he received the information for his syndicated column on July 14, 2003, from Richard Armitage, the then deputy secretary of state, and that the Armitage source was corroborated by Karl Rove.

Scooter Libby was eventually convicted of perjury, lying to a grand jury, and of obstruction of justice—felonies that carried with them one-and-a-half to three years of prison time. He appealed and was eventually sentenced to thirty months in prison for lying. That punishment was commuted by President Bush in 2007.

Valerie Plame emerged as the victim in the court of public opinion. She wrote her memoirs, entitled *Fair Game*, and with a reported $2 million potential payoff from Simon and Schuster, entered the world of the glitterati. Plame's husband, Joe Wilson, wrote a tell-all book called *The Politics of Truth: Inside the Lies That Led to War and Betrayed My Wife's CIA Identity—A Diplomat's Memoir*.[37] And Warner Brothers Studios announced in March 2007 that it had bought the rights to the life stories of both Plame and Wilson. The whole saga will soon appear on the big screen. They, by the way, made their personal exits to Santa Fe, New Mexico, where they moved to get far away from the life inside the Beltway and its clandestine activity.

And Karl Rove? Although he was not indicted, "the Architect" was named in a civil suit by Plame and Wilson seeking damages for loss of career status and salary. The lawsuit has been dismissed, but Rove has suffered ignominy in the court of public opinion. The statement by Denis Collins, a member of the Libby jury, said it all: The jurors believed that the vice president's chief of staff had really been the "fall guy" for the administration. Collins asked rhetorically, "Where is Rove? Where are these other guys? I wish we weren't judging Libby."[38]

A few weeks after the Libby conviction, Rove was implicated again in a Washington brouhaha over an attempt to link him to the firing of a number of Republican federal prosecutors. E-mail messages surfaced that showed that Karl Rove had questioned how the Justice Department was going to proceed on certain judicial dismissals and whether or not the Department was going to replace some or all of them for "underperformance." However, the targeted prosecutors refused to leave their posts and cried foul. They contended that they were being fired in retaliation for having investigated some Republican lawmakers for corruption and for looking into voter fraud in a number of districts. The situation became more partisan when Rove responded by saying that their dismissal and the actions of the justice department were "entirely appropriate" and that "to my mind [this] is a lot of politics . . ."[39]

Rove was increasingly being skewered politically and beginning his slow descent into political limbo. Finally, in August 2007, "the Architect" resigned, simply saying that it was time to go. His departure raises significant strategic questions. Will the politics of values go with him? Will future political strategists for the Republicans continue to use his formerly effective means to win elections? Or will the appeal to wedge issues, the values voter, and the support for ideologically conservative candidates go by the board? Even more importantly, if this does occur, what will replace the politics of values in the future?

The handwriting is starting to appear on the wall. Some major Republican conservatives have already disappeared since the 2006 midterm election. Rick

Santorum, the powerful pro-life senator from Pennsylvania, lost his seat. Bill Frist, the majority leader of the Senate from Tennessee, decided not to run for reelection and then opted to pass on a run for the presidency in 2008 as well. Senator George Allen (R-VA) crashed in flames, losing his reelection campaign to Jim Webb, an opponent of the Iraq war and all things Bush. These were major loses for the party and for Karl Rove, the fading "architect."

In a direct challenge to the politics of values, some Democrats changed their campaign tactics, proud to show their liberal religious colors and to speak with their newly found religious voices. Ted Strickland, a Democrat who was also an ordained Methodist minister, defeated J. Kenneth Blackwell, the Republican candidate for governor in Ohio. Some Democrats even won major duels with their religious, political rivals. For example, in North Carolina, Heath Schuler, a former National Football League quarterback who was a member of the evangelical organization Fellowship of Christian Athletes, ran for Congress as a Democrat. His views on abortion and gun control have been described as "far out of step with the prevailing views of the Democrats"[40] but represented the new type of centrist Democrat. Beating the Republican incumbent Charles Taylor, 54 percent to 46 percent, Schuler appealed to a large segment of the voting population who were simply disaffected with the Republican Party.

Every Democrat who sought reelection to the Congress in 2006 won. Thus, running on values came back to bite the Republicans on the butt, not because values were an unimportant issue—they were, and remain so—but because the Republicans were more concerned with the values that *separated* people rather than the values that *united* them. Chief among these has always been the question of character—the virtue and measure of a man (or a woman).

After six years of almost unbridled rule, the Republicans let the worst part of their aggregated character show: They became arrogant rather than "compassionate" conservatives, they took their eyes off the prize, and they abrogated the right to be a vital force for keeping and making America great. Worse, their alliance with the evangelicals became the final coffin nail of what was, for the Republicans, the debacle of the 2006 midterm election.

Can the Republicans regain their political composure? It is possible for them to take the White House again in 2008? Or have they made so many mistakes, from abusing their base to making poor choices of issues, values, and policies, that it will be impossible to recover? The next chapter looks at the road ahead and looks at the future of the Republican Party and the viability of the politics of values as the best strategy recovery for the GOP's political dominance in the future.

Notes

1. "Survey of Voters," *New York Times*, November 9, 2006, P7.
2. Susan Schmidt and James V. Grimaldi, "Abramoff Pleads Guilty to 3 Counts," *Washington Post*, January 4, 2006, A1.
3. He had met the lobbyist through Italia Federici, with whom he was romantically involved during his tenure at the Interior Department. She has recently been named in a two-count criminal document that usually implies that a guilty plea has been negotiated. See Associated Press, *New York Times*, June 7, 2007, A29.
4. Edmund L. Andrews, "Ex-Interior Aide Pleads Guilty to Lying in Lobbying Case," *New York Times*, March 24, 2007, A9.
5. Tom DeLay with Stephen Mansfield, *No Retreat, No Surrender: One American's Fight* (Sentinel: New York, 2007), 87.
6. Letter of the House Ethics Committee to Tom DeLay, October 6, 2004, www.house.gov/ethics/Delay-letter.html.
7. DeLay, *No Retreat*.
8. DeLay, *No Retreat*, 102.
9. Neil Volz, "Ohio Congressman Ney Admits to Conspiracy, False Statements," *North Country Gazette*, October 16, 2006, www.northcountrygazette.org.
10. Jesse McKinley, "Incumbents on the Ropes over Ties to Abramoff," *New York Times*, October 27, 2006, A14.
11. Matt Kelley, "Lobbying Restrictions Are Ineffectual, Critics Say," *USA Today*, February 22, 2007, 7A.
12. Neil A. Lewis and David D. Kirkpatrick, "F.B.I. Searches Home of California Lawmaker," *New York Times*, April 19, 2007, A13.
13. "A Blame Game," *New York Times*, October 20, 2006, A19.
14. David D. Kirkpatrick, "Republican Woes Lead to Feuding by Conservatives," *New York Times*, October 20, 2006, A1.
15. Kirkpatrick, "Republican Woes Lead to Feuding by Conservatives," A19.
16. Joel C. Hunter, *Right Wing, Wrong Bird: Why the Tactics of the Religious Right Won't Fly with Most Conservative Christians* (Longwood, Florida: Distributed Church Press, 2006).
17. Laurie Goodstein and Neela Banerjee, "Minister Denies Gay Tryst, but Admits Buying Drugs," *New York Times*, November 4, 2006, A13.
18. Catherine Tsai, "Key Evangelical Quits Amid Gay Sex Claim," *Associated Press*, November 11, 2006, http://news.yahoo.com.
19. Text of Haggard's message to the New Life Church Family, New Life Church, November 5, 2006, no. 0494, l.
20. Mark Silk and John C. Green, "The GOP's Religious Problem," *Religion in the News*, Winter, vol. 9, no. 3, 2–4.
21. Neela Banerjee, "Gay and Evangelical, Seeking Paths of Acceptance," *New York Times*, December 12, 2006, A1.
22. Stephen Monsma and Mark Rogers, "In the Arena," in *Toward an Evangelical Public Policy: Political Strategies for the Health of the Nation*, eds. Ronald J. Sider and Diane Knippers (Grand Rapids: Baker Books, 2005), 326.
23. Monsma and Rogers, "In the Arena," 327.

24. Dan Frosch, "Layoffs Follow Scandal at Colorado Megachurch," *New York Times,* March 6, 2007, A3.

25. Deborah Solomon, "The Whistle-Blower," *New York Times Magazine,* June 3, 2007, 14.

26. Jim Rutenberg, "A Last Hurrah of Sorts for Bush-Rove Partnership," *New York Times,* November 7, 2006, 18.

27. Michael Abramowitz, "Midterm Vote May Define Rove's Legacy; Big Losses Could Dim Aura of Bush Adviser," *Washington Post,* October 30, 2006, A1.

28. Abramowitz, "Midterm Vote May Define Rove's Legacy."

29. Rutenberg, "A Last Hurrah of Sorts for Bush-Rove Partnership," 18.

30. Jim Vandhei and Dan Baltz, "Fall Elections Are Rove's Next Test, Reputation of Architect of Victory at Stake," *Washington Post,* June 17, 2006, A1, www.washingtonpost.com.

31. Dana Bash, "Rove Back to Basics in Reduced New Role," April 20, 2006, http://cnn.worldnews.com.

32. Transcript from "All Things Considered" on National Public Radio, October 24, 2006, www.npr.org/about/press/061024.rove.html.

33. Abramowitz, op. cit.

34. Mike Allen, "The Architect Speaks," *The Allen Report,* November 10, 2006, http://time-blog.com/allen_report/2006/11/the_architect_speaks.html.

35. Allen, "The Architect Speaks."

36. Neil A. Lewis, "Libby Defense Portrays Client as a Scapegoat," *New York Times,* January 24, 2007, A12.

37. Ambassador Joseph Wilson, *The Politics of Truth: Inside the Lies That Led to War and Betrayed My Wife's CIA. Identity—A Diplomat's Memoir* (New York: Graf Publishing Company, 2004).

38. "The View from the Jury Box," *New York Times,* March 7, 2007, A1. See also Eric Lipton, "Members of a Sympathetic Jury Describe an Emotional but Inevitable Conclusion," *New York Times,* March 7, 2007, A17.

39. David Johnston and Eric Lipton, "Rove Is Linked to Early Query over Dismissals," *New York Times,* March 16, 2007, A19.

40. Shaila Dewan and Anne E. Kornblut, "In Key House Races, Democrats Run to the Right," *New York Times,* October 30, 2006, A1.

8

Looking Forward:
Can the Politics of Values Surive?

Introduction

WILL VALUES BE A SIGNIFICANT driving force in the 2008 election? No doubt, but the answers to "how" and "to what extent" will be determined by voter interest, intensity, and specificity. Will values be *the* issue or only part of a bigger voter search for peace and prosperity?

The person who wins the presidency after George W. Bush will be expected to end the war, make America safe from terrorists, provide universal health care, increase prosperity, deal with immigration reform, and wipe out poverty. That individual will need to have a plan to bring about environmental change and deal with the plethora of cultural and social problems that continue to divide the country. How can voters find any mere political mortal who will be able to accomplish such goals?

The answer is clear but difficult: They must elect someone who will replace the politics of values with a virtuous vision for America, a candidate who will be capable of creating policies to create a more just, moderate, and humane United States for the future. Republicans must move away from using values as a partisan means to win elections and embrace a positive strategy that will rally Americans around a new type of politics that is inclusive, pragmatic, and based on the common good. And Democrats must understand the criticality of acknowledging values and be willing to articulate them in the context of their party's political choices as well. It is time for everyone to deemphasize those issues that divide people and instead begin to stress those concerns that unite them. These include better educational opportunities, ending economic disparities, assuring living wages, and making sure that all Americans can find jobs, buy a home, be safe, and get affordable health care. Candidates must have the courage to go against the tide of zero-sum moral political choices, be willing to compromise, and be ready to stress tolerance and civility. It is time to find common ground, to end the use and abuse of values during campaigns, and to rebuild voting coalitions based on the broad principles that have made America great rather than on the divisive values that have made it vulnerable to the culture wars and the fissures within its political process.

Fueling the Politics of Values

George W. Bush and the cadre of powerful people who surround him have ideologically taken hold of the Republican Party. Moderates and centrists have been pushed aside and replaced by a coalition of evangelicals and social conservatives who support traditional Christian values in economics, social policy, and international relations.

This is about more than faith-based initiatives, compassionate conservatism, or the war in Iraq. It is about stepping over the line—creating a fundamental shift in the relationship between church and state in America; it is about the deliberate destruction of the wall of separation that is supposed to exist between them; and about the creation of a partisan symbiosis between Republicans and evangelicals to implement Christian values in the public square.

What has been overlooked is that the president has legitimized this linkage by establishing public policies through executive actions and personal pressure, by crafting and controlling values legislation, by appointing conservative judges, and by taking military actions to advance democracy and capitalism. They are all part of the president's tactics designed to continue his strategic, conservative vision into the future. In short, under the president's direction, this country has shifted its domestic and foreign priorities, its values, and according to many observers, its credibility around the world.

A backlash is coming. But as long as evangelicals and social conservatives can continue to fan the fires of socially divisive issues and employ the politics of values, political change will only be able to occur incrementally. Take for example the question of abortion.

It remains the central issue at the top of the moral/political agenda, *the major matter of consideration in the minds of most values voters*. The example of how abortion is being contested in South Dakota serves as a bellwether for other states and illustrates how both sides are using the politics of values.

Abortion was a critical component in the midterm elections in South Dakota—and an extremely important one for evangelicals. In February of 2006, that state's legislature enacted a policy that would have made it a felony for a physician to perform an abortion except to prevent the death of the mother. Supported by the governor, Mike Rounds, the policy was meant to be a "full frontal attack"[1] on *Roe v. Wade*. It was placed on the ballot as a referendum several months later and became a significant issue, if not *the* issue, in the midterm congressional elections. The state's abortion ban would have eliminated all abortions, even those in cases of rape and incest.

Planned Parenthood became actively involved in South Dakota, trying to bring in money and organizers from outside to oppose the new policy. In response, the Reverend Jerry Falwell called on his followers through the Internet to "counter the propaganda"[2] of groups who were promoting the right to choose. Physicians for Life, Vote Yes for Life, and other pro-life advocates saw the opportunity to influence not only South Dakota but also other states as well, such as Oregon and California, that had parental notification for the abortions of minors on their ballots.

On Election Day, the voters of South Dakota rejected the total ban on abortions in their state. This action prompted Nancy Keenan, the president of NARAL, to characterize the failed policy as a "wake-up call to lawmakers in other states that America's pro-choice majority will not allow an assault . . . to go unanswered."[3]

But the battle did not end there. After the referendum was defeated, the South Dakota legislature passed another law requiring doctors to inform women seeking to terminate pregnancies that doing so would end the "life of a whole, separate, unique, living human being."[4] Planned Parenthood challenged the law immediately after, claiming that the definition of the term "human being" was actually a value judgment and unsupported by medical, scientific, theological, and philosophical proofs. Thus, restrictions on abortion continue and fuel the contentious battle in South Dakota.

In other states such as Pennsylvania, the Republican incumbent pro-life Senator Rick Santorum faced a Democrat, Bob Casey, who was also pro-life in the midterm elections. But Casey beat the sitting senator at his own game. He reportedly met with Catholic and evangelical clergy members and appeared to be willing to work with them politically to try to advance their pro-life views. While Santorum has been criticized for such actions in the past, Casey has not, showing that in close elections Democrats were as willing to engage in the politics of values as were their Republican counterparts. As a result, Casey was able to win over some of the conservative religious voters, defeating Santorum soundly 59 percent to 41 percent.[5]

Thus, Casey's election, the election of other Democrats on volatile values issues, and their ability to work with religious conservatives portends a possible Democratic move to the ideological center. Such a shift leads to the possibility, then, of more compromises on a variety of religious/political matters in the future.

While abortion remains the critical litmus test for many values voters, the Supreme Court further ignited the issue in 2007 when it heard the case of *Gonzalez v. Carhart*,[6] a challenge to the bipartisan Partial-Birth Abortion Ban Act that had been passed by Congress in 2003 and signed by President Bush with high public opinion approval. The law had forbidden late-term abortions and did not include an exemption for the health of the mother. Pro-choice opponents argued that the Partial-Birth Abortion Ban was vague, invalid, and imposed an undue burden on the mother. What should be remembered, however, is that the Democrats played the politics of values in passing the act. Sixty-three Democrats in the House voted for it along with seventeen in the Senate—some of them probably assuming that the Court would uphold the earlier Stenberg[7] decision, thus making it politically safe to vote for the bill.

In its decision, the Court rejected all of the pro-choice arguments. Most importantly, it held that the procedure known as Dilation and Extraction (D&E), which was usually used in most late-term abortions, was essentially the overt act of a physician that caused the death of the fetus. Further, it held that women were *properly* informed about the risks to their own physical or emotional health when seeking such late-term abortions.

The five conservative justices found the Partial-Birth Abortion Ban an acceptable, constitutional limitation on privacy and reproductive rights. And, in so doing, they have been able to further galvanize and give momentum to a variety of anti-abortion groups: the Justice Foundation, the National Right to Life Committee, Americans United for Life, Operation Outcry, and Feminists for Life. Reportedly these groups and other like-minded grassroots activists are expected to escalate their efforts to enact informed consent and mandatory counseling laws in state legislatures in the coming year. This issue is not going to go away anytime soon.

In the genre of the "culture of life," stem cell research was another values issue on the midterm ballot, a policy choice that was played out only in Missouri. Nevertheless, it is one that is still expected to have national implications for the future.

In Missouri, a referendum called for legalizing embryonic stem cell research, a policy that the incumbent Republican senator, Jim Talent, opposed. The measure, supported by his Democratic challenger Claire McCaskill, won and helped to elect her from the Show Me State.

Other states have responded quietly and without voter approval to the public's insistence to pursue advanced medical research involving embryonic stem cells. Legislatures have simply authorized funds, as in California, and set up multimillion dollar research centers, as in New Jersey.

One reason why this issue remains on the front burner is because the president sees it in moral rather than scientific or pragmatic terms. He has twice vetoed congressional attempts to fund stem cell research, but even more critically, he has been accused of compromising public health issues for political reasons.

The former Surgeon General, Dr. Richard H. Carmona, told a congressional panel in 2007 that top administration officials "repeatedly tried to weaken or suppress important public health reports because of political considerations."[8] These included information about stem cell research but also data about emergency contraception (Plan B, the morning-after pill), sex education, prison health problems, and global matters.

More scientists are arguing that the president's actions and policies are designed to make sure that conservative ideology and values trump medical research. Even more critically, this type of political behavior limits the potential for new experiments on Parkinson's disease, other debilitating illnesses, and chronic disabilities.

Just recently a medical breakthrough occurred that might be able to end the entire moral debate about stem cells. It could help to reconcile the religious concerns of the values voters with the need for scientific research. Religious conservatives contend that using embryonic stem cells for experiments is simply killing unborn life in favor of those who are living. But, biologists have recently reported on an experimental procedure that can use the skin cells of mice and convert them to an embryonic state by inserting just four genes. Should it be possible to replicate this procedure in human skin cells, it would make it unnecessary to use human embryonic cells to obtain stem cells. Reportedly, regenerative medicine could be a possibility in the future, a way to convert a patient's diseased heart, liver, or kidney tissues into healthy ones while also eliminating the need for costly and dangerous transplant procedures.

Although this and other breakthroughs are on the horizon, there is still a fear among religious conservatives that stem cell research will lead to attempts to create human life. Thus far, because the skin cell technique is not yet available, the president has vetoed a second piece of congressional legislation supporting embryonic stem cell research. Instead, he continues to hold to his policy of research only on stem cell colonies left over from fertility clinics and has tied his opposition to a federal financing plan designed to fund alternative techniques.

To no one's surprise, candidates for the 2008 presidency are being forced to deal with these kinds of scientific, medical, and technological questions. And, more often than not, values voters are demanding that those who are running for national office offer innovative stances on traditional, biblical responses to various types of breakthroughs, or reject them in the name of morality.

Other Responses to the Midterm Elections

Perhaps the most significant part of the fallout of the 2006 midterm elections has been the attempts by social and religious conservatives to identify new issues that might be used to create a new values agenda for the 2008 presidential race and beyond. The reasons for this reflect some significant changes in U.S. politics and demographics. For example, religious and social conservatives who had made major inroads into opposing same-sex marriage are now finding that people who are committed to such relationships are becoming more organized, active, and savvy about the importance of getting financial assistance from others who are willing to support their efforts. Second, some newspapers are reporting a curious phenomenon as well: that the emotional appeal and enthusiasm about wedge issues is beginning to wane. In short, people (or maybe just the media) are getting tired of fighting over (and possibly reporting about) polarizing values issues. And finally, the number of people identifying themselves as being in same-sex relationships has been growing, according to the Williams Institute at the University of California in Los Angeles.[9] Thus, if gays begin to attain a significant political mass and eventually become a more meaningful political constituency, same-sex marriage will become increasingly difficult to limit.

One can expect, then, that homosexuality will still be a contentious issue among values voters in the future. But it most likely will be approached from the legal perspective of civil rights and personal discrimination rather than the moral perspective of traditional family and personal values. This change has occurred ever so slightly with regard to the question of gays in the military.

In the spring of 2007, General John Shalikashvili, past chairman of the Joint Chiefs of Staff from 1993 to 1997, called on the Pentagon to reconsider former President Bill Clinton's policy of "don't ask, don't tell." In an op-ed piece in the *New York Times*, the retired general reacted to President Bush's long-term plan to increase the size of the armed forces as a strategy to fight the war on terror. Shalikashvili contended that the need, the times, and the change in military attitude were worth reconsidering and supported a new look at military service through the lens of nondiscrimination for sexual orientation. He was careful to call for a "measured, prudent approach to change."[10]

Shalikashvili's comments, however, prompted a new policy debate in military and policy circles, one that has the potential to escalate the whole question of homosexuality in America into an even larger wedge issue in the future. A month or so after the retired general's op-ed article, General Peter Pace, the marine general who was serving as chair of the Joint Chiefs of Staff, gave a completely different view of gays in the military during a newspaper interview with the *Chicago Tribune*. He equated homosexual sex with adultery and said that the military should not condone such behavior.

Claiming that his remarks were his personal views, Pace refused to apologize for his statement when originally challenged by a gay advocacy group. "As an individual," he said, "I would not want (the acceptance of gay behavior) to be our policy . . ." "We prosecute that kind of immoral behavior."[11] Later Pace said that he did believe that "don't ask, don't tell" should remain the policy of the military and recanted his stance. He admitted that he "should have focused . . . on his support for current Pentagon policy" rather than on his own personal views.[12] His apology, however, was too little and too late. For this, and a number of other political and military comments out-of-step with the Bush administration, the President did not reappoint General Pace as chair of the Joint Chiefs of Staff. In an unprecedented rebuff, Pace was effectively replaced by Marine Admiral Michael G. Mullen.

What the situation revealed was that though there are those within the military leadership who still oppose homosexuals in the armed services, their influence is waning in light of open, public opposition, military needs, and changing times. That is not to say that there are still many who may be willing to carry the issue further into the public arena if a possible policy change is contemplated. Thus, this matter may still emerge as a consideration for the values voter in the future.

On the radar scope, then, in view of the need to appeal to values voters with a more interesting and relevant agenda, are several "new" evangelical causes. These include, but are not limited to, AIDS in Africa, human rights and slavery in the Sudan, poverty in Third World countries, debt relief, and environmental issues.

Leading the call to bring attention to AIDS in Africa, for example, is Dr. Rick Warren and his wife Kay, who founded The Purpose-Driven Network, named after his bestselling book. They have hosted Global Summits on "AIDS and the Church" for the last two years at their Saddleback megachurch in Lake Forest, California. This year their meeting included speeches from U.S. senators Barack Obama (D-IL) and Sam Brownback (R-KS) along with sixty other high-ranking officials in the government and a variety of NGO's that deal with AIDS.

Obama came out strongly supporting the role that religious groups can play to stem the AIDS epidemic and approved their actions to inject the issue into the public debate. He said that churches must offer a moral framework for moral choices.

> "Let me say this loud and clear—I don't think that we can deny that there is a moral and spiritual component to prevention—that in too many places all over the world where HIV/AIDS is prevalent . . . the relationship between men and women, between sexuality and spirituality, has broken down, and needs to be repaired."[13]

Warren was quoted as saying that the church wanted to be compassionate and effective in its ministry toward those with AIDS. During the summit, the conference explored six ways to help and minister to those living with the disease: caring for and supporting the sick; handling testing and counseling; training volunteers; removing the stigma of the disease; encouraging healthy behavior; and helping with nutrition and medications. In addition, the summit planned a global effort to mobilize one billion church members to deal with other major global problems as well.[14]

Another subtle, new issue being considered among evangelicals besides AIDS has been the attempt to fund prisoner re-entry programs. This is a matter that received some Republican attention when Brownback, a primary candidate for the presidency, spent a night in the Louisiana State Penitentiary to address inmates during a Christian service.

The whole question of prisoner re-entry programs is bubbling up, partly due to the introduction of the Prison Rape Elimination Act. It brought together some Republicans and Democrats in the last Congress who introduced an obscure bill known as the Second Chance Act. Brought to the floor by two Democratic members of the Congressional Black Caucus, Stephanie Tubbs Jones (D-OH) and Danny Davis (D-IL), it called for the authorization of $100 million dollars over a two-year period to develop model programs for the 700,000 felons who will leave prison[15] and return to society in 2007. It has even caught the attention of Obama, but the issue is low on the Democratic House legislative agenda. It was championed by Senators Rick Santorum (R-PA) and Mike Dewine (R-OH), major conservative stalwarts who lost reelection in 2006, so the support of prisoner re-entry could go several different ways at this point.

Faith-based groups have quietly, and over a long period of time, been involved in providing social services such as drug treatment, continuing education, housing assistance, and mentoring programs to help prisoners adapt to civilian life. But President Bush upped the ante when his faith-based initiative in 2001 allowed federal monies to be expended for a variety of training programs inside jails and outside their walls, as well as funding projects designed to help the children of prisoners. Indeed, it was the first director of the Faith-Based and Community Initiative, John DiIulio, who had championed a variety of public and nonprofit programs during his academic career and policy time at the White House for such purposes.[16]

Many of these programs are conducted by Republican, Christian activists, of whom the most famous is Chuck Colson. A former special counsel to President Richard Nixon, Colson was involved in the committee to reelect the president and convicted of obstruction of justice in the Daniel Ellsberg Pentagon Papers case. He spent time in prison, where he found Jesus and was transformed.

In the 1970s, Colson founded Prison Fellowship, a discipleship that begins inside prison for the purpose of teaching inmates how to return to society as servants of Christ. Colson has spent the last thirty-plus years attempting to rehabilitate the felon population religiously, socially, and economically.

In 1997, the Inner Change Freedom Initiative (IFI) emerged out of Colson's efforts, becoming a separate 50lc(3) nonprofit organization two years later. IFI contracts with the Prison Fellowship organization for staffing and spiritual support services while states continue to provide the basic material needs of inmates. IFI fosters a respect for God's law and the rights of others and encourages the moral regeneration of prisoners.[17]

While his work has "compassionate" support, Colson's emphasis on the need for religious transformation makes the prisoner re-entry program problematic. There are those who contend that spending public money on prison re-entry programs with a religious basis is a violation of the separation of church and state. In June 2006, Judge Robert W. Pratt, a Clinton appointee, declared the program to be unconstitutional after a legal challenge from Americans United for Separation of Church and State. He ruled that IFI was pervasively sectarian.[18] But, the legal challenge has not stopped there. In 2007, the IFI was appealed to the 8th Circuit Court and a decision is currently pending.

Whatever happens, there is a caveat in this case specifically for those involved in faith-based social and charitable efforts. Both those on the right who want the wall between church and state to be serpentine rather than rigid and those on the left who want to preserve its high, protective posture must be aware of the dynamic tension that continually exists within the secular, constitutional, First Amendment principle that regulates the relationship between government and religion. The religious right is willing to challenge it, to seek greater state accommodation and to try to advance moral matters through the legal system. Members of the emerging progressive religious left, however, must consider how far and under what conditions their burgeoning movement is willing to test that dynamic—if at all—and whether or not they are willing to possibly jeopardize their own potential relationship with the Democratic Party if it does.

In this specific case, the prisoner re-entry issue is still being supported, as members of Congress continue to consider how to deal with this issue. Colson et al., undeterred, will still seek federal funding, and this will be an issue worth watching in the upcoming election.

As polarizing as questions of abortion, stem cell research, homosexual marriage, gays in the military, and prisoner re-entry funding are, the issue of affirmative action continues to bring even the most moderate people into heated debate. It brings moral questions of equity, equality, reconciliation, opportunity, access, and reparations into question—challenging values such as hard work and merit with the potential to ignite the 2008 presidential campaign.

Initially implemented as an executive order issued by President Lyndon Johnson in 1965, affirmative action was an attempt to remedy past discriminatory practices in the workplace. It required the federal government and those who did business with it to give preferential treatment to minorities, including blacks and women.

The first major judicial test of affirmative action came in 1978, when Allan Bakke, a white student who had been denied admission to medical school at the University of California, claimed reverse discrimination. The Supreme Court ruled[19] that in his case, race was the sole criterion for sixteen positions that had been put aside for minority students. Claiming that race could be considered as a factor, the justices held that it could not be the only reason for accepting students to universities.

Several other means of affirmative action were tried and challenges were mounted to those policies as well. In 2003, two cases involving the University of Michigan opened the question of affirmative action again.

At that time, the university granted a number of points for different acceptance criteria—class rank, race, extracurricular activities, and other considerations. Jennifer Gratz and Patrick Hamacher, two undergraduate students, challenged the university's policy of granting a more substantial number of points to minority students for race and a lesser number of points for merit-based criteria as a way to try to assure admissions diversity. Although the Supreme Court ruled that some points could be given for race, it contended that the use of an inordinate amount of points for race alone could not be used for undergraduate admissions.[20] In a separate ruling, the Court did allow Michigan's law school to consider race as part of the complete record of each student's application.[21]

This decision, which met with opposition from many quarters, resulted in a ballot initiative in Michigan during the 2006 midterm election. Proposition 2, as it was labeled, was a move to ban race and gender preferences totally in public education, employment, and contracting. With support from many sectors of Michigan's voting public, the Proposition passed 58 percent to 42 percent, reflecting a backlash against any type of affirmative action in that state.

Similar movements are occurring across the United States, with opponents expected to mount challenges in Arizona, Colorado, Missouri, Nebraska, Nevada, Oregon, South Dakota, Utah, and Wyoming.[22] Currently, California, Florida, Michigan, and Washington do not allow racial preferences to be used as the major consideration for acceptance into their state universities. Texas uses a top-10-percent plan, which allows students in the first tier of high school graduates to be admitted to its best state universities, while many other states such as Ohio and North Carolina are seeking creative ways to level the educational playing field.

In the summer of 2007, the Supreme Court decided to take a look at two similar programs to maintain school diversity: one in Seattle, Washington, and another in Louisville, Kentucky. In both school districts, transfers on the basis of race were used as the criterion for "tiebreakers" when it became necessary to limit the number of pupils able to attend a particular high school in order to prevent overcrowding it. In a five-to-four decision, Chief Justice John Roberts contended that "The way to stop discrimination on the basis of race is to stop discriminating on the basis of race."[23]

Opponents of the decision claimed that it set back all of the advances to equalize educational opportunity as decided and instituted by the activist Warren Court in 1954. In fact, Justice John Paul Stevens in his dissent said that the new decision in *Meredith v. Jefferson County Board of Education* "undermined" and threatened another round of race-related litigation. Thus, affirmative action in all its nuances can be expected to rear its head again as a variety of initiatives appear on future state ballots.

Another issue that will emerge for the values voter is the question of environmental justice. More and more, the religious left and center have been embracing the cause of global warming and other ecological matters from a biblical perspective—that of ethical "stewardship." Theirs is a concern over the responsibility of man to protect God's creation. But now, the religious right is becoming involved as well, with the religious notion of stewardship being revisited and expanded politically.

In January of 2007, the Reverend Rich Cizik, the public policy director of the National Association of Evangelicals, and Dr. Eric Chivian, a Nobel laureate who is the director of the Center for Health and the Global Environment at Harvard Medical School, drafted a statement calling for "changes in values, lifestyles and public policies to avert disastrous changes in climate."[24]

Coming together with twenty-eight other supporters of a fuller document that they drafted, both Cizik and Chivian maintained that science and faith can work together for "Creation Care." Part of their goal is to meet with congresspersons for help in developing a priority and agenda for environmental issues before the next presidential election.

While this partnership appears to be totally logical, it has come under fire from some powerful leaders within the evangelical network. Stemming from a different sense of moral priorities, Dr. James Dobson of Focus on the Family and Tony Perkins, the president of the Family Research Council, have reportedly sent a letter to the leadership of the NAE opposing the organization's emphasis on global warming and shift in its focus away from abortion, homosexuality, and sexual morality.[25] Others such as Jerald Walz, the representative for the Institute on Religion and Democracy, opposed the process by which the global warming campaign was announced and made public.

These complaints paled when, within a month of the new Evangelical-Environmental coalition, another event cemented the need for greater concern for the earth's ecology. In February 2007, the Intergovernmental Panel on Climate Change, which is administered by the United Nations Environment Program, reported that global warming exists, that it is "unequivocal," and that it is most likely caused by man's activities and the climate conditions that he has created in the wake of industrialization.[26]

The mainstream media reported the story widely, and within policy circles there was a sudden epiphany that higher temperatures, rising sea levels that will continue for centuries, and continued greenhouse emissions might require immediate political action. Recognizing the significance of the findings and their policy implications, the Bush administration was quick to emphasize that the U.S. had "played a leading role in studying and combating climate change, in part by an investment of an average of almost $5 billion a year for the past six years in research and tax incentives for new technologies."[27] This view is, of course, open to interpretation, and those within the religious and political arenas concerned with the ethical obligation of earthly stewardship and public responsibility for sustainable development seemingly have a clear priority on which to work in the coming elections.

Finally, values also will come into play in the presidential election with regard to foreign policy. The only united foreign policy stance of evangelicals is their approval of U.S. support for Israel. Most see that political commitment as the basis of "God's foreign policy." In July of 2006, the Reverend John Hagee of San Antonio came to Washington with over 3,000 evangelicals to hold a conference of his newly founded organization, Christians United for Israel.[28]

This support is based on the belief that Christ will return to Israel for his Second Coming to fulfill the prophecies of the last days. Evangelicals believe that the state of Israel must be protected for this purpose and that the Jewish state must be supported in its attempts to rid the Middle East of Hezbollah, Hamas, and any others who might be a threat to their continued existence. Currently the Iranian president, Mahmoud Ahmadinejad, who questions the Holocaust, has nuclear power, has called for the abolition of Israel, and continues to expand his sphere of influence in the Middle East, is the focus of evangelical attempts to influence American foreign policy to isolate and take a hard line with Iran. Pat Robertson even went so far as to say that Prime Minister Ariel Sharon's stroke might have been God's punishment for withdrawing from territory that belonged to biblical Israel.[29]

But values voters are also increasingly split on other aspects of the role of the United States in international affairs. This includes everything from the war in Iraq to how to fight terrorism at home and abroad. Within the last year, Robertson announced on his television station that God told him that a major terrorist catastrophe would occur in the United States by the end of 2007. Such predictions have the potential to raise insecurities within the minds of evangelicals and to reinforce the warnings of many inside the Bush administration who were also saying the same thing during the summer of 2007.

With such statements, it is difficult to see the evangelical voice as being taken seriously in the foreign policy arena. But, religion can have a credible role to play in international relations, if it is based on broad values such as human rights and social justice.

Former Secretary of State Madeleine Albright, for example, sees the impact of religion on foreign policy in a nuanced way. She believes that Americans must look at what religion can inspire people to do. The challenge, she says, is for "policymakers to harness the unifying potential of faith, while containing its capacity to divide."[30] Faith-based diplomacy, according to her, can be a useful, yet supplemental, tool to traditional diplomacy. She maintains that religion, at its best, can reinforce core beliefs among peoples of diverse cultures and provide some harmony.[31]

These issues, however, will have to compete with other pressing policy concerns: the war in Iraq, comprehensive immigration reform, social security privatization, and numerous other social problems that will require government attention in the coming years. The struggle for meaningful issues will always be a source of introspection for the religious right and the Republican Party, and such challenges have been met with new insights often in the past. Losses in the educational arena on school prayer gave way to support for vouchers and school choice. The rejection of evolution sparked activism on behalf of intelligent design. Abortion rights led them to policy stands on stem cell research and physician-assisted suicide. Liberal public policies for welfare gave impetus for reform with Charitable Choice and faith-based initiatives. The loss of the White House to Bill Clinton led to the Contract with America and a sweep of religious and social conservatives to power in 1994.

Many on the right believe that it is too soon to be writing the obituary of either social/religious conservatism or the Republican Party. Even David Kuo, who criticized the Bush administration and White House staffers for being disrespectful to the Christian conservatives, argues that evangelical political activism is not dead, nor is it gravitating toward the Democrats in any kind of meaningful way. He believes, along with others, that evangelicals are in a state of social and political transition, a period of re-examination about their roles in society.[32] This has always animated the evangelicals in America and given meaning for their spiritual and social stances.

At the same time, however, it is also too soon to be sending out the wedding invitations for the marriage of the religious left and center with the Democratic Party, even though they have so many things in common. The courtship continues, but the marriage is still quite a way off.

The Candidates

What is critical to the religious right and the Republican Party, as well as the spiritual progressive and the Democratic Party, however, are the candidates who will represent them in the presidential election of 2008 and beyond. This is a much more serious problem for the Republicans. They prefer to frame their candidates in terms of values, character, and personal integrity that are in synch with their religious beliefs. Democrats are more willing to infuse their moral values with spirituality than dogmatism and by whatever means can be used to serve their sense of the common good.

In the spring of 2007, the Council for National Policy, a conservative social/religious organization founded by Reverend Tim LaHaye about twenty-five years ago, met in Florida to discuss and strategize who might best represent the views of religious and social conservatives in America. Attending were individuals such as Dr. James Dobson, head of Focus on the Family, Reverend Jerry Falwall of Liberty University, and Grover Norquist, head of Americans for Tax Reform. According to the *New York Times*, the group has become a "pivotal stop for Republican presidential primary hopefuls"[33] and a place where George W. Bush had come to gain support before his presidential bid in 1999.

The Council for National Policy, however, has had a very different view with regard to the acceptability and electability of the Republican Party's announced candidates during the 2008 election cycle. The Council admitted early in the primary process that the morale of the values voter could be characterized as "anxious"; that there were no real choices among the candidates, and that if "neither of the two parties" ended up nominating an individual with a pro-choice stance, it might even consider supporting a third party candidate![34] The Republican front-runners represented a challenge to their religious, social, and political agendas.

Former New York City Mayor Rudolph Guiliani, for instance, has been married three times, is estranged from his son, supports gun control, and is more liberal than his Republican challengers on abortion, stem cell research, and gay marriage. To further complicate matters, Guiliani, as a Catholic, finds himself unable to be "morally coherent" in his personal and political life as demanded by his religion.

In a speech at the Houston Baptist College, Guiliani explained the two "pillars" of his moral and political thinking; that is, his personal opposition to abortion and his unequivocal toleration for opposing views that are as personal, and equally decent, moral, and religious as his.[35] He contends that the reversal of *Roe v. Wade* would be acceptable, that he would not spend public funds to pay for abortions, and that although he personally opposes abortion he respects a woman's right to choose. Voters are still trying to internalize his nuanced thinking and figure out what he really means.

In some ways, Guiliani is taking the Kerry 2004 stance, and because he is, some members of the Catholic American hierarchy are already accusing him of being fragmented, without moral coherence, and a questionable candidate. In June 2007, Bishop Thomas J. Tobin of Providence, Rhode Island, became the first Catholic official to publicly condemn the former mayor. He compared Guiliani to Pontius Pilate, saying that hizzoner's stance on abortion could be paraphrased like the Roman ruler's claim: "I'm personally opposed to crucifixion, but I don't want to impose my belief on others."[36] Tobin considers Guiliani's position on abortion "preposterous," maintaining that Catholics are required to be pro-life, and that Catholic politicians have a "special obligation"[37] in that regard.

Senator John McCain has not fared so well, either. He has been married twice. He opposes abortion. He is calling for greater involvement of U.S. troops in the Iraq war. It is this latter stance that worries many members of his party who are standing for reelection. As the U.S. position in Iraq weakens and more soldiers are killed, the way that the war is being waged and its probable outcome are being questioned by party naysayers. McCain is standing with the few shaky Bush loyalists on the military "surge," backing the president's insistence that the only way to defeat the terrorists is on their own turf. As a result, he has lost needed financial support and important members of his staff. Further, McCain has moved himself ideologically to the center—working with Hillary Clinton, Ted Kennedy, and Russ Feingold on key legislation, making his credentials and commitment to the conservative base of the party suspect on a number of reform issues.

Former Governor Mitt Romney also poses a problem to values voters. As a Mormon, he is not recognized as a "real" Christian since many of the beliefs of his faith community reflect ideas that come from the Book of Mormon rather than the Bible. Further, Romney has personally opposed abortion but switched his stance in his gubernatorial role as the governor of Massachusetts. He is therefore considered culturally and politically suspect.

Romney, however, has been able to weather the attacks of his opponents thus far. This is mainly due to his own stable family life, his personal wealth, the financial donations of other Mormons, and the monetary support of many of his corporate connections.

Romney played a key role in fundraising for the Republican Governors Association, helping to put about $26 million[38] into the party's coffers in the past and used his critical networking skills to lock up some important donors for his own presidential primary bid. In one of his early fundraising efforts, he was able to enlist the support of wealthy donors to the tune of $6.5 million[39] in just one day. He has also been able to tap the likes of J. Willard Marriott, Jr., and Richard Marriott of hotel fame—Mormon members and part of a group of other donors from the Church of Latter-Day Saints.

The other early announced contenders, Governor Mike Huckabee of Arkansas, Representative Duncan Hunter of California, and Senator Sam Brownback of Kansas, were essentially nonstarters during the Republican presidential primary. Indeed, the primary challenger in the shadows, former Senator Fred Thompson, seemed to best represent the values of the religious and social conservatives as the presidential primaries heated up.

Thompson has made a "strong pitch"[40] to the conservative wing of the party. In early speeches, he praised Barry Goldwater and Ronald Reagan, opposed the death tax, and criticized the Democrats for ostensibly surrendering on Iraq. He called for securing the borders as the basis for meaningful immigration reform and has taken clearly traditional stands on life, marriage, and family values.

The major contenders, in fact, have all been courting the religious right. The Christian Broadcasting Network, the television station founded by Pat

Robertson, has been providing a forum for Republican candidates to win over evangelical Christians. With a reported audience of one million viewers, the station's chief political reporter, David Brody, has been able to interview all the Republican primary candidates. In fact, he recently bragged to the press that Fred Thompson gave him an advanced copy of the videotaped message that he would be delivering to the National Right to Life convention for his "Brody File" rather than to CNN or Fox.

The Christian media, it is clear, reinforces the politics of values in its own way, specifically by reaching a targeted, religious, conservative audience; continually discussing wedge issues; and attacking liberal candidates. But the Republican values voters are finding themselves with choices that are becoming more and more narrow—in terms of authentic religious, conservative candidates and issues. How can they support candidates who do not live the values that they espouse? How can they support a candidate from a stable family but who is a member of a religion that they believe is more of a cult rather than an authentic progeny of Christianity, a religion that sees its revealed truths as an adjunct to the Holy Scripture, a less-than-literal understanding and commitment to the message of Jesus as delivered in the Bible? How can they vote for candidates who change their minds on moral issues such as abortion, who acknowledge the importance of stem cell research, and who are ambivalent, in many cases, about school prayer, gay marriage, and intelligent design? Given less-than-ideal candidates, in their eyes, might values voters simply vote strategically—for a divorced man or a pseudoconservative—rather than for a centrist, a liberal, or another Clinton?

The Pew Forum on Religion and Public Life has reported a number of significant findings on American voters and their values. Its statistics show that above all else, Americans are *pragmatic*; that is, that "they cannot be easily categorized as conservative or liberal on today's most pressing social questions," and that they do not favor any clear ideological approach to most social issues.[41]

According to the Forum's data, each contentious social concern reflects a different response within the electorate. On gay marriage and gay adoption, the public is more conservative, while on gays in the military, in schools, or in the workplace they are more liberal/centrist. On cloning they are conservative, while on embryonic stem cell research more liberal. And, on abortion, most want some sort of a national public policy that reflects a moderate position—embracing neither extreme.

The politics of values, as a divisive electoral strategy of the Republican-evangelical symbiosis, must end and be replaced with a new way to respond to the subtle, changing values of hardworking, sensible Americans. The exploitation of wedge issues, the party support for only the most conservative of political leaders, the tactic of framing as many issues as possible within moral parameters, and the exploitation of the moral flaws of others must stop if Republicans hope to remain relevant and in political power in the future.

The polarization among U.S. voters and the culture wars are undermining America's potential to help its citizens attain a virtuous society based on social justice, economic opportunity, and freedom—the life that they envisioned for themselves and their families. Just as importantly, the political and religious divide fragments the country and militates against it playing a role to advance human rights, economic globalization, and a role in the moral leadership of the world.

To regain such a position, the politics of values must be replaced by a positive vision and virtuous approach to politics if America is to move beyond its current ideological and partisan polarization. This change must include public programs and policies that pursue social justice and economic needs—a virtuous vision that will unify people rather than exploit wedge issues and be advanced by centrist leaders committed to the pragmatic common good. Civility and tolerance must replace personal attacks, particularly as they jeopardize the future candidacies of decent individuals who might be considering public service to help their fellow citizens. It is time to once again recognize the Greek ideal: that politics is the extension of ethics in the public realm. This can only happen when values are recognized for their intrinsic worth and a virtuous vision becomes the moving force of American politics in the future.

Denominational belongers, who have morphed into partisan religious activists, need to be challenged by progressive spiritual believers—by those who have strong principles but who do not see the right or the need for specific religious churches or groups to force those values on others politically. They are the citizens who espouse a sense of transcendence rather than doctrine or dogma; people who do not need to be in a megachurch to say their prayers in order to live meaningful lives and to work for social justice.

The pendulum is swinging, and in 2008 the presidential election could be won by that individual who can rally people of good will and common sense. If Republicans do not grasp this notion—if they remain unwilling to become more pluralistic and inclusive, if they cannot or will not embrace the marginalized in society, if they lose sight of their party's own virtue and integrity, if they forget their primary responsibilities—they will continue to lose political ground in America in the long term.

Democrats, too, must grasp the need to make strategic political change and be willing to replace the politics of values. They must learn from the mistakes of its tacticians, embrace the moral imperative in politics, and be courageous enough to articulate a more relevant relationship with their party and the values voter for the future in order to regain the moral high ground that they have championed in the past.

The values voter will always be important, and both political parties need to remember this. But the values that he or she votes for may very well change in the future as Americans tire of the negative use of politics of values and seek a better, more tolerant and more civilized life for their children, themselves, and the rest of the world.

Notes

1. Monica Davey, "National Battle over Abortions Focuses on a Referendum in South Dakota," *New York Times*, November 2006, A20.

2. Davey, "National Battle over Abortions."

3. "South Dakota Votes Against Ban of Almost All Abortions," November 8, 2006, http://cnn.worldnews.

4. Susan Saulny, "Full Federal Appellate Court Will Revisit Abortion Issue in South Dakota," *New York Times*, April 11, 2007, A13.

5. See *New York Times* official election results, November 9, 2006, P8 and 9.

6. *Gonzalez v. Carhart*, Nos. 03-380 and 05-1382. Decided April 18, 2007.

7. *Stenberg v. Carhart* 530 U.S. 914 (2000).

8. Gardiner Harris, "Surgeon General Sees 4 Year Term as Compromised," *New York Times*, July 11, 2007, A1.

9. Kirk Johnson, "Gay Marriage Losing Punch as Ballot Issue," *New York Times*, October 14, 2006, A10.

10. John M. Shalikashvili, "Second Thoughts on Gays in the Military," *New York Times*, January 2, 2007, www.nytimes.com/2007/01/02.

11. Pauline Jelinek, "Aides, Pace Won't Apologize for Gay Remark," *Associated Press*, March 13, 2007, http://news.yahoo.com/s/ap/20070313.

12. Thom Shanker, "Top General Explains Remarks on Gays," *New York Times*, March 14, 2007, A15.

13. Michael Finnegan, "Obama Discusses AIDS Epidemic with Orange Country Evangelicals," *Los Angeles Times*, December 2, 2006, www.barackobama.com.

14. "Dr. Rick and Kay Warren Bring HIV/AIDs Leaders to Church," www.redorbit.com.

15. Chris Suellentrop, "The Right Has a Jailhouse Conversion," *New York Times Magazine*, December 24, 2006, 48.

16. See Jo Renee Formicola, Mary Segers, and Paul Weber, *Faith-Based Initiatives and the Bush Administration: The Good, the Bad, and the Ugly"* (Lanham, Maryland: Rowman & Littlefield, 2003). See Chapter 3 for in-depth information on John DiIulio.

17. See the Prison Fellowship website, www.ifiprison.org/site.

18. *Americans United for Separation of Church and State v. Prison Fellowship Ministries.* Case: 4:03-cv-90074-RP-TJS. Dec. 367. Filed 06/-2/2006.

19. See *Regents of the University of California v. Bakke*, 438 U.S. 265 (1978).

20. See *Gratz v. Bollinger*, 539 U.S. 244 (2003).

21. See *Grutter v. Bollinger*, 539 U.S. 306 (2003).

22. Tamar Lewin, "Colleges Regroup After Voters Ban Race Preferences," *New York Times*, January 26, 2007, A15.

23. *Meredith v. Jefferson County Board of Eduction*, No. 05-915. Decision June 28, 2007.

24. John Heilprin, "Evangelicals, Scientists Join on Warming," *Associated Press*, January 17, 2007, http://news.yahoo.com.

25. Laurie Goodstein, "Evangelical Group Rebuffs Critics on Right," *New York Times*, March 14, 2007, A15.

26. Elisabeth Rosenthal and Andrew C. Revkin, "Science Panel Says Global Warming Is 'Unequivocal,'" *New York Times*, February 3, 2007, A1.

27. Rosenthal and Revkin, "Science Panel Says Global Warming Is Unequivocal."

28. David D. Kirkpatrick, "For Evangelical, Supporting Israel Is 'God's Foreign Policy,'" *New York Times*, November 14, 2006, A1.

29. Kirkpatrick, "For Evangelical, Supporting Israel is 'God's Foreign Policy,'" A6.

30. Madeleine Albright, "Faith and Diplomacy," in *Faith and International Affairs*, vol. 4, no. 2, Fall 2006, 3.

31. Albright, "Faith and Diplomacy," 9.

32. David Kuo, "Putting Faith before Politics," *New York Times*, November 16, 2006, A35.

33. David D. Kirkpatrick, "Christian Right Labors to Find '08 Candidate," February 24, 2007, www.nyutimes.com/2007/02/25/us/politics.

34. Kirkpatrick, "Christian Right Labors to Find '08 Candidate." See also: Dr. James Dobson, "The Values Test," *New York Times*, October 4, 2007, A29.

35. Rudolph W. Giuliani, "Speech at the Houston Baptist College," *New York Times*, May 10, 2007, A12.

36. Marc Sanotra, "Rhode Island Bishop Condemns Giuliani's Position on Abortion," *New York Times*, June 8, 2007, A20.

37. Sanotra, "Rhode Island Bishop Condemns Giuliani's Position on Abortion."

38. David D. Kirkpatrick, "Romney Used His Wealth to Enlist Richest Donors," *New York Times*, April 6, 2007, A17.

39. Kirkpatrick, "Romney Used His Wealth to Enlist Richest Donors."

40. Katharine Q. Seelye, "Thompson Makes Strong Pitch to Conservative Republicans," *New York Times*, June 3, 2007, A33.

41. Pew Forum, "Pragmatic Americans Liberal and Conservative on Social Issues," http://pewforum.org/docs/index,php?Doc = 150.

Works Cited

Abington Township School District v. Schempp, 374 U.S. 203 (1963).

Abramowitz, Michael. "Midterm Vote May Define Rove's Legacy; Big Losses Could Dim Aura of Bush Adviser." *Washington Post*, October 30, 2006, A1.

"ACLU Challenges Misuse of Taxpayer Dollars to Fund Religion in Nationwide Abstinence-Only-Until-Marriage Program." Available from www.aclu.prg/repro ductiverights/gen/12602prs200050516.html.

ACLU of Massachusetts v. Leavitt, No. 1:05-cv-11000-JLT, February 23, 2006.

Administrative Board of the United States Catholic Conference. *Faithful Citizenship: A Catholic Call to Political Responsibility*. Available from www.usccb.org/faithful citizenship/bishopStatement.html.

Albright, Madeleine. "Faith and Diplomacy." In *Faith and International Affairs* (Fall 2006), vol. 4, no. 2, 3.

Allen, Mike. "The Architect Speaks." *The Allen Report*, November 10, 2006. Available from http://time-blog.com/allen_report/2006/11/the_architect_speaks.html.

American Family Association Journal. "Evangelical Strategy Statement Gains Approval." May 2005. Available from www.afajournal.org/2005/may/5.05evangeli cals.asp.

Americans United for Separation of Church and State v. Prison Fellowship Ministries. Case: 4:03-cv-90074-RP-TJS. Dec. 367.

Anderson, Lisa. "Christian Middle Seeking a Turn at Bully Pulpit." *Chicago Tribune*, September 21, 2006. Available from www.chicagotribune.com.

Andrews, Edmund L. "Ex-Interior Aide Pleads Guilty to Lying in Lobbying Case." *New York Times*, March 24, 2007, A9.

Associated Press. "Commissioner Under Fire for Vioxx Scandal, 'Morning After' Pill Delay." September 23, 2005. Available from www.msnbc.msn.com/id/9455426.

Bai, Matt. "Democratic Moral Values?" *New York Times Magazine*, April 24, 2005, 25.

———. "The Framing Wars." *New York Times Magazine*, September 17, 2005, Sec. 6, 44.

———. "The Inside Agitator." *New York Times Magazine*, October 1, 2006, 55–60.

Banerjee, Neela. "Black Churches Struggle over Their Role in Politics." *New York Times*, March 6, 2005, A23.

———. "For Some Black Pastors, Accepting Gay Members Means Losing Others." *New York Times*, March 27, 2007, A12.

———. "Gay and Evangelical, Seeking Paths of Acceptance." *New York Times*, December 12, 2006, A1.

———. "Religious Left Struggles to Find Unifying Message." *New York Times*, May 10, 2006, A17.

Bash, Dana, "Rove Back to Basics in Reduced New Role," April 20, 2006. Available from http://cnn.worldnews.com.

Bash, Dana and Deirdre Walsh. "Bush Vetoes Embryonic Stem-Cell Bill." September 4, 2006. Available from www.CNN.com.

Battle, Michael. *The Black Church in America.* Malden, Massachusetts: Blackwell, 2006.

Bell, Daniel. *The End of Ideology.* Cambridge: Harvard University, 2000.

Benedetto, Richard. "Faith-Based Programs Flourishing, Bush Says." *USA Today*, March 10, 2006, 5A.

Benedict XVI, Pope. *Sacramentum Caritatis.* February 22, 2007. Available from www.usccb.org.

"A Blame Game." *New York Times*, October 20, 2006, A19.

Blumenthal, Ralph. "A Preacher's Credo: Eliminate the Negative, Accentuate the Prosperity." *New York Times*, March 30, 2006.

"Catholics and Political Responsibility." June 12, 2007. Available from www.usccb.org.

Cohen, Cathy J. "The Church? A response to "Beyond the Civil Rights Industry" in *Boston Review* (April/May 2001). Available from www.bostonreview.com.

Congregation for the Doctrine of the Faith. "Doctrinal Note on Some Questions Regarding *The Participation of Catholics in Political Life.*" sec. l, para. 2. Available from www.vatican.va/roman_curia//congregations/cfaith/documents/re_con/c faith.doc_2000.

Connolly, Ceci. "Teen Pledges Barely Cut STD Rates, Study Says." *Washington Post*, March 19, 2005, A3.

Connelly, Phoebe. "Contraception in the Crosshairs." *In These Times*, March 26, 2006. Available from www.inthesetimes.com/article/2558.

Copeland, Libby. "With Gifts from God." *Washington Post*, March 25, 2001, F1.

Danforth, John. *Faith and Politics: How the "Moral Values" Debate Divides America and How to Move Forward Together.* New York: Penguin Books, 2006, 29.

Davey, Monica. "National Battle over Abortions Focuses on a Referendum in South Dakota." *New York Times*, November 2006, A20.

DeLay, Tom and Stephen Mansfield. *No Retreat, No Surrender: One American's Fight.* Sentinel: New York, 2007.

Dewan, Shaila and Anne E. Kornblut. "In Key House Races, Democrats Run to the Right." *New York Times*, October 30, 2006, A1.

DiIulio, John. Interview by Joe Renee Formicola and Mary Segers. *Faith-Based Initiatives and the Bush Administration.* Lanham, Maryland: Rowman & Littlefield, 2003.

Dionne, E. J., Jr. "The End of the Right?" *Washington Post*, August 4, 2006, A17.

Dowd, Matthew. "Karl Rove: The Architect." Interview with Matthew Dowd. Available from www.pbs.org/wgbh/pages/frontline/shows/architect/interviews/dowd.html.

Eckstrom, Kevin. "Broadest-Ever U.S. Church Unity Group Launched." *Religion News Service*, April 5, 2006. Available from www.socialpolicyandreligion.org/news/article.cfm?id_4071.

Edwards v. Aguillard, 482 U.S. 578 (1987).

Engle v. Vitale, 370 U.S. 421 (1962).

Epperson v. Arkansas, 393 U.S. 97 (1968).

Epstein, Edward. "Stem Cell Bill Veto Is First by Bush." *San Francisco Chronicle*, July 20, 2006, A11.

"Excerpts of the President's Speech to National Association of Evangelicals," *New York Times*, March 9, 1983, A18.

Finder, Alan. "Matters of Faith Find a New Prominence on Campus." *New York Times*, May 2, 2007, A16.

Fineman, Howard. "Rove Unleashed." Available from www.msnbc.msn.com/id/6596809/site/newsweek.

Finnegan, Michael. "Obama Discusses AIDS Epidemic with Orange Country Evangelicals." *Los Angeles Times*, December 2, 2006. Available from www.barackobama.com.

Formicola, Jo Renée. "The Reverend Al Sharpton: Pentecostal for Racial Justice." in Jo Renee Formicola and Hubert Morken eds., *Religious Leaders and Faith-Based Politics*. Lanham, Maryland: Rowman & Littlefield, 2001.

Formicola, Jo Renée, Mary Segers, and Paul Weber. *Faith-Based Initiatives and the Bush Administration: The Good, the Bad, and the Ugly*." Lanham, Maryland: Rowman & Littlefield, 2003.

Fowler, Robert Booth, Allen D. Hertzke and Laura R. Olson. *Religion and Politics in America*, 2nd ed. Boulder: Westview, 1999, 43.

Frosch, Dan. "Layoffs Follow Scandal at Colorado Megachurch." *New York Times*, March 6, 2007, A3.

Fukuyama, Francis. *The End of History and the Last Man*. New York: Free Press, 1992.

Gailey, Phil. "Reagan, at Prayer Breakfast, Calls Politics and Religion Inseparable." *New York Times*, August 24, 1984, A2.

Goldsmith, Stephen. *The Twenty-First Century City: Resurrecting Urban America*. Washington, D.C.: Regnery, 1997.

Gonzalez v. Oregon, 546 U.S. 243 (2006).

Goodnough, Abby. "Husband Takes Schiavo Fight Back to Political Arena." *New York Times*, August 16, 2006, A15.

Goodnough, Abby and Carl Hulse. "Judge in Florida Rejects Effort by House." *New York Times*, March 19, 2005, A1, A12.

Goodstein, Laurie. "Evangelical Group Rebuffs Critics on Right." *New York Times*, March 14, 2007, A15.

———. "Faith Has Role in Politics, Obama Tells Church Convention." *New York Times*, June 24, 2007, A22.

———. "Fearing the Loss of Teenagers, Evangelicals Turn Up the Fire." *New York Times*, October 6, 2006, 1.

———. "Living Day to Day by a Gospel of Green." *New York Times*, March 8, 2007, F1 and 10.

———. "Schiavo Case Highlight an Alliance between Catholics and Evangelicals." *New York Times*, March 24, 2005, A20.

Goodstein, Laurie and Neela Banerjee. "Minister Denies Gay Tryst, but Admits Buying Drugs." *New York Times*, November 4, 2006, A13.

Gorski, Eric and Karen E. Crummy. "Democrat's Goal: Demonstrate Values." *Denver Post*, August 6, 2006.

Gratz v. Bollinger, 539 U.S. 244 (2003).

Grutter v. Bollinger, 539 U.S. 306 (2003).

Green, John C. "Seeking a Place" in *Toward an Evangelical Public Policy*, ed. by Ronald J. Sider and Diane Knippers. Grand Rapids: Baker Books, 2005, 15.

Greenhouse, Linda. "Justices Reject Suit on Federal Money for Faith-Based Office." *New York Times*, June 26, 2007, A8.

Giuliani, Rudolph W. "Speech at the Houston Baptist College." *New York Times*, May 10, 2007, A12.

Gushee, David P., ed., *Christians and Politics Beyond the Culture Wars: An Agenda for Engagement*. Grand Rapids, Michigan: Baker Books, 2000.

Harris, Fredrick C. *Something Within: Religion in African American Political Activism*. New York: Oxford University Press, 1999.

Harris, Gardiner. "Surgeon General Sees 4 Year Term as Compromised." *New York Times*, July 11, 2007, A1.

Healy, Patrick D. "Clinton Seeking Shared Ground over Abortions." *New York Times*, January 25, 2005, A1.

Heilprin, John. "Evangelicals, Scientists Join on Warming." *Associated Press*, January 17, 2007. Available from news.yahoo.com.

Henriques, Diana B. "As Religious Programs Expand, Disputes Rise Over Tax Breaks." *New York Times*, October 10, 2006 and October 1–20, 2006.

———. "Sharing the Health Bills." *New York Times*, October 20, 2006, C1.

Henriques, Diana B. and Andrew W. Lehren. "Religious Groups Reaping Share of Federal Aid for Pet Projects." *New York Times*, May 13, 2007, A1.

Hernandez v. Robles, 2006 NY Slip Opinion 05239.

Holmes v. Bush, FSC Case Nos. SC04-23323/2324/2325 (2006).

Hulse, Carl and David D. Kirkpatrick. "Even Death Does Not Quiet Harsh Political Fight." *New York Times*, April 1, 2005, A1

———. "Moving Quickly, Senate Approves Schiavo Measure." *New York Times*, March 21, 2005, A14.

Ignatieff, Michael. "Democratic Providentialism." *New York Times Magazine*, December 12, 2004, 29.

Institute of Politics, John F. Kennedy School of Government. *Campaign for President: The Managers Look at 2004*. Lanham, Maryland: Rowman & Littlefield, 2006, ch. 3.

Jelinek, Pauline. "Aides, Pace Won't Apologize for Gay Remark." *Associated Press*, March 13, 2007. Available from news.yahoo.com/s/ap/20070313.

Johnson, George. "For the Anti-Evolutionists, Hope in High Places." *New York Times Week in Review*, October 3, 2005, wk 3.

Johnson, Kirk. "Gay Marriage Losing Punch as Ballot Issue." *New York Times*, October 14, 2006, A10.

Johnston, David and Eric Lipton. "Rove Is Linked to Early Query over Dismissals." *New York Times*, March 16, 2007, A19.

Kelley, Matt. "Lobbying Restrictions Are Ineffectual, Critics Say." *USA Today*, February 22, 2007, 7A.

Kirkpatrick, David D. "Book Says Bush Aides Ridiculed Christian Allies." *New York Times*, October 13. 2006.

———. "Bush Sought Vatican Official's Help on Issues, Report Says." *New York Times*, June 13, 2004, A38.

———. "Christian Right Labors to Find '08 Candidate," February 24, 2007. Available from www.nyutimes.com/2007/02/25/us/politics.

———. "Democrats in 2 Southern States Push Bills on Bible Study," *New York Times*, January 27, 2006, A20.

———. "For Evangelical, Supporting Israel Is 'God's Foreign Policy.'" *New York Times*, November 14, 2006, A1.

———. "Republican Woes Lead to Feuding by Conservatives." *New York Times*, October 20, 2006, A1.

———. "Romney Used His Wealth to Enlist Richest Donors." *New York Times*, April 6, 2007, A17.

Kirkpatrick, David. D. and Joel C. Hunter. *Right Wing, Wrong Bird: Why the Tactics of the Religious Right Won't Fly with Most Conservative Christians*. Longwood, Florida: Distributed Church Press, 2006.

Kirkpatrick, David D. and Sheryl Gay Stolberg. "How Family's Cause Reached the Halls of Congress." *New York Times*, March 22, 2005, A1.

Kitzmiller v. Dover Area School District, Case No. 04cv2688, Cited as: 2005 WL 578974 (MD Pa. 2005).

Krager, Aaron. "Faith, Values, Poverty: Sojourner's Forum—Barak Obama." Available from http://faithfullyliberal.com/?p = 45.

Kuo, David. "Interview with John Edwards." Available from www.beliefnet.com/story/213/story_21312.html.

———. "Putting Faith before Politics." *New York Times*, November 16, 2006, A35.

Larson, Bob. *Larson's Book of Rock*. Wheaton, Illinois: Tyndale Publishers, 1987.

Leland, John. "'Christian Diets' Fewer Loaves, Lots of Fishes." *New York Times*, April 28, 2005, G2.

———. "The Word in Bubbles." *New York Times*. August 26, 2006, 5.

Lerner, Michael. *The Left Hand of God: Taking Back Our Country from the Religious Right*. San Francisco: HarperCollins, 2006.

———. *Spirit Matters: Global Healing and the Wisdom of the Soul*. Hampton Roads, 2000.

———, ed., *Tikkun Reader: Twentieth Anniversary*. Lanham, Maryland: Rowman & Littlefield, 2006.

Lewin, Tamar. "Colleges Regroup After Voters Ban Race Preferences." *New York Times*, January 26, 2007, A15.

Lewis, Neil A. "Libby Defense Portrays Client as a Scapegoat." *New York Times*, January 24, 2007, A12.

Lewis, Neil A. and David D. Kirkpatrick. "F.B.I. Searches Home of California Lawmaker." *New York Times*, April 19, 2007, A13.

Lichtblau, Eric. "Bush Plans to Let Religious Groups Get Building Aid." *New York Times*, February 23, 2002, A1.

Lindsley, Joseph. "Finding Religion: Democrats Try to Talk Like God-fearing Folk." *Weekly Standard*, April 17, 2006. Available from www.weeklystandard.com.

Lipton, Eric. "Members of a Sympathetic Jury Describe an Emotional but Inevitable Conclusion." *New York Times*, March 7, 2007, A17.

Luo, Michael. "For Clinton, Faith Intertwines with Political Life." *New York Times*, July 7, 2007, A1.

Magnet, Myron. *The Dream and the Nightmare: The Sixties Legacy to the Underclass.* New York: William Morrow and Company, 1993.

McGraw, Barbara A. and Jo Renee Formicola, eds., *Taking Religious Pluralism Seriously: Religious Pluralism on America's Sacred Ground.* Waco: Baylor University, 2006.

McKinley, Jesse. "Incumbents on the Ropes over Ties to Abramoff." *New York Times*, October 27, 2006, A14.

———. "A Youth Ministry Some Call Antigay Tests Tolerance." *New York Times*, September 9, 2007, A12.

Meredith v. Jefferson County Board of Eduction, No. 05-915.

Mitchell, Alison. "Bush Draws Campaign Theme from More Than 'The Heart.'" *New York Times*, June 12, 2000, A1.

Monsma, Stephen and Mark Rogers. "In the Arena." In *Toward an Evangelical Public Policy: Political Strategies for the Health of the Nation*, eds. Ronald J. Sider and Diane Knippers. Grand Rapids: Baker Books, 2005.

Morken, Hubert. "Bishop T. D. Jakes: A Ministry for Empowerment." In Jo Renee Formicola and Hubert Morken, eds., *Religious Leaders and Faith-Based Politics* Lanham, Maryland: Rowman & Littlefield, 2001, 28.

Morken, Hubert and Jo Renee Formicola. *The Politics of School Choice.* Lanham, Maryland: Rowman & Littlefield, 1999.

Nagourney, Adam. "Democrats Weigh De-emphasizing Abortion as an Issue." *New York Times*, December 24, 2004, A25.

———. "In a Polarizing Case, Jeb Bush Cements His Political Stature." *New York Times*, March 25, 2005, A1.

National Association of Evangelicals. *For the Health of the Nation: An Evangelical Call to Civil Responsibility.* Available from www.nae.net/images/civic-responsibility2pdf.

Neal, Terry M. "Midwestern Mayor Shapes Bush's Message." *Washington Post*, June 5, 1999, A6.

Neuhaus, R. J. "Evangelicals and Catholics Together." *First Things* 43 (May 1994): 15–22.

Obama, Barak. *The Audacity of Hope.* New York: Crown Publishers, 2006, 38–39.

———. "Barack Obama Speaks Out on Faith and Politics: 'Call to Renewal' Keynote Address." Available from http://obama.senate.gov/podcast/060628-call.to.renewal.

Olasky, Marvin. *Compassionate Conservatism.* New York: The Free Press, 2000, xii.

———. *The Tragedy of American Compassion.* Washington, D.C.: Regnery Publishing, 1992.

Osteen, Joel. *Becoming a Better You: 7 Keys to Improving Your Life.* Simon and Schuster: New York, 2006.

———. *Your Best Life Now: Seven Steps to Living at Your Full Potential.* Waynesboro, Georgia: Faithworks, 2004.

de Parle, Jason. "Passing Down the Legacy of Conservatism." *New York Times,* July 31, 2006, A13.

Parry, Sam. "Bush's 'Incredible' Votes Tallies." *Consortiumnews.com.* November 9, 2004. Available from www.consortiumnews.com/Print/2004/110904.html.

Paul, Pope John, II. *The Gospel of Life (Evangelium Vitae).* Boston: The Daughters of St. Paul, 1995.

———. "Life Sustaining Treatments and Vegetative State: Scientific Advances and Ethical Dilemmas." March 20, 2004. Available from www.vatican.va.

Perdue v. O'Kelley et al., Georgia State Supreme Court S06Al574.

Pew Forum, *Religion in Public Life.* Section IV. Available from www.people-press.org/reports/display.php3?pageID = 115.

———. "Pragmatic Americans Liberal and Conservative on Social Issues." http://pewforum.org/docs/index,php?Doc = 150.

Pew Forum on Religion in Public Life. "United States Demographic Profile." Available from pewforum.org/world-affairs/countries/?CountryID = 222.

Phillips, Kevin. *American Theocracy.* New York: Viking, 2006, 121.

Regents of the University of California v. Bakke, 438 U.S. 265 (l978).

Riemer, Neal. *The Future of the Democratic Revolution: Toward a More Prophetic Politics.* New York: Praeger, l984.

"Rocking for Jesus." December 8, 2004. Available from www.cbsnews.com/stories2004/12/01/60II/printable658590.shtml.

Roe v. Wade 410 U.S. 113 (l973).

Rosenthal, Elisabeth and Andrew C. Revkin. "Science Panel Says Global Warming Is 'Unequivocal.'" *New York Times,* February 3, 2006, A1.

Rutenberg, Jim. "A Last Hurrah of Sorts for Bush-Rove Partnership." *New York Times,* November 7, 2006, 18.

———. "Bush Calls for an Amendment Banning Same-Sex Nuptials." *New York Times,* June 4, 2006, A30.

Sanotra, Marc. "Rhode Island Bishop Condemns Giuliani's Position on Abortion." *New York Times,* June 8, 2007, A20.

Sargent, Lyman Tower. *Contemporary Political Ideologies.* Belmont, California: Thompson, Wadsworth, 2006, ch. l.

Saulny, Susan. "Full Federal Appellate Court Will Revisit Abortion Issue in South Dakota." *New York Times,* April 11, 2007, A13.

———. "U.S. Gives Charter Schools a Big Push in New Orleans." *New York Times,* June 31, 2006, A19.

Schaefer Riley, Naomi. *God on the Quad.* New York: St. Martin's Press, 2005.

Schiavo, Michael and Michael Hirsh. *Terri: The Truth.* New York: Dutton, 2006.

Schmidt, Susan and James V. Grimaldi. "Abramoff Pleads Guilty to 3 Counts." *Washington Post,* January 4, 2006, A1.

Schori, Katharine Jefferts. "Interview with Katharine Jefferts Schori." *Time Magazine,* July 17, 2006, vol. 168, no. 3, 6.

Schwartz, Frederick D. Review of *Phyllis Schlafly and Grassroots Conservatism: A Woman's Crusade,* by Donald Critchlow. *American Heritage Magazine,* November 2, 2005. Available from www.americanheritage.com.

186   *Works Cited*

Selman v. Cobb County School District, Civil Action No. 1:02-CV-2325-CC (December 20, 2005).

Seelye, Katharine Q. "Thompson Makes Strong Pitch to Conservative Republicans." *New York Times*, June 3, 2007, A33.

Shalikashvili, John M. "Second Thoughts on Gays in the Military." *New York Times*, January 2, 2007. Available from www.nytimes.com/2007/01/02.

Shanker, Thom. "Top General Explains Remarks on Gays." *New York Times*, March 14, 2007, A15.

Shorto, Russell. "With God at Our Desks," *New York Times Magazine*, October 31, 2004, 42.

Sider, Ronald J. "The Radical Religious Middle." *The Review of Faith and International Affairs*. Winter 2006, vol. 4, no. 3, 44.

———. *Rich Christians in an Age of Hunger: A Biblical Study*. Dallas: Word Publishing, 1977.

Silk, Mark and John C. Green. "The GOP's Religious Problem." *Religion in the News* (Winter), vol. 9, no. 3, 2–4.

Smith, Ashley and Stacy Mattingly. *Unlikely Angel: The Untold Story of the Atlanta Hostage Hero*. Zondervan/HarperCollins, 2005.

Solomon, Deborah. "The Whistle-Blower." *New York Times Magazine*, June 3, 2007.

———. "You Listening to Me?" *New York Times Magazine*, January 28, 2007.

Solomon, Lois K. "Political Voices of Religious Left." *South Florida Sun-Sentinel*. July 24, 2006.

"South Dakota Votes Against Ban of Almost All Abortions." November 8, 2006. Available from http://cnn.worldnews.

Sprenglemeyer, M. E. "Dobson: Rallying Family Values Voters." *Rocky Mountain News*, September 23, 2006. Available from www.rockymountainnews.com.

St. John, Warren. "Sports, Songs and Salvation on Faith Night at the Ballpark." *New York Times*, June 2, 2006, A1.

Stenberg v. Carhart, 530 U.S. 914 (2000).

Stolberg, Sheryl Gay. "A Collision of Disparate Forces May Be Reshaping American Law." *New York Times*, April 1, 2005, A18.

Stolberg, Sheryl Gay and Carl Hulse. "Negotiators Add Abortion Clause to Spending Bill." *New York Times*, November 20, 2004, A1.

Suellentrop, Chris. "The Right Has A Jailhouse Conversion." *New York Times Magazine*, December 24, 2006, 48.

"Survey of Voters." *New York Times*, November 9, 2006, P7.

Suskind, Ron. "Faith Certainty and the Presidency of George W. Bush." *New York Times Magazine*, October 17, 2004. Available from www.nytimes.com/2004/10/17/magazine/17Bush.

Toner, Robin. "Cheney Addresses Anti-Abortion Group." *New York Times*, April 21, 2004, A21.

Toner, Robin and Carl Hulse. "A Family's Battle Brings Life's End into Discussion." *New York Times*, March 20, 2005, A1.

Tsai, Catherine. "Key Evangelical Quits Amid Gay Sex Claim." *Associated Press*, November 11, 2006. Available from http://news.yahoo.com.

U.S. Public Law 104-193, August 22, 1996. *Personal Responsibility and Work Opportunity Reconciliation Act*.

Vandhei, Jim and Dan Baltz. "Fall Elections Are Rove's Next Test, Reputation of Architect of Victory at Stake." *Washington Post*, June 17, 2006, A1. Available from www.washingtonpost.com.

"The View from the Jury Box." *New York Times*, March 7, 2007, A1.

Volz, Neil. "Ohio Congressman Ney Admits to Conspiracy, False Statements." *North Country Gazette*, October 16, 2006. Available from www.northcountrygazette.org.

Walker, Rob. "Consumed." *New York Times Magazine*, March 6, 2005, sec.6, 28.

———. "God Is in the Distribution," *New York Times Magazine*, November 13, 2005, 38.

Wallis, Jim. *God's Politics: Why the Right Gets It Wrong and the Left Doesn't Get It*. San Francisco: HarperCollins, 2005.

Walzer, Michael. "All God's Children Got Values." *Dissent* (Spring 2005). Available from www.dissentmagazine.org.

Warren, Rick. *The Purpose-Driven Life: Reflections on What on Earth Am I Here For*. Grand Rapids, Michigan: Zondervan, 2002.

Waxman, Sharon. "The Passion of the Marketers." *New York Times*, July 18, 2005, C1.

———. "Sony Effort to Reach Christians Is Disputed." *New York Times*, November 2, 2005, E1.

Wilson, Joseph. *The Politics of Truth: Inside the Lies That Led to War and Betrayed My Wife's CIA Identity—A Diplomat's Memoir*. New York: Graf Publishing Company, 2004.

Winzenburg, Stephen. "National Religious Broadcasters" in *Museum of Broadcast Communications Encyclopedia of Radio: 2004*, vol. 2, 1007–8.

Young, Yolanda. "Black Clergy's Silence Hurts Gays." *USA Today*, March 10, 2006, A16.

Zapor, Patricia. "End of 'Catholic Vote.' Other Categories May Predict Election Better." Available from www.catholicnews.com/data.

Zelman v. Simmons-Harris, 536 U.S. 639 (2002).

Websites

hirr.hartsem.edu.
www.christianradio.com/network.asp.
www.extremeclothing.com.
www.fca.org.
www.focusonthefamily.com/aboutus/A000000408.
www.goldstars.com/speakers/display.
www.gospelmusicchannel.com.
www.ifiprison.org/site.
www.leftbehind-worldatwar.com/churchtheatricalrelease/howitworks.php.
www.reliancebankltd.com.
www.silverringthing.com.
www.tikkun.com.
www.webelieveohio.org.

Index

abortion: Bush, George W.'s, actions against, 11–13; Catholics differing with Guiliani on, 173; Clinton, Hillary's, views on, 111; the Democratic Party's rethinking of position on, 110–11; Falwell on propaganda and, 161; South Dakota and battles over, 161; voter separation over issue of, 11, 19–20, 160–62. *See also* Global Gag Rule; *Gonzalez v. Carhart*; National Right to Life Committee; Partial Birth Abortion Ban Act; *Roe v. Wade*; Unborn Victims of Violence Act

Abramoff, Jack, 136; DeLay and scandal with, 138, 140; Doolittle and scandal with, 141–42; Griles and scandal with, 138; Ney and scandal with, 141; Norquist mentoring, 137; Pombo and scandal with, 141–42; success and ascension of, 137–38

ACCB. *See* American Chamber of Christians in Business

ACLU. *See* American Civil Liberties Union

Adams, John Quincy (President), 79

affirmative action, 168–69

Africa, 165–66

Ahmadinejad, Mahmoud (President), 171

AIDS: Obama on religious groups efforts towards controlling, 166; Warren, Rick, Reverend, and Warren, Kay's, efforts for Africa and, 165–66

Albright, Madeline (Secretary of State), 171

American Chamber of Christians in Business (ACCB), 62

American Civil Liberties Union (ACLU), 57–58

American Theocracy (Phillips), 31

Arterburn, Stephen, 59–60

assisted suicide, 18

Association of Christian Financial Advisors, 62

Augustine (saint), 78

Bai, Matt: on Dean's leadership, 103; on the Democratic Party's problem with values, 102

Bakke, Allan, 168

Ball, Jim, Reverend, 60

Bauer, Gary, 37

Bolten, Josh, 152

Brody, David, 175

Bush, George W. (President), 7; abortion and counter actions of, 11–13; Catholic activism encouraged by, 50; Catholics and Kerry versus, 51; DiIulio working with, 46–47; on environ-

About the Author

Jo Renée Formicola is professor of political science at Seton Hall University. She is the author of *The Catholic Church and Human Rights* (New York: Garland, 1988) and *John Paul II: Prophetic Politician* (Washington, D.C.: Georgetown University Press, 2002). She is the co-author of *The Politics of School Choice* (Lanham, Maryland; Rowman & Littlefield, 2003) with Hubert Morken, and *Faith-Based Initiatives and the Bush Administration: The Good, the Bad, and the Ugly* (Lanham, Maryland: Rowman & Littlefield, 2003) with Mary Segers and Paul Weber. She has edited and contributed chapters to *Everson Revisited: Religion, Education, and Law at the Crossroads* (Lanham, Maryland: Rowman & Littlefield, 1997) with Hubert Morken, *Religious Leaders and Faith-Based Politics: Ten Profiles* (Lanham, Maryland: Rowman & Littlefield, 2001) with Hubert Morken, and *Taking Religious Pluralism Seriously: Spiritual Politics on America's Sacred Ground* (Waco: Baylor University Press, 2005) with Barbara A. McGraw. She has also written extensively on issues of religion and politics in the *Journal of Church and State*, *Momentum*, and other peer-reviewed periodicals.